Polygons Feel No Pain

Volume 1

Ingemar Ragnemalm

Course book in modern Computer Graphics

Foreword

Why would anyone name a computer graphics book "Polygons feel no pain"? In case you wonder, here are the reasons:

- Computer graphics is very much about polygons.
- Computer games tend to be violent and I am *aiming for gaming*!
- A major point with it is to inflict less pain (in your back) than the others do.
- It is a whole lot more fun than yet another book entitled "Computer Graphics with OpenGL".

So the message is that computer graphics is fun, computer games are fun too, and blasting some grunts in Quake doesn't hurt anyone.

Let's start the game. INSERT COIN(S) TO CONTINUE...

Cover image by Susanne Ragnemalm, based on the original Candide model.

Related web pages:

http://www.computer-graphics.se

http://www.isy.liu.se

http://www.ragnemalm.se

1. Introduction

This book was written as course material for my course in Computer Graphics at Linköping University. There are many computer graphics books, including the Hearn&Baker book [6] that was course book for our course for many years. That book is excellent in many areas, low-level algorithms and splines in particular. However, the amount of material that was missing for my needs kept growing, and whatever book I considered as replacement seemed to miss just as much. And they are all big books that don't slip as easily into the backpack as they should.

And that is why this book was created: I wanted to create a small, portable book that you can bring with you without any pain in the shoulders, and that fits the course well at the same time.

1.1 Who should read this book?

Since this book is written for the course TSBK07 Computer Graphics at the University of Linköping, attendants of that course and similar courses are the target audience. That means students at 2nd to 4th grade with some experience in algebra and programming.

The course does not demand any prior knowledge of computer graphics, so it will start from the bottom. The tempo will, however, be pretty high.

1.2 What should you expect to learn from this book, and its course?

Computer graphics is the art of creating images from a description. You will learn how computer graphics works, including the math and programming behind it. There will be some 2D graphics algorithms, but most of the course is about 3D graphics, real-time graphics in particular. We will go reasonably far into the subject, including methods for working with very large worlds, but more advanced topics are left for volume 2, "So How Can We Make Them Scream?". Computer graphics has many applications, and we focus on what I think is most challenging: Real-time graphics, including games. We focus on modern hardware (modern GPUs), and modern programming methods, which includes shader programming.

1.3 A few words about the past

Most of the book is based on my lecture material for the computer graphics course, much of it first appearing in the "Devil in a book" supplements from 2000-2007.

The Computer Graphics course I am leading, currently with the name TSBK07 Computer Graphics, has a long history. It was started in the mid-80's by professor Per-Erik Danielsson and associate professor Björn Gudmundsson. I attended the course as a student, so it was my first formal training in computer graphics. I have been course leader and lecturer for it since 2000. As is natural for a fast-moving subject like this, the course is revised from year to year. This book is created as a part of that process. The changes for 2008 were larger than usual, important material moved down from the advanced course.

This was a good time to write this book. I hope that I am offering a course and a book that are fairly up-to-date and that cover the subject fairly well, for being a first course on computer graphics. And with volume 2, I believe we have a neat book set that covers much of the essentials for graphics and game programmers.

1.4 A book using OpenGL, not an OpenGL book

Note that this text is about computer graphics, not OpenGL or any other specific API. OpenGL will be used for examples, but you may want to get some other book for learning OpenGL as such. However, I would advise you to avoid books that discuss OpenGL up to version 2.1, since, we will aim at the more modern OpenGL 3.2 and beyond.

This book tries to avoid any code that is heavily language- or operating system dependent. Code examples are in C, but that does not mean that you have to use C, with or without OO extensions (e.g. C++). There are other ways and I want to encourage you to explore them. Operating system dependency is avoided, so what you find in this book should work anywhere. There is no language or OS that is the only way.

So what you have here is a computer graphics book with focus on OpenGL and game programming. Let us get started with chapter 3, a short chapter about some groundwork, subjects that I hope most readers know about already. We start to get the speed up in chapter 4 and chapter 5, with chapter 6 being the chapter where we take off, in full 3D. What you will find most interesting and enjoyable depends on you.

Some last words before leaving the introduction. After the revisions, I hope most errors are gone. But if you still find any, please let me know when you find them. I wish to give special thanks to Richard Åklint, Arvid Kongstad, Kristofer Krus and Marcus Wallenberg, who did exactly that, and more than anyone else found and reported many of the errors in the earlier printings.

2. Table of contents

3. Graphics systems

This chapter covers the very basics. It starts with the question of what a graphics system is, and why. Then we come to the question of what a pixel is and how the image is stored in memory, how colors are represented and how you can access single pixels. Finally, I say a few words about graphics libraries, including OpenGL.

3.1 Graphics hardware

The first computer displays were hardwired for displaying text. Modern PCs still have character display systems built-in, a feature with little meaning today, mostly used for "safe mode" tricks, for primitive command-line work. But let us turn to graphics.

The minimal graphics system is a computer with a video controller connected to its system bus, as in Figure 1:

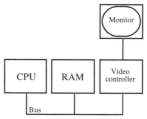

FIGURE 1. A primitive graphics system

Either the CPU has to feed the video controller with data (an unwanted burden, mildly speaking) or the video controller must access some part of RAM, where the image is located that it is supposed to display. If the video controller must do that over the system bus, it will cause collisions where the CPU must wait.

A more efficient system is shown in Figure 2. Here, we have dedicated VRAM, that the video controller can access without collisions with the CPU.

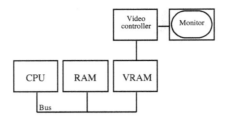

FIGURE 2. A graphics system with dedicated VRAM

However, modern systems are usually equipped with a co-processor that takes care of some graphics operations. It is called a Display Processor, Graphics Accelerator or Graphics Processing Unit (GPU). Older graphics accelerators were either for 2D or 3D graphics. Modern GPUs, however, are so good at both that you only need one.

Any modern desktop computer, as well as laptops, come with a GPU as part of their video circuitry. At the time of writing this, the leading accelerators comes from NVidia (the GeForce 700 series), with AMD (the Radeon series, formerly ATI) as the main competitor. The development of these components is extremely fast, although the turbulence among manufacturers seems to have calmed down and NVidia and AMD have been the leaders for some time now. This system is illustrated by Figure 3.

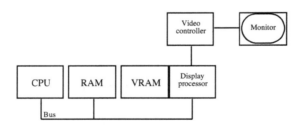

FIGURE 3. A modern graphics system

These steps through the development of graphics system has one thing in common: They all work towards reducing the communication on the main system bus, and reducing the CPU involvement in the graphics. On modern systems, it is possible to upload not only textures but also geometry to the GPU, and much rendering can be done with fairly simple control calls from the CPU. Furthermore, the on-board processing is highly programmable by using *shader programs*, small programs computing certain parts of the graphics pipeline. We will return to that shortly, in chapter 3.7.2.

3.2 Image formats

The image buffer is generally one block of consecutive memory. The first pixel (typically the top-left one) is stored at the first byte of memory. In some older systems the image was separated into "bit planes", so to draw one pixel, you had to look up three different places.

Graphics systems

This is not used any more. Rather, each pixel is stored as one small consecutive block of memory. This is known as *chunky pixels*, see Figure 4.

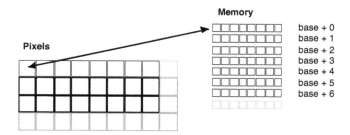

FIGURE 4. With chunky pixels, each pixel is one single chunk of memory

The pixel size is measured in bits, since it can be less than a full byte (8 bits). What pixel size that is used has varied over time, and it varies with different systems and settings. On early systems, one to three bits per pixel was normal, where three bits typically implied that the system had separate bit planes. Nowadays, the most common setting is a full four bytes (32 bits) per pixel. Table 1 lists the pixel sizes used for chunky pixel systems (modern systems). All these alternatives except 2 bits have been commonplace at some time.

TABLE 1. Pixel sizes

Pixel size (bits)	Number of colors	Note	Interest
1	2	Mostly used for masking	Some
2	4	Very uncommon even in the past	None
4	16	Almost non-existent today	None
8	256	Always available, but avoided	Some
16	Thousands	"High color"	Fair
24/32	Millions	"True color"	Standard
Up to 256 (4x64)	Billions	Floating-point formats	On-board

Out of these, only the last are of much interest today, plus that 1-bit images are also often used as masks or other kinds of binary data, often off-screen. 8-bit color (256 colors) is marginally useful, as a minimum that you can safely demand, but new applications should take advantage of 16- or 24-bit colors.

The first three depths are packed several pixels in one byte, which is impractical but space-efficient. The 24/32 depth really only uses three bytes (24 bits) for displaying the color, but a fourth byte is used to make the space required a power of two. That byte may be used as alpha channel, used for transparency operations.

The last row represents capabilities of modern graphics boards which can work with floating-point pixel data, which changes the picture altogether. Although output is still 24 bits, the improved internal precision and range open new possibilities like high dynamic range rendering. These floating-point buffers support from 16 to 32 (or even 64) bits floating-point numbers per channel, which means that the once "forever perfect" precision of 32 bits per pixel is being replaced by 128-256 bits per pixel!

A discussion of image formats could also deal with disk-based formats like JPEG and PNG, but that it is mainly an image coding question. For graphics, disk-based formats is mainly a question of unpacking them into memory so they can be used as textures. I recommend libraries like libjpeg and libpng, or QuickTime, for handling this. Some formats are so simple that you can easily write your own loader, but those formats are space-inefficient and mostly interesting for educational use.

3.3 Displaying color

Color is not the same thing as electromagnetic radiation frequencies, but a mapping of it. The human eye senses color information with sensors with three different frequency intervals, giving us a three-dimensional color space. If I claim that these three intervals are *red, green and blue*, then I am simplifying things a little bit, but not too much really. The XYZ color space, which is the true color space of the eye, is very close to RGB so we can consider them identical most of the time.

So, the eye detects three primary colors, red, green and blue. Linear combinations of these form a 3D space, with all perceivable colors, including the secondary colors, that are combinations of two primary colors: cyan = green+blue, magenta = red+blue and yellow = red + green. Also, white = red + green + blue and black = zero in all three primary colors. This way to combine color is called *additive color mixing*, typically used in color displays (including television sets). We note that yellow, which is often claimed to be a primary color in kindergarten, is *not* a primary color. So please forget what you were told in kindergarten, it is simply incorrect.

Maybe you know that your inkjet printer uses cyan, magenta, yellow and black? What you have there are filters that take away one color. Cyan removes red, magenta removes green, yellow removes blue. Thus, mixing cyan and magenta will remove both red and green and only leave the blue light reflecting from the paper. This is known as *subtractive color mixing*. See Figure 5 for an illustration of additive and subtractive color mixing.

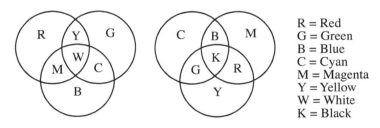

R = Red
G = Green
B = Blue
C = Cyan
M = Magenta
Y = Yellow
W = White
K = Black

FIGURE 5. Additive (left) and subtractive (right) color mixing

So, color is best represented as a vector (R, G, B). The components should be floating-point as far as possible, to avoid round-off errors, but once you reach the display, it is likely to take integers, usually 8 bits per channel.

When the video controller displays a pixel, it will need to be translated to a red, green and blue component, which is then passed to a D/A converter. We can assume, for now, that the D/A takes 8 bits per channel.

When using 8-bit color, the value is passed to a color look-up table (CLUT), which returns the three components. This is a mode that you rarely use today.

16-bit color is usually implemented as a fixed-color system, where a fixed number of the 16 bits are used for each channel. A color table is possible, but usually not used. Since 16 is not divisible by 3, the number of bits used for each color varies. You may find 5-5-5, 6-6-4, 6-5-5 etc. No matter what is used, the three parts must be separated (shifted and masked), and the missing bits are filled with zeros. Then we have three channels to pass to the D/A converter.

The 24-bit case is also fixed-color, and the most simple and comfortable one. You just take the three bytes and pass them to each channel of the D/A converter.

When assuming up to 8 bits per channel, I don't claim that this is the absolute maximum forever. Floating-point is used deeper and deeper into the systems. So you should assume that colors are floating point except when explicitly stated otherwise.

3.4 Accessing the image buffer

The simplest operation you can do in computer graphics is to draw one pixel. Given an image buffer, and granted that you are allowed to access it directly (not always the case), what you need is the following information: The *image width* in number of bytes (row-Bytes), the *base address* (base), the pixel size in bits (pixelSize) and the *pixel coordinates* (x, y). Then you find the address of the pixel like this:

```
p = base + x * pixelSize/8 + y * rowBytes
```

For pixel sizes 8 or larger, you can use this pointer to simply read out or write the pixel.

In practice, you rarely access the screen image buffer directly, but you often access other image buffers in this way. That can be image buffers that you modify before passing them to the graphics package, like when you unpack an image from disk to memory.

3.5 The graphics pipeline and shader programs

Instead of accessing frame buffers directly, this is done by the GPU. What you do from the CPU side is to pass geometry, image data (textures), and geometric transformations to the GPU, and then this data is rendered using *shader programs*.

A shader program is a small program kernel, running on the GPU, computing some specific task. It is executed in parallel as GPU native code. The GPU itself is a massively parallel processor, providing very high throughput of parallel tasks, of which there are many in graphics. Shaders are executed at specific points in the graphics pipeline. Let us take a closer look at the pipeline.

It all starts with *3D models*, which we can consider being polygons for now, built from points in space, the corners of the polygons, *vertices*. The various steps that have to be done form the graphics pipeline. It roughly consists of the following steps:

- Vertex processing. (Calculate screen positions from model coordinates.)
- Primitive assembly and geometry processing. (Combines vertices)
- Clip and cull. (Take away data that won't be visible.)
- Rasterization. (Find all pixels in a polygon.)
- Fragment processing. (Calculate pixel values. *Fragments* are "candidate pixels", they are not pixels yet but might be,)
- Frame buffer operations. (Write to actual pixel in frame buffer.)

Out of these steps, vertex, geometry and fragment processing can be programmed in detail by the application programmer (that means you). Shader programs are particularly vital, and an integral part of all modern computer graphics. The most important shaders are the *vertex* and *fragment* shaders (the latter also known as pixel shaders). A shader is a short program that is executed for every vertex (vertex shader) and for every fragment (fragment shader). This short program specifies how data is placed in the scene (vertex shaders) and how pixels are colorized (fragment shader). See page 19 for an example with shaders.

3.6 Graphics libraries

Ever since computers got any graphics capabilities whatsoever, a natural component of any operating system is a graphics library. This is particularly true since the Xerox PARC, Apple Lisa and Apple Macintosh arrived, the systems that broke with the character display tradition.

The pure minimum is, as mentioned before, to control single pixels. The next step is to draw lines. But a complete graphics package include a lot more: Lines, rectangles, circles/ovals, polygons, text, regions, colors, patterns... These calls are typical for 2D libraries like QuickDraw, GDI or Core Graphics.

Each kind of primitive can also be modified to be drawn in many different ways. A primitive can be filled (with colors or patterns), erased, framed, and lines and frames may have different thickness, style etc.

It may seem that many of these primitives are easy to implement. In reality, the only thing that is easy to do is to do a careless and more or less faulty implementation. We will later return to some aspects of this.

Graphics systems

3.7 OpenGL

A 3D graphics library will focus differently than a 2D one. Transformations play a bigger role, and much work will focus solely on rendering polygons. OpenGL [17] is one such library, the open industry standard that is available on most platforms. That is the library that this book focuses upon. However, as stated before, this is not an OpenGL book, and you are expected to use a separate text about OpenGL available for learning the API.

There are other 3D libraries. Many live on top of either OpenGL or Microsoft DirectX - often both. OpenGL, together with its close cousin OpenGL ES (OpenGL for embedded systems) and WebGL (OpenGL in web browser), is portable and vendor-neutral.

A few words on OpenGL as such. GL simply means Graphics Library. "Open" does not mean open source, although open source solutions exists (most notably the Mesa library). OpenGL is a cross-platform API, but since it must cooperate with various platform specific systems, window systems in particular, there are parts that are made specifically for that. Those parts are separate from the platform independent parts.

OpenGL is highly focused on its task, rendering polygons. It is so focused that you will sometimes wonder why some features are not in there, like text rendering, user interface, gaming input devices etc. This is a question of focus as well as portability. All nonportable and non-graphics features must stay out of the main library.

We will be using OpenGL 3.2. As of spring 2012, this was new for the course, since we have been using OpenGL 2.1 up to then. OpenGL versions are a bit confusing. You may ask, why do we switch to OpenGL 3.2 when the latest is 4? Why didn't we switch to 3 when it arrived two years earlier? The reason is that it takes time for each version to propagate. Version 4 requires the very latest boards, and will not work on many boards that are perfectly current. The big step was to move to OpenGL 3.2, which is modern without having unreasonable hardware demands. As late as autumn 2011, 3.2 was finally available on all major platforms, which makes this the right time to take this move, and today it is still a very good baseline.

The main part of OpenGL is called GL, and uses the prefix **gl** or **GL** on all calls, types and constants. It is tightly connected to its shading language, *GLSL* (OpenGL Shading Language). It comes with various extra libraries, like the now obsolete utility library called GLU, OpenGL Utilities, and you will often find GLext, OpenGL extensions. On every platform, there will be one or more platform dependent libraries, with the routines needed to communicate with that specific operating system:

- GLX for X-windows, that is Linux and most other Unixes

- AGL, CGL and NSOpenGL for OS X on Apple Macintosh

- WGL for Microsoft Windows

Although these OS interfaces are fairly simple, so your platform dependent code can generally be easily isolated, their use still makes you code less than fully portable. Thus, there are solutions that hide the platform dependency under a platform independent layer. There are two that I particularly want to mention: GLUT/FreeGLUT and SDL.

GLUT, OpenGL Utility Toolkit [18] is a popular and easy to use cross-platform API for OpenGL, nowadays mainly through its free clone FreeGLUT. It handles user interface, event and windowing, but is focused on graphics alone, so it has no calls for sound etc. *MicroGlut* is a GLUT subset which removes all deprecated solutions.

SDL, Simple Directmedia Layer, [19] is a popular open source package for high-performance cross-platform media applications, games in particular. It has a much wider scope than GLUT, and is thus very interesting for writing cross-platform games.

A third option has gained popularity recently, the GLFW library, and there are a number others listed on the OpenGL home page.

All too often, programmers find these cross-platform APIs insufficient and turn to platform dependent solutions instead. This is understandable; the cross-platform packages must restrict themselves to least common denominator solutions with no platform specific features. On the other hand, you will lose portability. My advice is to start with a cross-platform API. GLUT is great up to a point. But when you need to move on, package your system dependent calls in some way to isolate the parts you may need to rewrite.

A special note concerning Mac OSX: There are no less than three OpenGL APIs for the Mac, AGL, CGL and NSOpenGL. Avoid AGL, it is obsolete. CGL is for full-screen animations, while NSOpenGL is for NextStep/Cocoa views. Concerning the latter, you can ignore the NSOpenGLView, and create the OpenGL context into a general NSView yourself. It is just as easy, and avoids some problems reported by game programmers.

Concerning MS Windows, there is another important thing to note. You need an extension manager to access the modern features of OpenGL. There are two such managers to consider: glee and GLEW. I have good experience with glee so I can recommend it. All it takes for your program is to #include the manager and making a single initialization call. Then it will run shaders and all the rest you need.

I mentioned programming languages in the beginning. OpenGL is primarily presented having an API for C, but do not let that make you think that it can only be used from C. Just like OpenGL is available for most platforms, there are also interfaces for most programming languages that you may wish to consider.

I could recommend you my own favorite, but when you do projects in my courses, you should feel free to use just about any tool you like. You do the work, so you make the decision. You may not have that privilege in your future work, but you have it here.

3.7.1 Shader programming languages

As previously mentioned, shader programs are an essential part of a graphics program. There are a few different languages for shader programming. As mentioned above, OpenGL uses GLSL, OpenGL Shading Language. The main alternatives are the very similar Cg (from NVidia) and HLSL (from Microsoft). The similarities are bigger than the differences. I find shaders rather easy to port. There are also assembly languages for shaders, but they are hardly used any more.

3.7.2 A simple OpenGL example

I will round off this introduction with a minimal working example of modern OpenGL.

Any modern OpenGL program should be based on shaders, and it should also use onboard vertex buffers to minimize the amount of data transfers from CPU to GPU. It is quite a challenge to make a small and simple OpenGL program these days, but using some pretty reasonable utility code a minimal example can look like the one below.

First, here is the main program (mostly portable save some differences in includes):

```
#include "MicroGlut.h"
#include "GL_utilities.h"

// Globals
// Data would normally be read from files
GLfloat vertices[] = {-0.5f,-0.5f,0.0f, -0.5f,0.5f,0.0f, 0.5f,-0.5f,0.0f };

// vertex array object
unsigned int vertexArrayObjID;

void init(void)
{
    // vertex buffer object, used for uploading vertex data
    unsigned int vertexBufferObjID;
    // Reference to shader program:
    GLuint program;

    // GL inits
    glClearColor(0.2,0.2,0.5,0);
    glEnable(GL_DEPTH_TEST);

    // Load and compile shader
    program = loadShaders("minimal.vert", "minimal.frag"); // In our GL_utilities
    glUseProgram(program);

    // Allocate and activate Vertex Array Object
    glGenVertexArrays(1, &vertexArrayObjID);
    glBindVertexArray(vertexArrayObjID);
    // Allocate Vertex Buffer Objects
    glGenBuffers(1, &vertexBufferObjID);

    // VBO for vertex data
    glBindBuffer(GL_ARRAY_BUFFER, vertexBufferObjID);
    glBufferData(GL_ARRAY_BUFFER, 9*sizeof(GLfloat), vertices, GL_STATIC_DRAW);
    glVertexAttribPointer(glGetAttribLocation(program, "in_Position"),
                          3, GL_FLOAT, GL_FALSE, 0, 0);
    glEnableVertexAttribArray(glGetAttribLocation(program, "in_Position"));
}

void display(void)
{
    // clear the screen
    glClear(GL_COLOR_BUFFER_BIT | GL_DEPTH_BUFFER_BIT);

    // Draw the triangle
```

```
    glBindVertexArray(vertexArrayObjID);// Select VAO
    glDrawArrays(GL_TRIANGLES, 0, 3);// draw object
    glFlush();
}

int main(int argc, const char *argv[])
{
    glutInit();
    glutCreateWindow ("GL3 white triangle example");
    glutDisplayFunc(display);
    init ();
    glutMainLoop();
}
```

Here is the vertex shader (a minimal pass-through vertex shader):

```
#version 150
in  vec3 in_Position;
void main(void)
{
    gl_Position = vec4(in_Position, 1.0);
}
```

Finally, here is the fragment shader (sets the output to white):

```
#version 150
out vec4 out_Color;
void main(void)
{
    out_Color = vec4(1.0);
}
```

This will draw a white triangle, as in Figure 6.

FIGURE 6. Output of the simple OpenGL example

This example uses a package with reusable code, with some calls similar to GLUT for event processing plus shader loading (not in GLUT). A few comments about what it does:

The main program creates a window and installs some callbacks. This is not part of OpenGL but looks different in different libraries.

Graphics systems

The initialization uploads geometry (a triangle) to a *Vertex Buffer Object* (VBO), which is a reference to the buffer on the GPU. Such buffers are referred to in groups (here containing only a single one) by a *Vertex Array Object*. Thus, consider the VAO to be a container for several VBOs. With this structure we can activate a whole set of buffers at once through the VAO. This makes the initialization complex but the drawing much easier.

Note how small the drawing code is, in the display() procedure. The drawing is done by glDrawArrays. This is not quite the call we will use in the future (we will rather use glDrawElements) but close to equivalent.

The shader programs are truly minimal, doing almost nothing. The vertex shader is just "pass-through", passing on the geometry with no change. What you usually do there is to apply transformations specified by the host program. We will see how that is done in chapter 6.2. Concerning the fragment shader, its most common tasks are to calculate lighting effects (see chapter 7) and texturing (chapter 10). We will also make a more general discussion about shaders in chapter 6.11.

The example may seem complex for drawing a single triangle, and in a way it is. If all we wanted was to draw single triangles, it could be a lot simpler. However, the same code can be used to draw big models with thousands of triangles with minor changes, and efficiently. That is where the strength lies.

Throughout the book, we will frequently return to OpenGL and see how specific techniques can be implemented. Before that is meaningful, we will need some linear algebra, in particular its use for representing transformations by matrix multiplication. Thus, that comes next, and you will see that these operations map directly to OpenGL.

4. Linear algebra toolbox

Before we can continue, I must mention the most vital linear algebra operations that we will end up using. Although this course will not use any advanced math at all, the math that we are using are the basic building blocks of graphics, and of highest importance. Once we move to 3D space, a big challenge is to get used to expressing 3D in mathematical terms. At the end of this chapter, I will take a step up to some geometrical toolbox operations that are common in computer graphics.

You should consider the operations that are summarized here your best friends and treat them as such. Then they will be friendly and helpful and help you out of many hard problems, although you will have to be gentle at times. But if you don't, they might scream and bite you in your nose.

4.1 Vectors

A *vector* in N-dimensional space is an array of scalar values, one for each dimension. In 2 dimensions, a vector may be expressed as $\mathbf{v} = <v_x, v_y>$.

A vector may be a *positional vector*, denoting a specific location in space, or it may be a *directional vector*.

A number of important operations can be applied to a vector, and let us list the most important ones. Vector addition hardly needs mentioning:

$$\mathbf{a} + \mathbf{b} = (a_x+b_x, a_y+b_y, a_z+b_z)$$

It should be noted that we usually work with column vectors, but here the row vector is more practical.

A vector can be scaled by multiplication by a scalar value:

$$s \cdot \mathbf{a} = (s \cdot a_x, s \cdot a_y, s \cdot a_z)$$

The *magnitude* is the length of a vector:

$$|\boldsymbol{a}| \;=\; \sqrt{a_x^2 + a_y^2 + a_z^2}$$

Normalization is used to create a vector with the same direction as the original but with unit length, length 1:

$$\hat{a} \;=\; \frac{a}{|a|}$$

4.2 Vector products

The *dot product* (or scalar product) is defined as:

$$\boldsymbol{a} \bullet \boldsymbol{b} \;=\; |\boldsymbol{a}| \cdot |\boldsymbol{b}| \cdot \cos\varphi \;=\; a_x \cdot b_x + a_y \cdot b_y + a_z \cdot b_z$$

The dot product has a number of important properties:

- A dot product is a scalar value!
- **a** • **b** = 0 if a and b are orthogonal
- **a** • **b** = **b** • **a** (commutative)
- **a** • (**b** + **c**) = **a** • **b** + **a** • **c** (associative)

The value of the dot product as a tool in 3D graphics simply can not be overstated. As you will see, there are dot products literally everywhere. The most obvious interpretation of the dot product is that it projects one vector onto another, but there is more to it than that.

The *cross product* (or vector product) is really only meaningful to us in 3D and is defined as:

$$\boldsymbol{a} \times \boldsymbol{b} \;=\; \hat{n} \cdot |\boldsymbol{a}| \cdot |\boldsymbol{b}| \cdot \sin\varphi \;=\; \langle a_y \cdot b_z - a_z \cdot b_y,\, a_z \cdot b_x - a_x \cdot b_z,\, a_x \cdot b_y - a_y \cdot b_x \rangle$$

Like the dot product, the cross product has some important properties, but not the same ones:

- A Cross product is a vector, orthogonal to both a and b
- **a** x **b** = (0,0,0) if **a** and **b** are parallel
- **a** x **b** = - **b** x **a**

4.3 Matrices and matrix multiplication

Let me also remind you of the concept of matrices and matrix multiplication.

A matrix is a 2D-array of scalar values. We will mostly care about matrices with the same number of rows and columns. A 2D vector can be multiplied by a 2x2 matrix, producing a

---

vector. A 2x2 matrix can be multiplied by another 2x2 matrix, producing a new 2x2 matrix.

$$M \cdot a = \begin{bmatrix} M_{11} & M_{12} \\ M_{21} & M_{22} \end{bmatrix} \cdot \begin{bmatrix} a_x \\ a_y \end{bmatrix} = \begin{bmatrix} M_{11}a_x + M_{12}a_y \\ M_{21}a_x + M_{22}a_y \end{bmatrix}$$

$$M \cdot N = \begin{bmatrix} M_{11} & M_{12} \\ M_{21} & M_{22} \end{bmatrix} \cdot \begin{bmatrix} N_{11} & N_{12} \\ N_{21} & N_{22} \end{bmatrix} = \begin{bmatrix} M_{11}N_{11} + M_{12}N_{21} & M_{11}N_{12} + M_{12}N_{22} \\ M_{21}N_{11} + M_{22}N_{21} & M_{21}N_{12} + M_{22}N_{22} \end{bmatrix}$$

And matrices, too, have some properties that we should be aware of:

- They are associative: $A \cdot B \cdot C = (A \cdot B) \cdot C = A \cdot (B \cdot C)$
- They are non-commutative: $A \cdot B$ and $B \cdot A$ not guaranteed to be equal!

We generally only use symmetric matrices (2x2, 3x3, 4x4) here, but matrix multiplication is defined for non-symmetric matrices as well, as long as the first operand has as many columns as the second has rows.

The identity matrix, often called I, is a matrix which is 1 along the diagonal and 0 elsewhere, like this:

$$\begin{bmatrix} 1 & 0 \\ 0 & 1 \end{bmatrix}$$

Multiplication with an identity matrix has no effect.

Two more operations on matrices should be mentioned: *transpose* and *inverse*. Transposing a matrix is simply to flip it over the diagonal, making rows to columns and columns to rows. The transpose of M is denoted M^T.

The inverse of a matrix is a matrix that multiplied with the original matrix produces the identity matrix: $MM^{-1} = I$. A popular method of finding the inverse (if it exists) is *gaussian elimination*. Only symmetrical matrices can be inverted.

You may notice that a matrix multiplication is really nothing else than a set of dot products. A matrix multiplication between a matrix and a vector turns into a set of dot products if you consider the matrix to be a set of row vectors, and a multiplication between matrices are all possible dot products between two sets of vectors. But with a reverse reasoning, a dot product is a matrix multiplication between a transposed vector and another vector: $\mathbf{a} \cdot \mathbf{b} = A^T B$ (where A and B are $\mathbf{a}$ and $\mathbf{b}$ viewed as 1x3 matrices).

4.4 Typographic conventions for vectors and matrices

Although not always strictly followed, I have some typographic conventions in this book.

Scalar symbols are lowercase and in normal style: a

Symbols for vectors are usually lowercase and boldface: $\mathbf{a} = (a_x, a_y, a_z)$

Unit vectors are sadly non-standardized in this book. A symbol with a circumflex is always a unit vector: $\hat{a}$, but for practical reasons (they are only easy to write in equation boxes) you will find many cases where unit vectors are written in other ways.

Matrices are always given as uppercase, normal type: A

For historical reasons, you may find cases where vectors or scalars are, too, given as uppercase, normal type, but these should be rare.

Symbols in *italic* are nothing special; italic symbols denote nothing more than that they are in a equation box.

Finally, I know some of you may be used to the vertical bar | as symbol for the dot product. In this book, dot product is denoted a dot, just as the name says. We simply can't rewrite all course material everywhere because a linear algebra teacher changes a book. Since dot product tends to have the name it has, I personally hope that we are soon back to normal. However, both small dots · and fat dots • may appear for dot product. As with other inconsistencies, I am trying to eliminate them as far as possible, but that is sometimes hard for technical reasons (word processor limitations). Fat dots are supposed to be dot products, small are scalar multiplications.

4.5 3D space

Now, some fundamental 3D concepts:

We need to add one more axis, the Z axis. Let the X and Y be screen coordinates, that is right and up. Then Z is the depth... but should it point into the screen or out from it?

The most intuitive answer is that you want it to point inwards, away from you. Alas, that is not as suitable as it seems. That would make the coordinate system a *left-handed system*, which would make many operations different from what we are used to (e.g. cross products). Rather, we choose to point out from the screen, that is backwards, which makes the system *right-handed*. This is the very first example of a fundamental law of computer graphics:

Computer graphics people do it backwards!

If you ever wonder whether you have a right-handed system or a left-handed system, put your thumb along the X axis. If the other fingers hit Y before Z, the hand matches the handedness of the coordinate system. See Figure 7.

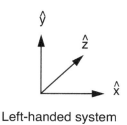
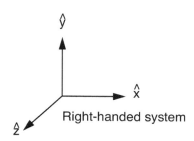

Left-handed system

Right-handed system

FIGURE 7. Left- and right-handed coordinate systems

Just like in 2D, vectors can be position vectors (points) or directional vectors.

A 3D line can be defined in several ways, either by two points on the line, or by one point on the line and one directional vector. In the latter case, we can write a formula with a variable μ that defines all points on the line:

$$\mathbf{p'} = \mathbf{p} + \mu\,\mathbf{d}$$

A 3D line segment can be defined by its two endpoints, or, equivalently, by one point and one directional vector, plus an interval. Then any point on the line fulfills this criterion:

$$\mathbf{p'} = \mathbf{p} + \mu\,\mathbf{d}, 0 < \mu < 1$$

A 3D plane is defined by the plane equation:

$$Ax + By + Cz + D = 0$$

where (A, B, C) is a vector that is orthogonal to the plane, the normal vector to the plane.

4.6 Orthonormal basis

We will often work in different coordinate systems. A 3D coordinate system uses three basis vectors.

$$\hat{x}, \hat{y}, \hat{z}$$

These should form an *orthonormal basis*. A conversion between two bases is done by expressing one basis in the other, with three vectors $\mathbf{u}, \mathbf{v}, \mathbf{w}$. This is an orthonormal basis if

$$|u| = 1, |v| = 1, |w| = 1$$

and

$$u \bullet v = 0, u \bullet w = 0, v \bullet w = 0$$

which means that all three are unit vectors and they are all orthogonal to each other. From these three vectors we can build a matrix that converts any point in the old basis to a point the new one:

$$p' = \begin{bmatrix} u_x & v_x & w_x \\ u_y & v_y & w_y \\ u_z & v_z & w_z \end{bmatrix} p$$

This means that the vector $(1, 0, 0)$ should be mapped to (u_x, u_y, u_z).

Orthonormal bases will appear frequently in the following, for example in the form of rotation matrices.

Finally, it should be noted that an orthonormal matrix is inverted simply by transposing it:

$$M^{-1} = M^T$$

That was a little reminder of some things you should remember from linear algebra. Let us continue with some typical computer graphics toolbox operations, operations that will turn out to be useful in many different computer graphics problems.

4.7 On what side of a plane is a point?

The plane equation specifies what points are in the plane, but the definition doesn't explicitly tell whether a point that is not in the plane is on the side that the normal vector points to (the front side), or the other side. However, that information *is* in the plane equation's data. We just have to check how to get it.

Consider a plane with plane vector **n**, a point **a** in the plane, and a point **p** on the positive side, the side where the plane vector points. See Figure 8.

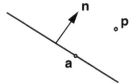

FIGURE 8. On which side is p?

The plane is defined by $Ax + By + Cz + D = 0$, that is $\mathbf{n} \cdot \mathbf{a} + D = 0$, where $D = -\mathbf{n} \cdot \mathbf{a}$, using any point **a** in the plane. That is, the plane equation really just says that $\mathbf{n} \cdot \mathbf{a}$ is the same for all points in the plane.

$\mathbf{p} - \mathbf{a} = \mathbf{ap}$ is a vector from the plane to $\mathbf{p}$. By definition of the dot product, $\mathbf{ap} \cdot \mathbf{n} > 0$ when the angle between $\mathbf{n}$ and $\mathbf{ap}$ is $< \pi/2$. That is true when $\mathbf{p}$ is on the positive side of the plane!

$$\mathbf{ap} \cdot \mathbf{n} = (\mathbf{p} - \mathbf{a}) \cdot \mathbf{n} = \mathbf{p} \cdot \mathbf{n} - \mathbf{a} \cdot \mathbf{n} = \mathbf{p} \cdot \mathbf{n} + D.$$

Thus, $\mathbf{p} \cdot \mathbf{n} + D > 0$ on the positive side, as expected!

4.8 Intersection between a line segment and a plane

Take two points, $\mathbf{a}$ and $\mathbf{b}$. They define the line segment $\mathbf{p} = \mathbf{a} + \mathbf{ab} \cdot \mu, 0 < \mu < 1$

The plane is defined by the normal vector $\mathbf{n}$ as: $\mathbf{n} \cdot \mathbf{p} + D = 0$ for any $\mathbf{p}$ in the plane.

Get the intersection by inserting the segment equation into the plane equation.

$$\mathbf{n} \cdot \mathbf{p} + D = \mathbf{n} \cdot (\mathbf{a} + \mathbf{ab} \cdot \mu) + D = 0 =>$$

$$\mu = (-D - \mathbf{n} \cdot \mathbf{a}) / (\mathbf{n} \cdot \mathbf{ab})$$

Calculate μ using this equation. If $0 < \mu < 1$, then the segment intersects the plane. Insert μ into the line segment equation to get the intersection.

4.9 Splitting a polygon

When building a BSP tree, you frequently have to split a polygon by a plane. To do that, you calculate the intersections between line segments and the plane, and build two polygons from the vertices of the original polygon and the intersections.

Algorithm outline (see Figure 9):

```
for all source polygon segments p, q
    if the segment pq intersects the plane
        find the intersection s
        put the intersection s in both polygons
    put the end point of the segment (q) in the proper polygon
```

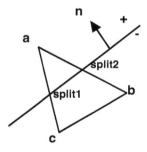

FIGURE 9. A polygon split by a plane

In order to split the polygon in the figure above, the following steps are done:

```
Init:previous := last(inpoly) = c
p=a:Different sides! Split! => find split1
    put split1 on outnegative
    put split1 on outpositive
    put a on outpositive
    previous := a
p = b:Different sides! Split! => find split2
    put split2 on outpositive
    put split2 on outnegative
    put b on outnegative
    previous := b
p = c:Same side!
    put c on outnegative
    previous := c
```

Throughout the algorithm, "previous" is updated to be the previous point, so the current segment is always from previous to p.

The result is that the following polygons (outpositive and outnegative) are built from inpoly:

inpoly	outpositive	outnegative
a	split1	split1
b	a	split2
c	split2	b
		c

Compare the lists to the operations above, to see how outpositive and outnegative are built, vertex by vertex.

4.10 Intersection ray-triangle

The problem of finding the intersection of a line (ray) and a triangle is obviously relevant to ray-casting, but also to collision detection and other problems.

There are several methods to solve this problem. The following is the method I use, which also appears in the literature:

Consider a triangle $\mathbf{a}, \mathbf{b}, \mathbf{c}$. You can calculate the normal vector by taking the cross product of $\mathbf{ab}$ and $\mathbf{ac}$.

Then, find the intersection between the ray and the plane, as done in section 4.8 on page 29. This gives you a μ value for the line equation, and thereby the intersection point $\mathbf{i}$ = (i_x, i_y, i_z). The question is, is this inside the triangle $\mathbf{a}, \mathbf{b}, \mathbf{c}$?

You can express the point $\mathbf{i}$ as a linear combination of $\mathbf{ab}$ and $\mathbf{ac}$! Then, $\mathbf{i} = \mathbf{a} + \mu_1 \cdot \mathbf{ab} + \mu_2 \cdot \mathbf{ac}$. We get three equations, one for every axis, and seek μ_1 and μ_2. This is an over-determined system, due to the demand that $\mathbf{i}$ is in the plane. See Figure 10.

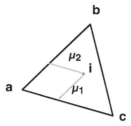

FIGURE 10. Checking if the point i is inside the triangle abc.

Solve this equation system (e.g. by Gaussian elimination)! If the following three conditions are fulfilled, then **i** is in the triangle, and the ray does intersect with the triangle.

$$0 < \mu_1$$

$$0 < \mu_2$$

$$\mu_1 + \mu_2 < 1$$

Each condition defines one side of the triangle. On equality, the ray hits a side of the triangle.

What I used here is called *Barycentric coordinates*. The usual definition of Barycentric coordinates is

$$\mathbf{i} = \alpha\mathbf{a} + \beta\mathbf{b} + \chi\mathbf{c}$$

where $\alpha + \beta + \chi = 1$. You are inside the triangle if

$$\alpha > 0, \beta > 0, \chi > 0$$

This is actually equivalent to the formula above. Since this is the common mathematical definition, let is show that this is the case: Our formula above is the same as

$$\mathbf{i} = \mathbf{a} + \mu_1 \cdot (\mathbf{b}\text{-}\mathbf{a}) + \mu_2 \cdot (\mathbf{c}\text{-}\mathbf{a})$$

which we can rewrite to

$$\mathbf{i} = (1\text{-}\mu_1\text{-}\mu_2)\mathbf{a} + \mu_1\mathbf{b} + \mu_2\mathbf{c}$$

which means that

$$\alpha = 1\text{-}\mu_1\text{-}\mu_2$$

$$\beta = \mu_1$$

$$\chi = \mu_2$$

Same thing! We just used one variable and one condition less. But what about the test for being inside the triangle?

$$\alpha > 0 \Leftrightarrow 1-\mu_1-\mu_2 > 0 \Leftrightarrow \mu_1 + \mu_2 < 1$$

$$\beta > 0 \Leftrightarrow \mu_1 > 0$$

$$\chi > 0 \Leftrightarrow \mu_2 > 0$$

Definitely the same thing! So the test above was indeed using barycentric coordinates, but in a simplified way. Note that this simplification is possible for three points, which is all we need for a triangle, but barycentric coordinates work with any number of points, as well as higher dimensions. As long as the sum of all weights are one and all are positive, we are guaranteed to be in the *convex hull* of the points. This fact will have some importance later, when drawing splines.

4.11 Intersection line-sphere

Finding the intersection between a line and any quadric (see chapter 8) is a matter of inserting the line equation into the equation for the shape. This has some relevance for ray-tracing, and may also be useful when working with quadrics as bounding shapes.

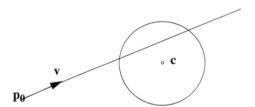

FIGURE 11. Intersection between a line (ray) and a sphere

Take a sphere with center c and radius r as in Figure 11. A point p is on the sphere if

$$|p - c|^2 = r^2$$

With a line expressed as $p = p_0 + \mu v$, you insert the line into the sphere formula and get

$$|p_0 + \mu v - c|^2 = r^2$$

The squared distance can be rewritten as a dot product.

$$(p_0 + \mu v - c) \bullet (p_0 + \mu v - c) = r^2$$

Define $\mathbf{a} = \mathbf{c} - \mathbf{p_0}$ and rewrite to

$$(\mu\mathbf{v} - \mathbf{a})\bullet(\mu\mathbf{v} - \mathbf{a}) = r^2$$

Perform the dot product and we get

$$\mu^2(\mathbf{v}\bullet\mathbf{v}) - 2\mu(\mathbf{a}\bullet\mathbf{v}) + \mathbf{a}\bullet\mathbf{a} = r^2$$

Assume that assume that $|\mathbf{v}| = 1$ and we have

$$\mu^2 - 2\mu(\mathbf{a}\bullet\mathbf{v}) + |\mathbf{a}|^2 - r^2 = 0$$

which is a simple quadratic equation, and we arrive to the solution

$$\mu = a \bullet v \pm \sqrt{(a \bullet v)^2 - |a|^2 + r^2}$$

This gives us two μ values, which gives two points, unless the discriminant is negative, in which case there is no intersection.

4.12 Splitting and mirroring a vector

The task of mirroring a vector is vital in many computer graphics operations, in shading, ray-tracing and other purposes. In Figure 12, similar to the figures we will use in the shading chapter (chapter 7),

$\mathbf{l}$ is the vector towards the light source.

$\mathbf{n}$ is the normal vector of the surface.

$\mathbf{r}$ is the reflection of $\mathbf{l}$ in the surface.

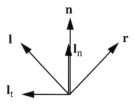

FIGURE 12. Reflection of a vector by projection on the normal vector

Consider two vectors, $\mathbf{l}$ and $\mathbf{n}$. To begin with, we don't assume anything about their lengths. They may be 2D or 3D. How can you find the vectors $\mathbf{l_n}$ (normal component of $\mathbf{l}$) and $\mathbf{l_t}$ (tangent component), as shown in the figure? This is solved using the dot product:

$$\mathbf{l}_n = \mathbf{n}/|\mathbf{n}| \cdot |\mathbf{l}| \cdot \cos\theta = \mathbf{n} \, / \, |\mathbf{n}| \cdot (\mathbf{n} \bullet \mathbf{l}) \, / \, |\mathbf{n}| = \mathbf{n} \cdot (\mathbf{n} \bullet \mathbf{l}) \, / \, |\mathbf{n}|^2$$

$$|\mathbf{n}|^2 = n_x^2 + n_y^2 + n_z^2$$

$$\mathbf{l}_t = \mathbf{l} - \mathbf{l}_n$$

This is the general vector splitting method. Note that we did not need any square root for vector lengths.

If the goal is to calculate the mirroring vector $\mathbf{r}$, that is then done like this (Figure 13):

$$\mathbf{r} = \mathbf{l}_n - \mathbf{l}_t = 2\mathbf{l}_n - \mathbf{l}$$

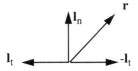

FIGURE 13. Calculating r

But, the normal vector $\mathbf{n}$ is generally given as a unit vector! Then $|\mathbf{n}| = 1$, and $\mathbf{l}_n$ is simplified to:

$$\mathbf{l}_n = \mathbf{n}(\mathbf{n} \bullet \mathbf{l})$$

which gives us the final $\mathbf{r}$:

$$\mathbf{r} = \mathbf{l}_n - \mathbf{l}_t = 2\mathbf{l}_n - \mathbf{l} = 2(\mathbf{n} \bullet \mathbf{l})\mathbf{n} - \mathbf{l}$$

4.13 Decomposing a polygon to triangles

Many 3D algorithms take triangles as input. You may find 3D models where some polygons are not triangles. Then you want to convert your polygons to triangles, decomposing them. For convex polygons, this is a straight-forward operation, illustrated by Figure :

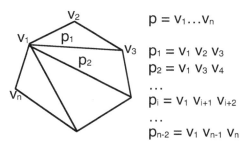

$$p = v_1 \ldots v_n$$

$$p_1 = v_1\ v_2\ v_3$$

$$p_2 = v_1\ v_3\ v_4$$

$$\ldots$$

$$p_i = v_1\ v_{i+1}\ v_{i+2}$$

$$\ldots$$

$$p_{n-2} = v_1\ v_{n-1}\ v_n$$

FIGURE 14. Decomposing a convex polygon to triangles

The algorithm is one of the simplest so far:

```
for i = 1 to n-2 do
    build a polygon from v₁, vᵢ₊₁, vᵢ₊₂
```

Decomposing a non-convex polygon is slightly more complex. One method for dealing with it is the *vector method*. It works as follows:

Step 1: Identify concave polygon parts

Find concave vertices by using the cross product of the vectors between three consecutive vertices, e.g. $(v_3 \text{-} v_2) \times (v_4 \text{-} v_3)$. See Figure 15.

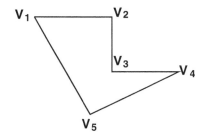

FIGURE 15. A concave polygon to be decomposed

At v_3, the sign of the cross product will differ from the others!

Step 2: Choose a splitting vector and split the polygon.

Use one of the sides near the conflicting vertex as splitting vector, and split along it, shown in Figure 16.

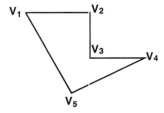

FIGURE 16. The vector methods uses a polygon branch near a concave vertex as splitting vector

Repeat step 1 and 2 until all polygons are convex.

Step 3: If triangles are wanted (rather than any convex polygons), split into triangles with the method at the beginning of this section.

This does not necessarily produce an optimal result. Rather, it will introduce new vertices and result in a higher number of polygons than necessary. In any event, it will eventually produce convex polygons.

5. Two-dimensional transformations

For now, we will forget most drawing primitives, and put our attention to one: drawing shapes from lines or polygons. Our goal is to introduce geometric transformations in 2D, and then expand that to 3D, where it is of extreme importance.

5.1 The need for transformations

Consider a set of points, $\mathbf{p_1}..\mathbf{p_n}$, defining a complex polygon. This polygon can, with a little artistic talent, describe some meaningful, useful shape. For example, by only four points we can make an Asteroids-style spaceship, like Figure 17:

FIGURE 17. An Asteroids-style spaceship can be created by a very simple polygon

Note that I have picked a suitable location for the origin. This is quite important when you start rotating the spaceship.

Handling a small shape like this is not much of a challenge, but consider a more complex case, a polygon which happens to be the picture of a tree. A tree is a complex shape that needs many, hundreds or thousands of segments in order to look good, as in Figure 18.

We now assume that we have a graphics package that can draw lines. We can draw this shape by a simple algorithm, looking somewhat like this:

```
moveTo(p[n])
for i := 1 to n do
    lineTo(p[i])
```

(although we will more likely pass the whole array to a call that renders entire polygons, like the example in chapter 3.7.2).

FIGURE 18. A polygon shaped like a tree requires much detail

Great, we can draw a tree! Now we want to draw a forest!

By translating the set of points in different ways, we can place the tree in many different places. If we can also scale the set of points, we can make trees of different size, creating an illusion of depth. And finally, if we can also rotate the set of points, we can create trees that are not straight and that are even laying down (in case there has been a storm recently). This is not all we need to create a really pretty-looking forest, but it is a start.

So, we need three transformations, translation, scaling and rotation. Each of these transformations can be defined as follows:

Translation is so trivial:

$$\mathbf{p'} = \mathbf{p} + \mathbf{v} = (p_x, p_y) + (v_x, v_y) = (p_x + v_x, p_y + v_y)$$

A simple vector addition. Scaling is equally simple:

$$\mathbf{p'} = s \cdot \mathbf{p} = s\,(p_x, p_y) = (s \cdot p_x, s \cdot p_y)$$

Rotation is the most complex of these three:

$$\mathbf{p'} = R(\mathbf{p}, \phi) = (p_x \cdot \cos(\phi) - p_y \cdot \sin(\phi)\,, p_x \cdot \sin(\phi) + p_y \cdot \cos(\phi))$$

These are all rigid body transformations. The tree-shaped polygon described by $p_1..p_n$ will translate, scale and rotate but always keep the same shape. With those tools, we can assign a few suitable transformation for each tree, and easily draw a forest like in Figure 19.

Two-dimensional transformations

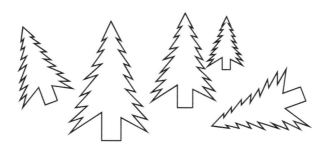

FIGURE 19. Making a forest by transforming a single tree shape

There are a few issues that I ignore here, like filling rather than framing, and most of all making sure that the frontmost is drawn on the top. We will return to that in later chapters.

Now let's note one detail. The rotation is nicely represented by a matrix:

$$\boldsymbol{p}' \;=\; R(\phi)\cdot\boldsymbol{p},\, R(\phi) = \begin{bmatrix} \cos\varphi & -\sin\varphi \\ \sin\varphi & \cos\varphi \end{bmatrix}$$

This matrix reveals a possibility for combining operations. If we can write the others as matrices, the problem of transforming the shape changes dramatically. Let's write scaling as a matrix:

$$\boldsymbol{p}' \;=\; S(s)\cdot\boldsymbol{p},\, S(s) = \begin{bmatrix} s & 0 \\ 0 & s \end{bmatrix}$$

That's a silly matrix, but it will make sense soon. We have matrix representations for two out of three. But how about translation? That is one of the most commonly needed transformations you can think of. It is *impossible* to make an addition by a multiplication!

Sort of. Hang on...

5.2 Homogeneous coordinates

Adding by multiplication is indeed possible, by extending our coordinate system to what is called *homogeneous coordinates*. Simply put, what we do is to add one extra coordinate, a "fake" coordinate which does not represent any spatial degree of freedom. This extra coordinate is defined like this:

A point in homogeneous coordinates for 2D space consists of three coordinates, the spatial coordinates X and Y, plus the third, the homogeneous coordinate H:

$$\mathbf{p_h} = (x_h, y_h, h)$$

where $p_x = x_h/h$ and $p_y = y_h/h$. This definition seems meaningless for the moment. For now, let us consider the case h=1. Then, $p_x = x_h$ and $p_y = y_h$ and all that has happened is that we add a constant 1 to the end of the vector, which becomes $\mathbf{p} = (p_x, p_y, 1)$.

So, all vectors for 2D space are now three-component vectors. Consequently, matrices need to be 3x3. I claim that I can perform a translation by multiplying a vector by a matrix in this system. This is how it works:

$$\mathbf{p'} = T(v_x, v_y) \cdot \mathbf{p} = \begin{bmatrix} 1 & 0 & v_x \\ 0 & 1 & v_y \\ 0 & 0 & 1 \end{bmatrix} \cdot \begin{bmatrix} p_x \\ p_y \\ 1 \end{bmatrix} = \begin{bmatrix} p_x + v_x \\ p_y + v_y \\ 1 \end{bmatrix}$$

If we measure performance by multiplications, this only makes matters worse, it costs multiplications for something that only used to need additions, but it will still come for free for models with large number of points.

To make this compatible with rotation and scaling, we must adapt the latter to 3x3 matrices. Rotation becomes:

$$R(\varphi) = \begin{bmatrix} \cos\varphi & -\sin\varphi & 0 \\ \sin\varphi & \cos\varphi & 0 \\ 0 & 0 & 1 \end{bmatrix}$$

and scaling, here extended to separate values for x and y, becomes:

$$S(s_x, s_y) = \begin{bmatrix} s_x & 0 & 0 \\ 0 & s_y & 0 \\ 0 & 0 & 1 \end{bmatrix}$$

5.3 Composite transformations

Right, now we have everything represented as 3x3 matrices. This means that we can scale and rotate the points by

$$\mathbf{p'} = R(\phi) \cdot S(s) \cdot \mathbf{p}$$

So we can take each point, multiply by S, and then multiply by R.

$$\mathbf{p'} = R(\phi) \cdot (S(s) \cdot \mathbf{p})$$

OK, but since matrix multiplication is associative, we can just as well multiply the two matrices together first, once and for all, and then multiply the resulting matrix R·S to each and every point in the shape!

$$\mathbf{p'} = (R(\phi) \cdot S(s)) \cdot \mathbf{p}$$

Is this important? One important point is that it gives us a compact representation, but it is also a performance booster. Let us look at the 2x2 matrix case, where we use matrices for rotation and scaling. Each matrix to vector multiplication costs four multiplications. Each matrix to matrix multiplication costs eight multiplications. The scaling, applied without matrix, costs only two multiplications.

So for a single point, the transformation costs $2 + 4 = 6$ multiplications without matrices, and $8 + 4 = 12$ multiplications with matrices, a clear loss. With a large number of points, say N, the first case will scale linearly to 6N, while for the latter you do a single matrix multiplication for 8 multiplications, and then one vector-to-matrix multiplication for each point, ending up at $8 + 4N$, which will be a better choice already for N>4! And that was for only two transformations! When you need more - and you will - then each added transformation is practically for free. In 3D the problem grows by, literally, an order of magnitude.

When making composite transformations, the rules for matrix multiplications must be kept in mind. Matrix multiplication is associative, but not commutative! You can not expect that $A \cdot B = B \cdot A$! It can be true for special cases, but generally it is incorrect. As a practical example, consider the translation and scaling of a tree (Figure 20):

The tree is translated by the vector t, and scaled uniformly by 2. If the transformations are applied as $T(t) \cdot S(2) \cdot \mathbf{p}$, then the scaling is applied first, then the translation, and the result is the tree in the middle of Figure 20. If, on the other hand, you apply $S(2) \cdot T(t) \cdot \mathbf{p}$, then you get the rightmost tree, where the translation itself has been scaled to double! You can get similar effects when combining with rotation.

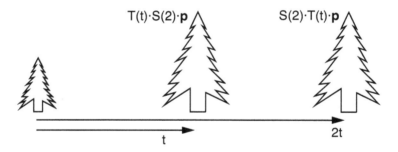

FIGURE 20. Different results depending on the order of transformations

5.4 Inverse transformations

Since all these transformations are represented as matrices and applied by matrix multiplication, it is possible to negate them, to apply the inverse transformation, by multiplying by the inverse of the matrix. However, finding the inverse does not always have to be done by finding the inverse the general way. For all the three transformations that we have worked with, there are intuitive inverses that you can find from the definition.

The inverse of translation is simply to translate in the opposite direction, by negating the translation vector:

$$T^{-1}(t_x, t_y) = T(-t_x, -t_y) = \begin{bmatrix} 1 & 0 & -t_x \\ 0 & 1 & -t_y \\ 0 & 0 & 1 \end{bmatrix}$$

The inverse of scaling by s is to scale by 1/s:

$$S^{-1}(s_x, s_y) = S\left(\frac{1}{s_x}, \frac{1}{s_y}\right) = \begin{bmatrix} \dfrac{1}{s_x} & 0 & 0 \\ 0 & \dfrac{1}{s_y} & 0 \\ 0 & 0 & 1 \end{bmatrix}$$

The inverse of rotation is obviously to rotate in the opposite direction. However, we should note something important here: cos(-ϕ) = cos(ϕ), so only the sin(ϕ) changes sign. If you look at the rotation matrix, the cos(f) is on the diagonal of the matrix, and the sin(ϕ) are on opposing places. Thus, inverting the rotation matrix is equivalent to transposing it, flipping it over the diagonal:

$$R^{-1}(\varphi) = R(-\varphi) = \begin{bmatrix} \cos-\varphi & -\sin-\varphi & 0 \\ \sin-\varphi & \cos-\varphi & 0 \\ 0 & 0 & 1 \end{bmatrix} = \begin{bmatrix} \cos\varphi & \sin\varphi & 0 \\ -\sin\varphi & \cos\varphi & 0 \\ 0 & 0 & 1 \end{bmatrix} = R^T(\varphi)$$

This property comes from the fact that a rotation matrix is actually an *orthonormal basis*; its rows, as well as columns, form a set of basis vectors that are orthogonal and have unit length. Any such matrix can be inverted by transposing it! That means that even combinations of several rotations around different axes can be inverted that way. We will take advantage of this property when doing rotation around an arbitrary axis in 3D. But first, let us do that very thing in 2D.

5.5 2D rotation around arbitrary point

Let us continue with composite transformations. Take this case: You have a shape placed somewhere in 2D space (the space ship, but not centered on origin for whatever reason), as in Figure 21. Now, we want to rotate the ship around a chosen point, which is in this example where the origin should have been. Let us call that point of rotation **p**. Note that this point itself is not being transformed, by the points forming the shape, that is the vertices of the polygon.

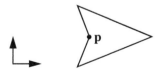

FIGURE 21. Spaceship model to be rotated around an arbitrary point p

Two-dimensional transformations

This is fairly easy to do with composite transformations. The first thing we do is to apply a translation, which moves the model from being around **p** to be around origin, using the center of rotation as a vector, but negated, that is T(-**p**). This translation may seem like something we really don't want to do, but wait, we will put it back at the end. (Figure 22.)

FIGURE 22. After translation to origin

Now the model is located around the origin. Apply the desired rotation, R(ϕ)! Then we get Figure 23:

FIGURE 23. Rotated shape

Finally, apply the inverse of the first translation, T(**p**). The model ends up around the original point, but rotated, Figure 24.

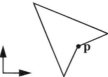

FIGURE 24. Final result

And you do not have to make each transformation one by one to your model. You can multiply them all together and get the entire rotation as one single, composite transformation!

$$T(\mathbf{p}) \cdot R(\phi) \cdot T(-\mathbf{p})$$

Note the order. The first transformation is to the right. Transformations are read right to left – backwards. This is another example of the "backwards" rule, and not the last one.

5.6 More 2D transformations

One more thing... There are other transformations that we can apply by matrices like the ones above. I will add two more: Mirroring and shearing.

Mirroring will negate one coordinate axis, flipping the model over that axis. This is a simple operation, but extremely useful. The matrix in Figure 25 performs mirroring along X, that is over the Y axis.

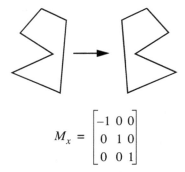

$$M_x = \begin{bmatrix} -1 & 0 & 0 \\ 0 & 1 & 0 \\ 0 & 0 & 1 \end{bmatrix}$$

FIGURE 25. Mirroring along the X axis

Shearing (Figure 26) will deform an object like when a deck of cards goes from being a straight pile to a slanted one. This is not as obviously useful as the other transformations, but it has its uses. For example, simple deformations can be made by shearing. As a commercial example, the game Weekend Warrior (by Pangea Software) uses shearing for the ghosts. It is a cheap effect, for better or worse. Somewhat cheap-looking, but cheap to implement too!

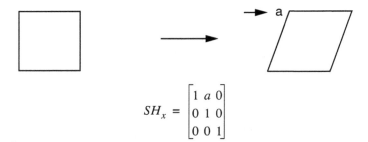

$$SH_x = \begin{bmatrix} 1 & a & 0 \\ 0 & 1 & 0 \\ 0 & 0 & 1 \end{bmatrix}$$

FIGURE 26. Shearing along the X axis

In this chapter you have read about how to perform transformations in 2D, but it is mostly theoretical so far. In chapter 6, you will see that when moving to the three dimensions and practical APIs, we will find the same concepts, and then we also do it with OpenGL.

Two-dimensional transformations

6. Three-dimensional transformations

In the chapter 5, we saw that transformations are important tools for graphics, and they are nicely represented as matrices. In this chapter, we will take these experiences with us into 3 dimensions. We will, however, not stop there. In 3D, we have much bigger need for transformations, and there is a whole chain of transformations for rendering a 3D model in a 3D environment. In particular, the problem of performing perspective projection will be covered here.

6.1 Transformations in 3D

Most of the 2D transformations trivially scale to 3D simply by adding the Z coordinate. Here are the most important ones, translation and scaling:

$$T(t_x, t_y, t_z) = \begin{bmatrix} 1 & 0 & 0 & t_x \\ 0 & 1 & 0 & t_y \\ 0 & 0 & 1 & t_z \\ 0 & 0 & 0 & 1 \end{bmatrix}$$

$$S(s_x, s_y, s_z) = \begin{bmatrix} s_x & 0 & 0 & 0 \\ 0 & s_y & 0 & 0 \\ 0 & 0 & s_z & 0 \\ 0 & 0 & 0 & 1 \end{bmatrix}$$

The rotation, however, becomes no less than three, and still they are less general than one was in 2D. The three matrices are for rotation around each axis, X, Y or Z:

$$R_x(\varphi) = \begin{bmatrix} 1 & 0 & 0 & 0 \\ 0 & \cos\varphi & -\sin\varphi & 0 \\ 0 & \sin\varphi & \cos\varphi & 0 \\ 0 & 0 & 0 & 1 \end{bmatrix}$$

$$R_y(\varphi) = \begin{bmatrix} \cos\varphi & 0 & \sin\varphi & 0 \\ 0 & 1 & 0 & 0 \\ -\sin\varphi & 0 & \cos\varphi & 0 \\ 0 & 0 & 0 & 1 \end{bmatrix}$$

$$R_z(\varphi) = \begin{bmatrix} \cos\varphi & -\sin\varphi & 0 & 0 \\ \sin\varphi & \cos\varphi & 0 & 0 \\ 0 & 0 & 1 & 0 \\ 0 & 0 & 0 & 1 \end{bmatrix}$$

Maybe you think that the rotation around the Y axis looks wrong? X and Z both has a minus in the top-right sin while Y has it in bottom-left. Well, it is not as inconsistent as it may seem. Look at how the non-zero elements shift when you move from Z to X. They shift diagonally. Where do they go as you move from X to Y? They wrap around, that is what happens. So the sin with the minus sign goes down-right, wraps around the left edge of the 3x3 part of the matrix, and ends up on the left side.

Finally, shearing and mirroring are equally simple to expand, although specific for an axis just like rotation:

$$Sh_z(sh_x, sh_y) = \begin{bmatrix} 1 & 0 & sh_x & 0 \\ 0 & 1 & sh_y & 0 \\ 0 & 0 & 1 & 0 \\ 0 & 0 & 0 & 1 \end{bmatrix} \qquad M_x = \begin{bmatrix} -1 & 0 & 0 & 0 \\ 0 & 1 & 0 & 0 \\ 0 & 0 & 1 & 0 \\ 0 & 0 & 0 & 1 \end{bmatrix}$$

Shearing and mirroring over other axes than shown should be obvious.

6.2 Rotation in OpenGL

In OpenGL, you can perform these transformations by creating a matrix like the ones described above, and upload it to a shader program. Building on the simple example from chapter 3.7.2, we add some code as follows:

We can hard code a matrix like this:

```
GLfloat rotationMatrix[] = {0.7f, -0.7f, 0.0f, 0.0f,
                            0.7f, 0.7f, 0.0f, 0.0f,
```

```
                0.0f, 0.0f, 1.0f, 0.0f,
                0.0f, 0.0f, 0.0f, 1.0f };
```

(What does this matrix do?) We can pass this matrix to a shader program with

```
glUniformMatrix4fv(glGetUniformLocation(program, "myMatrix"), 1,
GL_TRUE, rotationMatrix);
```

The second parameter states that it is one single matrix (not an array of several), and the third is a transposing flag. Be careful with that; if you enter matrices as above, it should be GL_TRUE, but that is not true for all math libraries.

The same matrix is applied to all vertices. When this is what we want, we use a so called *uniform* variable (uniform for all vertices), while we were using *attribute arrays* (individual attributes for each vertex) in the example in chapter 3.7.2. We will soon discuss these shader language details some more.

Then you can apply it to your vertices in the vertex shader by matrix multiplication, so the full vertex shader now looks like this:

```
#version 150

in  vec3 in_Position;
uniform mat4 myMatrix;

void main(void)
{
    gl_Position = myMatrix * vec4(in_Position, 1.0);
}
```

When inserted into the previous example from chapter 3.7.2, this results in a rotated triangle like in Figure 27.

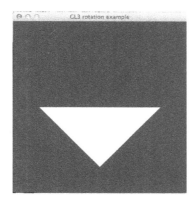

FIGURE 27. The example triangle rotated by a rotation matrix.

This is pretty straight-forward, but of course you would rarely hard-code matrices in a real program. You rather build them with a math library.

Rotating around a totally arbitrary axis is the subject for the next section, chapter 6.3.

6.3 Rotation around arbitrary axis

In 2D, rotation around an arbitrary point was a pretty easy thing to do. The problem was mainly interesting for the elegant use of composite transformations, not for being complicated.

In 3D, the same method can be used for rotating around any of the basis vectors X, Y or Z. But rotating around any given axis is significantly harder. As a matter of fact, I will present no less than two ways to do it:

- The geometrical method
- The change of basis method

Out of these, the former is easiest to understand if you have trouble with algebra, and the latter is a lot easier if you are comfortable with doing a change of basis.

Let us assume that the axis around which we want to perform rotation is given as two points, p_1 and p_2. Any way you do it, the algorithm structure is the same:

1) Translate the axis to pass through the origin. $T(-p_1)$

2) Rotate to align the axis with any of the basis axes. $R(?)$

3) Rotate around the axis $R_?(\phi)$

4) Inverse of 2) $R^{-1}(?) = R^T(?)$

5) Inverse of 1) $T^{-1}(-p_1) = T(p)$

The big problem is how to find step 2!

6.3.1 Geometrical method

This method is, compared to the method that follows later, somewhat awkward in that it requires more steps. On the other hand, it is easy to understand if you are not comfortable with a change of basis, and in particular we will see some elegant uses of dot and cross products to create rotation matrices.

First, let us form a unit vector for the direction of the axis.

$$ u = \frac{p_2 - p_1}{|p_2 - p_1|} = (u_x, u_y, u_z) $$

We project this vector onto the YZ plane (Figure 28) by setting its X component to zero.

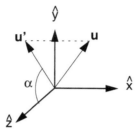

$$u' = (0, u_y, u_z)$$

FIGURE 28. u' is the projection onto the YZ plane

Thus, we get a help vector that has the same angle around the X axis, as in Figure 29. With it, we can find a rotation matrix that rotates the axis to a better place, that is the XZ plane.

From the dot and cross products we get

$$\cos\alpha = \frac{u' \bullet \hat{z}}{|u'| \cdot |\hat{z}|} = \frac{u_z}{\sqrt{u_y^2 + u_z^2}}$$

Define the constant d as

$$d = \sqrt{u_y^2 + u_z^2}$$

and we get

$$\cos\alpha = \frac{u_z}{d}$$

Continue with the cross product:

$$u' \times \hat{z} = (u_y, 0, 0) = \hat{x} \cdot |u'| \cdot |z'| \cdot \sin\alpha \Rightarrow \sin\alpha = \frac{u_y}{d}$$

With sin and cos of the same angle, we can form a rotation matrix:

$$R_x = \begin{bmatrix} 1 & 0 & 0 & 0 \\ 0 & \cos\alpha & -\sin\alpha & 0 \\ 0 & \sin\alpha & \cos\alpha & 0 \\ 0 & 0 & 0 & 1 \end{bmatrix} = \begin{bmatrix} 1 & 0 & 0 & 0 \\ 0 & \dfrac{u_z}{d} & -\dfrac{u_y}{d} & 0 \\ 0 & \dfrac{u_y}{d} & \dfrac{u_z}{d} & 0 \\ 0 & 0 & 0 & 1 \end{bmatrix}$$

and we did not even have to know the angle!

Three-dimensional transformations

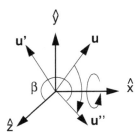

FIGURE 29. The vector u is rotated down onto the XY plane.

After that rotation, we know that the rotation axis must end up as

$$\mathbf{u}" = (u_x, 0, d)$$

that is, the X component is unchanged, while the Y component must be zero since it ends up in the XZ plane. Thus, the new Z component must have the length d!

The next step is to rotate around the Y axis, so that the rotation axis ends up along the Z axis. Since we have $\mathbf{u}"$, we can, again, find the sin and cos for the angle b (the angle between $\mathbf{u}"$ and the Z axis) by dot and cross products!

Dot product:

$$\cos\beta = \mathbf{u}" \cdot \hat{z} = d$$

Cross product:

$$\mathbf{u}" \times \hat{z} = (0, -u_x, 0) \Rightarrow \sin\beta = -u_x$$

That gives us a second rotation matrix:

$$R_y = \begin{bmatrix} \cos\beta & 0 & \sin\beta & 0 \\ 0 & 1 & 0 & 0 \\ -\sin\beta & 0 & \cos\beta & 0 \\ 0 & 0 & 0 & 1 \end{bmatrix} = \begin{bmatrix} d & 0 & -u_x & 0 \\ 0 & 1 & 0 & 0 \\ u_x & 0 & d & 0 \\ 0 & 0 & 0 & 1 \end{bmatrix}$$

So, step 2 above is $R_y R_x$, using these matrices, step 3 is a rotation around Z as specified, $R_z(\phi)$, and step 4 is the inverse of step 2, $R_x^{-1} R_y^{-1}$. This gives us a total solution in the form of a multiplication sequence of transformation matrices (replacing inverse of matrices by transposition):

$$T(\mathbf{p_1}) \cdot R_x^T \cdot R_y^T \cdot R_z(\phi) \cdot R_y \cdot R_x \cdot T(-\mathbf{p_1})$$

Three-dimensional transformations

And again, the order of multiplications is... did I tell you before? Backwards, yes.

Did you find this method a bit awkward? Finding rotation matrices from dot and cross products is pretty elegant, but it requires two such steps. Let us try another approach.

6.3.2 Change of basis method

Since a rotation is nothing but a change of basis anyway, performing it as such is straight-forward if you can only find the complete orthonormal basis defined in the current one.

To begin with, step 1 is the same as before, $T(-\mathbf{p_1})$. We also use the same u as before. The vector $\mathbf{u}$ will be our z axis, let us say that z' = $\mathbf{u}$. Now we need to find the x and y axes.

Let us assume that $\mathbf{u}$ is not parallel to the x axis. This is a special case that is easy to check for. Then we can find an up vector by the cross product:

$$y' = \frac{\mathbf{u} \times \hat{x}}{|\mathbf{u} \times \hat{x}|}$$

Finally, the side vector x' is found by another cross product:

$$x' = y' \times z'$$

The rotation matrix can now be assembled from these vectors as

$$R = \begin{bmatrix} x'_x & x'_y & x'_z & 0 \\ y'_x & y'_y & y'_z & 0 \\ z'_x & z'_y & z'_z & 0 \\ 0 & 0 & 0 & 1 \end{bmatrix}$$

And the total solution is the rather simple

$$T(\mathbf{p_1}) \cdot R^T \cdot R_z(\phi) \cdot R \cdot T(-\mathbf{p_1})$$

Now let me stress that this kind of operations is not a theoretical thing but something that you often do in practice.

Rotating around a specific point as above is easiest to do with some matrix multiplications on the CPU. This requires that we have some algebra package available. In languages like C++ or FPC, it comes natural to use operator overloading for vectors and matrices. For plain C, you need to use functions, which is more verbose but does the same thing.

In our algebra package VectorUtils3, we have the following functions:

ArbRotate(a, v) creates a rotation matrix for rotation by a around the vector **v**. (That is, implementing either of the two rotation methods above, usually a change of basis.)

T(v.x, v.y, v.z) creates a translation matris m for translation by the vector **v**.

Then the code could look like this, using C:

```
m = Mult(Mult(T(p.x, p.y, p.z), ArbRotate(a, v)), T(-p.x, -p.y, -p.z));
glUniformMatrix4fv(glGetUniformLocation(program, "myMatrix"), 1, GL_TRUE, m.m);
```

In C++ we use operator overloading to make it look slightly nicer but the difference is marginal:

```
m = T(p.x, p.y, p.z) * ArbRotate(a, v) * T(-p.x, -p.y, -p.z)
glUniformMatrix4fv(glGetUniformLocation(program, "myMatrix"), 1, GL_TRUE, m.m);
```

This method of transforming to one place, performing a transformation and then transform back can be used for other operations too, like mirroring. In that case, you translate and rotate the mirror to origin, aligned with proper axes, mirror over the suitable axis, and rotate and translate back again. All drawing done after that transformation will be mirrored. There is more to that problem, since objects behind the mirror will jump in front and objects beside the mirror will be mirrored in the wall beside it, if you don't take suitable measures to avoid such problems. Still, the fundamental operation is as above, move to the proper place, transform, move back.

6.4 3D viewing

In 2D, the problem of viewing was ignored since it is mostly trivial there. In 3D, we need to pay more attention to the problem.

We wish to render a 3D model in a scene. We have the model defined in its own, local coordinate system, the *model coordinates*. Its placement into the world must be defined, and moves it to *world coordinates*. But that is not all. The camera must be placed. But moving the camera in the world is actually not meaningful from a rendering perspective. Instead of moving the camera to the object that we wish to view, the object is moved in front to the camera. Or rather, the entire world is moved to the camera. This may seem backwards, but what did I say about computer graphics and backwards?

If Mohammed won't come to the mountain, the mountain must come to Mohammed!

That's CG in a nutshell!

Moving, transforming, from world coordinates to get in front of the camera brings us to *viewing coordinates*. Up to this point, it can all be done by the transformations described earlier, in particular translation and rotation. The next step is to get the data into the camera, to project the model to the image. That requires a new transformation, projection, that is the subject of the next section.

After the projection, we have X and Y projected to a 2D plane, and a Z value that will make sense later. Two rather simple steps remain: Normalization and device transformation. The normalization scales the projected coordinates to a cube with dimensions ±1 in all directions. The device transformation scales it to fit the physical size of the destination (the view port).

Three-dimensional transformations

In the Figure 30, the transformations are given right to left, since it will put the multiplications in the proper order, and we want it backwards anyway, don't we?

It should be noted that the transformation chain also contains a perspective division step.

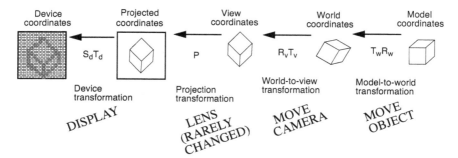

FIGURE 30. The transformation chain

So, when managing a 3D scene, you change the model-to-world transformation to move objects, the world-to-view transformation to move the camera (but you must transform *backwards*, since you really move the world and not the camera). The last two steps are usually set up once and for all and never changed. If you need to change the camera lens setting, like zooming, you do that by changing the projection transformation. Finally, if you want to change the viewport, typically since the user resizes the output window, you change the device transformation.

In OpenGL, all this information should be stored in matrices of your design, applied in your vertex shader as in the examples in chapter 6.2 and chapter 6.3. You may choose to keep projection (the camera lens) as well as world-to-view (camera placement) in global matrices, onto which you append a matrix for placing your model in the world. In classic OpenGL, this was done with two internal matrices, the *projection matrix* and the *model-view matrix*, where the latter was both model-to-world and world-to-view. Why? Because "world coordinates" doesn't exist from OpenGL's perspective.

6.5 Camera placement

A common way to set the world-to-camera transform is to set it so that the camera is placed in a specific place and looking in a specific direction. There even was an OpenGL call for that in the past, gluLookAt, now obsolete but well worth re-implementing. In this section, we will have a look at how such a call works.

The syntax for gluLookAt is gluLookAt($\mathbf{p}, \mathbf{l}, \mathbf{v}$), where $\mathbf{p}$ is the camera position in world coordinates, $\mathbf{l}$ is the point which the camera should "look at", and $\mathbf{v}$ is the up-vector. Let us pretend that we are implementing that call.

First, we form the vector $\mathbf{n} = \mathbf{p} - \mathbf{l}$, a vector pointing *backwards*, from the point $\mathbf{l}$ to the camera. The vectors $\mathbf{n}$ and $\mathbf{v}$ form an incomplete and non-orthonormal basis from which we can create an orthonormal basis. It should be noted that **v** is not required to be orthogonal to **n**. We normalize **n**:

$$\hat{n} = \frac{n}{|n|}$$

We can now get a vector pointing to the right with the cross product:

$$\hat{u} = \frac{v \times \hat{n}}{|v \times \hat{n}|}$$

Finally, we get the last vector in the basis by yet another cross product.

$$\hat{v} = \hat{n} \times \hat{u}$$

Now the vectors **u**, **v**, **n** are a complete orthonormal basis, usable as rotation matrix.

$$R = \begin{bmatrix} u_x & u_y & u_z & 0 \\ v_x & v_y & v_z & 0 \\ n_x & n_y & n_z & 0 \\ 0 & 0 & 0 & 1 \end{bmatrix}$$

Does it feel strange to form a rotation matrix by piling up three vectors like that? But what is a rotation matrix, but a change of basis? In this case, we specify the *new* basis in the *old* one, so the vectors are horizontal.

There's one more thing that we need to complete the gluLookAt function: the translation part. The camera should move to the point **p**, but, as stated before, since Mohammed (the camera) won't come to the mountain (the world coordinates)... we must translate in the reverse direction. Thus, we should translate by T(-**p**).

Finally, in what order should these matrices be applied? If they are applied as R·T, then the translation will be rotated. So it should be T·R...? No, since this is a camera positioning, you will translate and rotate the world, and then the translation really should be rotated. So the resulting world-to-view transform is

$$R \cdot T = \begin{bmatrix} u_x & u_y & u_z & 0 \\ v_x & v_y & v_z & 0 \\ n_x & n_y & n_z & 0 \\ 0 & 0 & 0 & 1 \end{bmatrix} \cdot \begin{bmatrix} 1 & 0 & 0 & -p_x \\ 0 & 1 & 0 & -p_y \\ 0 & 0 & 1 & -p_z \\ 0 & 0 & 0 & 1 \end{bmatrix} = \begin{bmatrix} u_x & u_y & u_z & -u \bullet p \\ v_x & v_y & v_z & -v \bullet p \\ n_x & n_y & n_z & -n \bullet p \\ 0 & 0 & 0 & 1 \end{bmatrix}$$

And as a little bonus, note that the matrix multiplication resulted in three dot products!

This is far from the only way you can aim the camera. You can, for example wish to rotate or translate the camera relative to its current position (e.g. when controlling an aircraft or a car). Then you don't care so much what it is looking at, you want to modify the world-to-view transform to do things like moving forward a certain distance, rotating a certain angle to the left etc. This can be done in a few different ways. One way is to keep a set of variables in your application, specifying position and orientation, and set the camera position according to these. Another method can be to work directly on the world-to-view matrix! From the matrix, you can directly read out things like the forward vector (as **-n** from the matrix above) or the position (p above, which requires an inverse rotation) or transforming it by matrix multiplication. The matrix representation is really quite powerful, not only for transforming but also for storing the information.

Now we know how to place the camera. The next step is to go into the camera and build the lens, the projection.

6.6 Projection

In order to project the scene onto an image plane, we need a camera model that describes how the light in the scene travels into the camera and arrives to a virtual image sensor.

There are a few ways to project the 3D data, but we rarely need to bother with more than one or at most two models. The simplest projection you can use is *parallel projection*, where size is unaffected by distance, and the projection operation simply uses x and y while z is discarded. There is also *oblique projection*, which is parallel projection plus shearing, which is popular with architects, but has little use for realistic animation.

What we are likely to use more or less all the time is, however, *perspective projection*, where size varies with distance.

The camera model that we use is a so called *pinhole camera*. That is a camera where the light arrives through an infinitesimally small hole. Figure 31 shows how we can envision this camera, as similar to a real camera as possible.

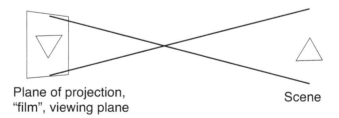

Plane of projection, "film", viewing plane

Scene

FIGURE 31. Intuitive camera model

A drawback with the pinhole camera, when applied strictly, is that it has infinite depth of field. In image analysis, a short depth of field can be a drawback. In image synthesis, however, a short depth of field is a highly desirable effect that is rather costly to achieve. We will return to that later (briefly, in chapter 17, and in more depth in part 2).

With this geometry, we get a first draft for the projection as in Figure 32.

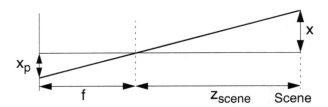

FIGURE 32. Projection geometry of a physical camera

In the figure, a distance in the scene, x, is projected to x_p. Simple geometry gives us:

$$\frac{x_p}{f} = \frac{x}{z_{scene}} \Leftrightarrow x_p = x \cdot \frac{f}{z_{scene}}$$

So perspective projection is essentially a division by z_{scene}. But let us look at this with more detail. Unlike above, we need a well-defined coordinate system, and we need a way to form a matrix that performs the projection.

While a real camera has the lens in the middle, the scene on one side and the sensor on the other, we will choose to place the lens in the origin, and the image plane, the sensor, as well as the scene, on the *negative* side of the XY plane, in negative Z. (Backwards!)

The origin, the lens, is the *projection reference point*, prp for short, and the *viewing plane*, vp for short, are illustrated in the Figure 33.

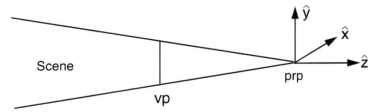

FIGURE 33. The camera model, with optical center prp and viewing plane vp

The *focal distance* is the distance between **prp** and vp, so if we use the symbols z_{prp} and z_{vp} as the Z component of their positions, knowing that X and Y components are zero, we get the focal distance

$$f = z_{prp} - z_{vp}$$

and since **prp** is usually in the origin that means that

$$f = -z_{vp}$$

So let us take a single point in the view, $\mathbf{a} = (x, y, z)$, and project it onto the viewing plane. It will be projected to the point $\mathbf{p} = (x_p, y_p, z_p)$, where $z_p = z_{vp}$.

Back to the geometry, and convert the informal distance to better values.

$$x_p = x \cdot \frac{f}{z_{scene}} = x \cdot \frac{f}{z_{prp} - z}$$

and similarly for y_p.

Now we need to put this in a matrix. Earlier, we noted that addition can not be done by multiplication, and then we did it anyway, using homogeneous coordinates. It turns out that we can use homogeneous coordinates to do division, too! Instead of deriving the matrix, I will suggest a preliminary draft for a projection matrix and show that it performs the proper task.

$$\begin{bmatrix} x_h \\ y_h \\ z_h \\ h \end{bmatrix} = \begin{bmatrix} f & 0 & 0 & 0 \\ 0 & f & 0 & 0 \\ 0 & 0 & -z_{vp} & z_{vp}z_{prp} \\ 0 & 0 & -1 & z_{prp} \end{bmatrix} \begin{bmatrix} x \\ y \\ z \\ 1 \end{bmatrix}$$

The -1 in the third column is what does the magic, the division. The homogeneous coordinate value h is no longer 1, so we must make a final step to get the projected coordinate.

$$x_h = f \cdot x$$

$$y_h = f \cdot y$$

$$z_h = -z \cdot z_{vp} + z_{vp}z_{prp}$$

$$h = z_{prp} - z$$

and according to the definition of homogeneous coordinates, that means

$$x_p = \frac{x_h}{h} = x \cdot \frac{f}{z_{prp} - z}$$

$$y_p = \frac{y_h}{h} = y \cdot \frac{f}{z_{prp} - z}$$

$$z_p = \frac{z_h}{h} = \frac{z_{vp} \cdot (z_{prp} - z)}{z_{prp} - z} = z_{vp} \cdot \frac{h}{h} = z_{vp}$$

which is exactly what we wanted! So now you know why the homogeneous coordinates had that division by h. It makes it possible to represent a division with a matrix, and we can do that with minimal performance penalty since it is only performed at the end, after an arbitrary number of transformations.

We are not quite done yet, though. The matrix above performs a perfectly fine transformation, but there are a few more things that we need to consider.

6.7 The viewing frustum

Since our view is limited by the edges of the viewport, we look into a sharply limited sub-section of space. On top of that, we must limit the viewing distance for reasons I will return to soon. All in all, the viewport, the distance limitations and the focal distance together define a six-sided polyhedron which contains all visible points, and is called the *viewing frustum* or *view volume*.

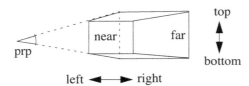

FIGURE 34. The viewing frustum

The frustum is conveniently defined by six scalars, left, right, top, bottom, near and far, as in Figure 34. All but the far value refers to the *near plane*, the side closest to the camera. Thus, top and bottom define the height of the near plane, left and right its width, and the near value tells how far it is from the camera, the prp. Finally, the far value tells the distance from prp to the far plane, and if we need the limits of that we can get them by projecting the near plane.

So, left, right, top and bottom are given by the fact that we must have limitations on the screen or window where the image is displayed, but how about near and far?

A practical reason to have near and far distances is that a maximum distance limits the amount of geometry that needs to be processed, and we must have a near value that is no less than zero, or geometry behind the camera will be displayed. Objects on distance zero are of little use too, and will cause divisions by zero when projecting them. But the real reason is that the rendering also includes distance information for determining which object to draw frontmost (by the so called Z-buffer method), and that information can not have infinite precision. I will return to that in chapter 12.

In OpenGL, you can specify the viewing frustum, and thereby the projection, with a matrix uploaded to the vertex shader as before. Note, however, that this needs to be in normalized coordinates, see below.

Three-dimensional transformations

6.8 Normalized coordinates

There is yet another coordinate system, but I choose to eventually make that a part of projection. Before going to device coordinates, we must have control over the range that the projected x and y values can have, or the device transformation will be hard to define. *Normalized coordinates* are projected coordinates that are scaled to fit in a cube from -1 to 1 along all coordinates.

To achieve this, we must modify the projection matrix to rescale properly. At this point, we will also drop the z row, which only mapped z to z_{vp}, and replace it with a row that will let us keep a z value, again for the visible surface detection. All we need to know now is that we do not want to flatten the z value, but keep some function of z for future needs.

Let us start with the scaling. The focal distance f = near. The point (left, bottom, -near) should be mapped to (-1, -1, -1). To do that scaling in x and y, to width and height 2, x must be scaled by 2/(right-left) and y by 2/(top-bottom). If we also once and for all decide that $z_{prp} = 0$, we get the following matrix:

$$\begin{bmatrix} x_h \\ y_h \\ z_h \\ h \end{bmatrix} = \begin{bmatrix} \dfrac{2near}{right-left} & 0 & A & 0 \\ 0 & \dfrac{2near}{top-bottom} & B & 0 \\ 0 & 0 & C & D \\ 0 & 0 & -1 & 0 \end{bmatrix} \begin{bmatrix} x \\ y \\ z \\ 1 \end{bmatrix}$$

Except for A, B, C and D, this is the final, complete projection matrix!

A and B can be zero when the viewing frustum is symmetrical, that is right = -left and top = -bottom, which is the typical case. In the case that the frustum is asymmetrical, a shearing is needed, which is what A and B perform.

C and D are needed to make the "projected" z values normalized instead of z_{vp}.

All these parameters turn out to be rather simple:

$$A = \frac{right + left}{right - left}$$

$$B = \frac{top + bottom}{top - bottom}$$

$$C = -\frac{far + near}{far - near}$$

$$D = \frac{-2 \cdot far \cdot near}{far - near}$$

Now, don't take this for granted (even though it is straight from the OpenGL Reference Manual). Let's insert (left, bottom, -near, 1) into the matrix and see what we get.

$$x_h = \frac{2near \cdot left}{right - left} - \frac{right + left}{right - left} \cdot near$$

$$z_h = \frac{far + near}{far - near} \cdot near - \frac{2far \cdot near}{far - near}$$

$$h = near$$

Division by h gives

$$x_p = \frac{2 \cdot left}{right - left} - \frac{right + left}{right - left} = \frac{left - right}{right - left} = -1$$

$$z_p = \frac{far + near}{far - near} - \frac{2far}{far - near} = \frac{near - far}{far - near} = -1$$

The same can be done for every corner of the viewing frustum.

So now we have a projection matrix that projects, scales to normalized coordinates, and also avoids flattening of Z for later purposes.

The matrix that we have thus found can be used in OpenGL shaders for perspective projection. A demo using such a matrix is given in chapter 8.4.

6.9 Picking

Picking is a common problem. It is the seemingly simple problem of selecting an object with a mouse. In a 2D scene this is usually trivial (possibly with some complications with complex shapes like splines), but in a 3D scene it is quite different, and there are several solutions to choose from. These include:

- Ray-casting in view coordinates
- Ray-casting in model coordinates
- Indexing models by color

Out of these, the first may seem like the most natural choice, the second is more efficient, and the third easiest to implement but least flexible in usage.

6.9.1 Picking by ray-casting

Ray-casting, as described in chapter 17.1, is the task of tracking a ray from the camera into a scene. We do it here almost the same way. Start from the camera, the projection reference point, through one pixel, into the scene. For picking, only one ray is cast, and it goes though the point where the user clicked the mouse.

However, this assumes that all models are transformed to view coordinates! See Figure 35. If we do that, we get *picking in view coordinates*. Doing all those transformations on the CPU can require considerable computations unless considerably optimized. However, it is also possible to do this on the GPU as part of the rendering. This would imply that we perform picking in the geometry stage. Then the actual picking is easy but it is less obvious how to pass the result to the CPU. (You can, for instance, use the write-to-texture feature of newer GPUs.)

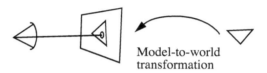

Model-to-world
transformation

FIGURE 35. Ray-casting in view coordinates

Another option is to perform picking in model coordinates! Then you transform the ray by the inverse model-to-view transform for *each model*. Since the models tend to be complex, this will be significantly faster. See Figure 36. Of course, we still have to make many ray-in-triangle checks so we have only optimized part of the problem.

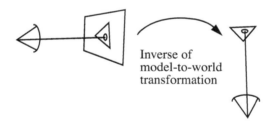

Inverse of
model-to-world
transformation

FIGURE 36. Ray-casting in model coordinates

Picking by ray-casting will give you an exact point within a specific triangle in a model, not only identification of a model. This gives you great possibilities in doing more than just identifying an object in the scene.

Considering how to optimize the raycasting in the models, I refer to the raytracing chapter. Basically, the usual principles apply with bounding shapes, and subdivisions. My first step would be a bounding sphere.

6.9.2 Picking by color index

A completely different way to perform picking, which is notably straight-forward, is to assign every separate model a unique color, a color that has no coupling to its look but is simply an identifier. The scene is then drawn with each model rendered in a single color, no shading or textures, like in Figure 37.

FIGURE 37. Three teapots rendered with distinctly different colors, making picking easy

This method is known as "The WYSIWYG method", and was, according to other publications, by Robin Forrest in the mid-1980's and used by Hanrahan and Haeberli for a 3D painting application [38].

Assuming that we render to a standard RGBA buffer with 8 bits per color, we have a maximum number of indices of $2^{32} = 4.3$ billions (including alpha), or 16 millions if we skip the alpha channel. However, I would advise a larger distance between the colors in order not to get accidents by interpolated values at edges. This will depend on the application, but in many cases you will be happy with a handfull of objects.

Once the image has been rendered, you can pick up the pixel at the mouse click by a call to glReadPixels. This call will get all pixels in a rectangle, so we choose a 1x1 pixel rectangle. Then we go through our list of color indices and see if we can find one that is within a small tolerance.

Now, you probably don't want the user to see your models drawn in flat colors like this. No problem, this can be avoided. You just draw the scene twice, once with indices and once with the ordinary look. You don't even have to render the color index image before the user clicks the mouse!

There are (at least) two options for doing this. Either you render to the ordinary image buffer, but without swapping buffers, pick up the color at the mouse pointer, and then erase the scene and render the image that the user should see, or you render the index color image off-screen, to a Framebuffer Object (i.e. render to a texture).

6.9.3 Old-style picking

It should also be mentioned that OpenGL had a built-in picking feature in the past. This is what you will usually find if you Google on the topic. However, that method is now obsolete and the methods described above are recommended.

6.10 Trackball-style controls

Trackball-style controls mean that we click-and-drag the mouse on an object in a scene in order to rotate it. This fits well with picking for manipulating one object out of several, or, as a simpler case, it can mean that we have a single object in the scene that is used for illustrating some effect.

This is a rather straight-forward application of rotation around an arbitrary axis, and just like in many other cases, the big thing is to keep track of the coordinate systems.

The user input, a click-and-drag of the mouse, gives us a movement on the screen, which translates to a vector in view coordinates. This should then be translated to rotation of an object (an instance of a model placed in the scene). However, this object may be rotated and translated, and the camera too. Thus, the transform should be applied in some way that the object is rotated in place, but not translated. The object rotation should be affected, but not the translation; we must apply a rotation so that no existing translation is rotated!

If, following my illustration of the transformation chain, the world-to-view transform is R_v*T_v, and the model-to-world is T_w*R_w (now, again, why do I use this order?), then the rotal model-to-view transformation is $R_v*T_v * T_w*R_w$. Now the rotation vector should cause a rotation somewhere in this chain.

And here is my solution: The mouse movement is a vector $\mathbf{v} = (v_x, v_y, 0)$. From this, I can find the orthogonal vector $\mathbf{u} = (u_x, u_y, 0) = (-v_y, v_x, 0)$. This is now transformed to world coordinates as $R_v^{-1}\mathbf{u}$. Then I use this vector as axis to rotate around, with its length for giving the rotation angle. This resulting rotation matrix is then inserted *between T_w and R_w*. This means that any existing model-to-world rotation is unaffcted, while any existing rotation is added upon by the new rotation matrix.

This approach is illutrated in Figure 38, As so often, you can reformulate the problem in other ways and work in other coordinate systems, but I find this solution reasonably straight-forward.

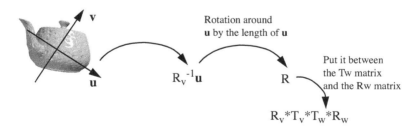

FIGURE 38. A way to implement trackball-style rotation from a mouse movement by v.

This simple problem is sometimes considered to hard that you need reusable code for it, but was it really that hard?

6.11 The OpenGL pipeline

Now we have the transformation chain, and it is time to put it in a wider perspective. You have already seen that we use shader programs not only for specifying transformations but also what should happen to the pixel later. Let us now have a look at how the whole system fits together.

The problem of displaying a 3D scene may seem simple since it is such a natural thing in real life, but the chain of operations that are needed is quite daunting at first glance.

You need a model of the 3D scene. This model includes many features:

- Each object must be represented somehow, its shape (chapter 8), color, position, and movement (chapter 14).

- The lighting of the scene must be defined (chapter 7). Where are the light sources, what propertied do they have, how should lighting be applied to the models?

- The camera must be placed and configured. How wide should the view be?

- How should the camera move? How do you avoid going too close to objects?

When rendering, a number of real-time tasks must be handled.

To each object, transformations must be applied that places them appropriately in the world.

- The transformed object should be rendered into the image buffer.

- When rendering, the proper object must be drawn, so far objects are not drawn on top of near objects. This is called *visible surface detection* (VSD, chapter 12).

- On a higher level, very large scenes need special processing to make the work manageable (chapter 13).

The OpenGL pipeline handles much of this, as shown in Figure 39.

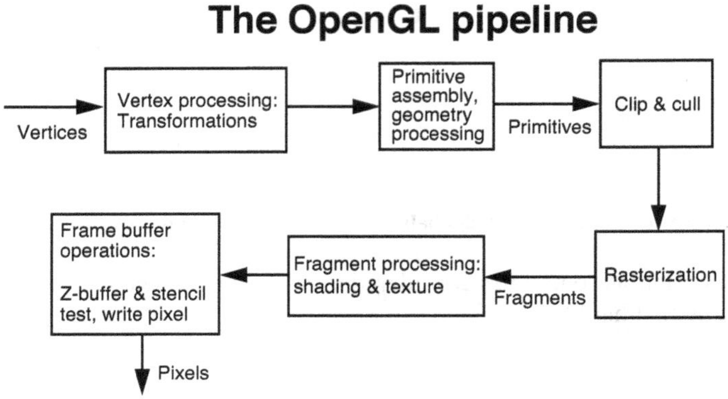

The OpenGL pipeline

FIGURE 39. The OpenGL pipeline (simplified)

Let us take a closer look at the OpenGL pipeline in the GPU, part by part.

6.11.1 Shader programs

Out of the boxes in the pipeline above, three are programmable, namely the vertex, fragment and geometry processors. The programs that run in them are called *shader programs*. Despite the name, they are not limited to lighting operations, but can also calculate texture and bump mapping, affect geometry and more. These are small programs that are executed either once per vertex or once per fragment, and they are executed on the GPU instead of the CPU.

Your minimum shader solution consists of two programs in cooperation, a vertex program and a fragment program. The geometry processing box allows no less than two more shaders, geometry and tesselation shaders, but these are optional and we skip them for now.

6.11.2 The vertex processor, vertex shader

The vertex processor is the first step in the pipeline, and also one of the fully programmable ones. It handles the following tasks:

- Vertex transformation (from model coordinates to screen coordinates)
- Transformation of normal vectors
- Generation and transformation of texture coordinates
- Lighting calculations by vertex

Vertex transformation should be obvious from other parts of this chapter. Slightly less obvious, since it has not been mentioned earlier, is normal vector transformations. Normal vectors should not be translated and not be projected, so only the rotation of the model-view matrix applies.

Generation of texture coordinates is as described in another place in this book. Transformation of texture coordinates is less obvious, and mostly beyond the scope of this book.

A vertex shader specifies the functionality of the vertex processor. In addition to what I said above, it can:

- set values for interpolation for use in a fragment shader

It knows nothing about:

- Perspective, viewport, frustum
- Primitives (!)
- Culling

6.11.3 Primitive assembly

Primitive assembly has nothing to do with "primitive" as in "simple". Rather, it assembles data for graphics primitives from connectivity data and the result of the vertex processor. The vertex processor knows nothing about connectivity, so here the appropriate data structures are put together, based on tables provided by the host program.

This box is optionally programmmable by the use of *geometry shaders*, the third kind of shader, which may add/modify geometry procedurally. Recent GPUs also have support for *tesselation shaders*, which also fits in the primitive assembly box from our perspective. These shaders are useful for operations like generating splines (see chapter 8). Although these operations are interesting and useful, they are beyond the scope of this book.

6.11.4 Clipping and culling

In this (non-programmable) step, the primitives are clipped to the edges of the screen, and back-face culling is applied.

Note that clipping must handle not only the simple clipping of the polygon as such, but also all data associated with the vertices. New vertices are created, and the other data, such as texture coordinates, must be interpolated properly.

6.11.5 Scan Conversion

This non-programmable step corresponds to what will be described in chapter 15.10. It is called rasterization, scan conversion or raster conversion. Polygons are converted to pixel coordinates of pixels that they cover, as in Figure 40. Note that although we get pixel coordinates, we use the term fragment as long as we do not write data to the actual pixel storage. A complete fragment is a candidate value for a specified pixel. At this point, we only have the coordinates.

FIGURE 40. Scan conversion

But this step does not only create pixel coordinates. It also interpolates other data, like texture coordinates, so that each fragment get its own, interpolated values.

6.11.6 The fragment processor

With pixel coordinates and interpolated values for color, texture coordinates etc., the fragment processor calculates a color value for the fragment, as illustrated by Figure 41.

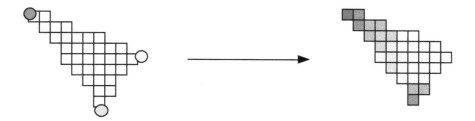

FIGURE 41. The fragment processor generates colors for each fragment

This handles several problems:

- Texturing
- Fog
- By-pixel light, including bump mapping

The *fragment shader* specifies this functionality. It is sometimes called pixel shader, although this name is arguable since the result is not necessarily written to a pixel due to later tests. It replaces the fixed functionality of the fragment processor. It can:

- set the fragment color
- get color values from textures
- use any kind of interpolated data from the vertices

It can not

- change the fragment coordinates
- write into textures[1]
- affect stencil, scissor, alpha, depth...

6.11.7 Fragment operations

Before the fragment can be written into the frame buffer (and thereby affect a real pixel) there are a few more operations that need to be done.

- Stencil test
- Z-buffer test

---

1. This is no longer true in OpenGL 4.2 and up, where the call *imageStore* was introduced

- The blend function (glBlendFunc etc.)

The stencil test checks the value of the stencil buffer (simply put, a mask buffer) to see if the fragment can be written at all. Although the stencil buffer is very useful, we choose not to elaborate on that here.

When I say that a certain kind of shader can or can not do something, my claims may turn incorrect over time. The technology is evolving all the time and limitations are worked on.

We are discussing shader programming all over the book. Some language details are not relevant for the discussions as such and are collected in chapter 18.

OpenGL pipeline does not solve all problems for us. It gives us the order of events for transformations and a few other operations, but there are many tasks that are more application-dependent, that OpenGL can not solve for us. Those problems are often addressed in the software parts of the 3D engine.

In this chapter, we covered transformations to different coordinate systems, the vertex processing. Now we need to continue with fragment processing, what to draw into the final pixels.

7. Light models and shading

Lighting is extremely important, and a hard problem since the exchange of light between objects in a real scene is an extremely complicated process depending on positions, light sources and not least materials. What makes it so hard is that lit objects emit light themselves, so the final light level is the result of an infinitely recursive process of light exchange. See Figure 42.

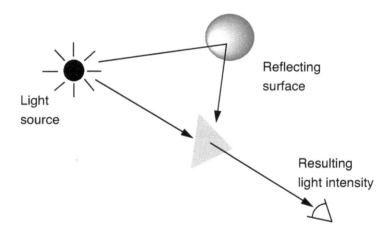

FIGURE 42. The exchange of light in a scene

The figure only hints at the complex process of real light exchange. A fully realistic model would have to integrate mutual light exchange between an infinite number of infinitesimal surfaces, each with different light levels and behavior, and include a detailed model of varying responses for different incoming and outgoing directions. For that reason, computer graphics always use fairly rough approximations of reality. With modern GPUs, the approximations are getting better and better even in real-time, but we will start with a simple and practical model that will do in most cases.

7.1 The three-component light model with the Phong model

We will start looking at a simple light model, the basic three-component model with *ambient*, *diffuse* and *specular* light components. This is a simple model that allows efficient implementation. Thus, it is the light model of choice if you want to do things the easy way.

We make two assumptions, both clearly incorrect:

- Light sources are point-shaped

- Light emitted from one surface gives no contribution to the light emitted from other surfaces, that is, only light sources contribute.

This is clearly unreasonable. No light sources are point-shaped, and even if that is a reasonable model for small sources like lightbulbs or candles, there are many distributed light sources. Also, in a lit room, every surface that is not pitch black is a light source, emitting parts of the light that hits it! Instead, all the exchange of secondary light is roughly modeled by the ambient light level, a constant level that contributes to all surfaces in the scene.

The light model works as follows: The light emitted from a point in a surface is the sum of the ambient light and contributions from all light sources from which light hits the surface. (This vaguely hints at a check for shadows, which we do not consider at this point.) The surface has a reflectivity, k_d, which we assume is constant for all directions. This reflectivity, as well as the light levels, should really be a three-component vector, R, G, B, but we ignore that too for now.

If the ambient light level is i_a, then the contribution from the ambient light to the light that is emitted from the surface is

$$i_{amb} = k_d i_a$$

This is the first component (out of three) in the light model. The other two components add contributions from direct illumination, modeling diffuse and specular reflections, respectively. Let us start with diffuse reflections.

Perfectly diffuse surfaces emit light with the same intensity in all directions. Such a surface is called a *Lambertian surface*. A surface which is fairly close to a perfect Lambertian surface is plain paper.

Even if Lambertian surfaces emit light uniformly in all directions, they do not accept light uniformly. The incoming light level depends on the angle with which the light hits the surface:

$$i_{diff} = k_d i_s \cos\theta$$

where i_s is the light level from the light source s and θ is the angle between the surface normal **n** and the direction towards the light source **s,** as shown in Figure 43. Thus, a diffuse surface will emit the most light when the light is parallel to the surface normal.

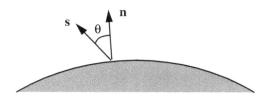

FIGURE 43. Diffuse reflections are calculated from the direction towards the light source and the surface normal.

We assume that both vectors are normalized, so they have length 1. The direction dependence is then easily calculated with the dot product.

$$\cos\theta = s{\cdot}n$$

This gives us the diffuse reflection component. If we only have those two components, ambient light and diffuse reflection, then we can calculate the total emitted light as:

$$i = i_{amb} + \sum i_{diff,s} = k_d i_a + \sum k_d i_s \cos\theta_s$$

where the sum is taken for all light sources s. (This formula does not take negative light into account. See below.)

The third component, *specular reflections*, add support for specular surfaces like metal. Note that this is something completely different from a mirroring surface since it will only reflect direct light from light sources.

The specular surface does not emit light uniformly in all directions, but will give higher light levels around a direction which is found by mirroring the incoming light direction in the surface.

From the geometry we have the direction towards the light source, s, and the surface normal vector n. From these we can calculate the mirrored vector r according to section 4.12:

$$r = 2n(s{\bullet}n) - s$$

The angle between r and the direction towards the camera, v, are used to calculate the light contribution. We call this angle ϕ. See Figure 44.

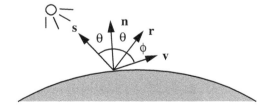

FIGURE 44. Vectors and angles involved in specular reflection

The contribution from specular reflection is calculated as

$$i_{spec} = k_{spec}i_s \cdot \cos^{\alpha}\phi_s$$

As before, we get the cos value from the dot product:

$$\cos\phi_s = \mathbf{r_s} \cdot \mathbf{v}$$

Note the exponent α! This parameter specifies how sharp the reflection should be, the *shininess*. At low α, say 1-5, the specular reflection will be fairly similar to the ambient one. To get really sharp reflections, α must be very high, 50-100. See Figure 45.

FIGURE 45. Shading of a sphere with diffuse reflection (far left) and specular reflection with shininess $\alpha = 1, 5, 25$ and 125 (remaining four).

The resulting light level must not be negative. There is no such thing as negative light. Therefore, we should eliminate that, and write the full formula as

$$i = k_d i_a + \Sigma \left(k_d \cdot i_s \cdot \max(0, \cos\theta_s) + k_{spec}i_s \cdot \max(0, \cos\phi_s)^{\alpha} \right)$$

This model for specular light is called the *Phong model*. This is not to be confused with Phong *shading*.

Finally, let me mention a similar, alternative way to calculate specular reflections, using the *halfway vector*. This is also known as the *Phong-Blinn model*. See Figure 46.

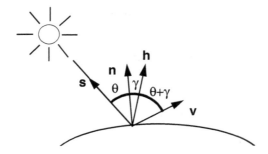

FIGURE 46. Specular reflection calculation using the halfway vector

The halfway vector **h** is calculated as the vector between **s** and **v**.

$$h_s = \frac{s + v}{|s + v|}$$

and then the specular reflection for a single light source is calculated as

$$i_{spec} = k_{spec} \cdot i_s \cdot \cos^\alpha \gamma_s = k_{spec} \cdot i_s \cdot (\mathbf{n} \cdot \mathbf{h_s})^\alpha$$

This opens possibilities for optimizations, e.g. when using directional light. In any event, the result is very similar.

7.2 Materials

The reflectivity of an object depends on its surface material. Materials do not only have different color, but also highly different reflectivity characteristics. The simplest way to distinguish materials is on a linear scale from diffuse (matte paper) to specular (shiny surfaces like metal). This is a very rough scale, but it handles most common materials fairly well. (If your task is to simulate materials as closely as possible, don't even think of a model this simple.)

With the three-component model, a material can thus be described by ten values, k_a, k_d and k_{spec} for each color channel (and possibly alpha although that complicates the matter a lot more) and the α value (shininess). It is common that k_a and k_d are the same.

7.3 Light attenuation

Above, we have only considered the incoming light level that reaches a surface. We should also consider the relation between the light source strength and the light level that reaches the surface, that is, we should have a way to specify the light attenuation, how much the light intensity drops with distance.

Since we are using point light sources, it seems as if the proper attenuation would be a quadratic falloff, right? Well, yes, in a way, but in a real situation we don't have point light sources, and much light is secondary light. A slower falloff will then be a good approximation for those factors that we can not model in other ways. So depending on the kind of scene, you may prefer a linear attenuation, or rather a combination of quadratic, linear and constant:

$$f(d) = \frac{1}{a + b \cdot d + c \cdot d^2}$$

where d is the distance and a, b, c are the desired attenuation parameters.

This is in no way a scientific and exact model. For higher precision, you should turn to methods like those in radiosity (see chapter 17) where attenuation is simply a question of what solid angle a surface fills when seen from another.

Attenuation can, to some extent, give the otherwise "dead" ambient light some life, since ambient light is associated with a light source, and can thus be affected by distance.

7.4 Other light models

The model described above is sufficient for many needs, but there are situations when you want more advanced models. An example is when drawing scenes in traffic. Traffic signs have a very different reflectivity, reflecting light back towards the light source rather than around a mirroring angle. Also, many materials vary the reflectivity depending on angle. For example, paper is close to Lambertian in most angles, but when viewed at very steep angles they suddenly look glossy. Gold has a similar variation, and glass is practically transparent at incoming angles near the normal, while it becomes very mirror-like near 90 degrees!

The first step towards a more general light model is to replace the constant k_s by angle-dependent functions.

$$I_{spec} = W(\theta) \cdot I_l \cdot \cos^{\alpha}\phi$$

This will model the variation from the incoming angle displayed in paper and glass well, but can not model traffic signs, for example.

A powerful tool for modeling reflections is the BRDF, the *bi-directional reflectance distribution function*. With such a function, you can model even behaviors like variable responses to different colors (frequencies), and dependencies of sideways angles (while we only considered elevation angles so far). All in all, the function takes five parameters, two incoming and outgoing angles plus the light frequency. This can be implemented by a formula or by a look-up table.

7.5 Shading

When we have decided on a light model, the next question is how to render it. On older systems, polygon rendering was a critical operation that had to be highly optimized. For those systems, the only reasonable way to render was to find a way to incrementally derive the shade of one pixel from its neighbor. On modern systems, we have a much bigger freedom to calculate each pixel separately. Three major ways to do shading can be identified, flat shading, Gouraud shading and Phong shading.

7.6 Flat shading

In flat shading, the shade for the entire polygon is calculated once and for all. We may simply take the surface normal for the polygon (which is easily calculated by a cross product) and do light calculation from that, as illustrated in Figure 47. This is fast enough for very slow systems, but the result is dull. Edges between polygons are highly visible and the shading is highly unrealistic.

Light models and shading

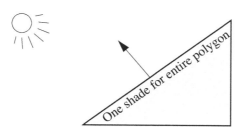

FIGURE 47. Flat shading, calculate one shade for entire polygon

Figure 48 shows two examples, an octahedron (eight-sided polyhedron) and the Stanford bunny model, both flat shaded. The octahedron looks perfectly natural, since the shape has so few polygons. However, we are usually using shading to make models look as round as possible, and flat shading can not help. The bunny looks really rough. (Concerning the model itself, see chapter 8.3.)

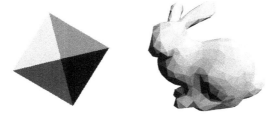

FIGURE 48. Flat-shaded octahedron, seen from corner, and the Stanford bunny model

You should hardly ever consider flat shading for normal rendering. However, there are different situations where flat shading is what you want, usually in the form of painting a whole object in a single color. Examples that will come later in this book include calculation of the potentially visible set (PVS) and form factors for radiosity.

7.7 Gouraud shading

Gouraud shading [12] is significantly better than flat shading. Gouraud shading is named after Henri Gouraud, who developed the method in the 70's. In Gouraud shading, the lighting calculations are performed once for each vertex, and shades are interpolated between vertices. This is simple, very efficient, and given polyhedra with enough detail it produces fairly good results. However, artifacts are visible and highlights (from specular reflections) are not rendered well.

Figure 49 shows an example with an octahedron seen from the corner. There are visible artifacts. The example shape is, of course, stretching the situation quite a bit since we try to make a low-polygon polyhedron look round, and that is why there is a second, more realistic example below.

FIGURE 49. Gouraud-shaded octahedron, seen from corner

For the bunny, we chose to make two different examples (Figure 50), with and without a specular component in the light calculation. The model has (barely) enough polygons to produce a decent result for diffuse reflections, but with specular reflections, polygons are too visible.

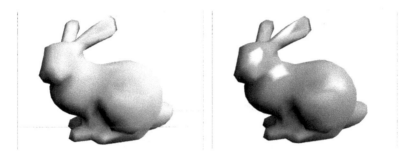

FIGURE 50. Stanford Bunny with Gouraud shading, diffuse only (left) and specular (right)

Figure 51 illustrates what happens. There is one normal vector in each vertex. Since we want to simulate a curved surface, these vectors are not necessarily parallel. For each vertex, lighting is calculated with its surface normal. Then these light values are interpolated over the surface.

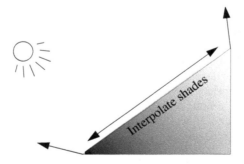

FIGURE 51. Gouraud shading, calculate light at vertices, interpolate shades

Gouraud shading was the method of choice for many years. After GPUs became commonplace in the late 90's, Gouraud shading came for free with the hardware, but since programmable shaders arrived, the world has turned to the higher quality of Phong shading. Even so, Gouraud shading is the fastest method. Thus it is often used despite being the second-class shading. Thus, Gouraud shading is:

- extremely fast
- renders curved surfaces fairly well, but with visible artifacts if the polygon count is low

7.8 Phong shading

Phong shading [11], not to confuse with the Phong model, is a high-performance shading method where lighting is calculated on a per-pixel basis. Like Gouraud shading, it is named after its inventor, in this case Dr. Bui-Tuong Phong. Instead of calculating shading values per vertex, and interpolating them to each pixel, the normal vector of the vertices is interpolated, so lighting can be calculated for each pixel with a unique normal vector.

Figure 52 shows the usual examples with an octahedron seen from the corner and the Stanford bunny. This is about as good as it can get when trying to make a low-polygon model like this look smooth. The bunny is rendered including the specular component, which gives some nice specular reflections.

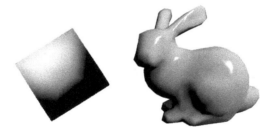

FIGURE 52. Phong shaded octahedron, seen from corner, and Phong shaded bunny

Figure 53 illustrates the calculations. Like before, each vertex has a surface normal, but this time the surface normals, and not the shades, are interpolated. Note that the normal vectors can not be used after linear interpolation alone, because if we do, the length of the vectors will be shorter in the middle. Thus, normalization is necessary in the fragment shader.

Phong shading features:

- renders curved surfaces with good results even for models with low polygon count
- supports nice specular reflections
- requires more computations, light calculations in the fragment shader rather than vertex, which means once for every pixel

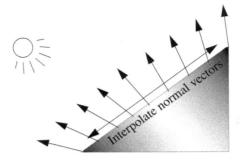

FIGURE 53. Phong shading; interpolate normals, calculate light by pixel

Note that any of these three shading methods can use the full three-component light model, so you can use the Phong model with flat shading, and you can render Phong shading with only diffuse reflection. However, coupling Phong shading to the Phong model for specular highlights is not unreasonable. According to their own publications, Valve software [32] calculates highlights separately with Phong shading, while diffuse shading appears to be computed by Gouraud shading. The simple logic is that the specular part is the only component that really needs Phong shading.

7.9 Light sources in OpenGL

When specifying light sources in OpenGL, this is mainly a matter of a position and a color (unless the light source is white, but even then the "color" may specify the strength of the light source). There are, however, a few more parameters to consider. Light attenuation, described in chapter 7.3, is easy to implement.

You can choose whether a light should be positional or directional. If the light source is very distant, like the sun, it can just as well be modeled as a direction vector, which will also make some optimizations possible. (Fewer calculations per pixel.)

A related issue is to specify materials, although that is not in the light source. A simple material description can specify material color for a separate diffuse and specular component, plus the shininess value, the shininess exponent in the Phong model. Just specify all components you need according to chapter 7.1, or implement some more sophisticated model when needed.

Note that you also sometime want a surface to be self-illuminated, which gives it a value to be added on top of the rest. This is just one more parameter to add in your fragment shader.

In order to calculate light, normal vectors must be included. (We skip light intensity, light color and material parameters for simplicity.). This adds one important detail. Most transformations that we perform on our models *must also be performed on the normal vectors*! If a model rotates, be it because it moves or the camera moves, the normal vectors must

Light models and shading

rotate exactly the same way. However, not all transformations should be applied, *not the translations*!

Likewise, positional light sources must also be transformed so they move appropriately with camera and object movements, and directional light sources should be rotated but not translated.

7.10 Shading in OpenGL

Once we get to shading, we can tie this together and make code of it. Gouraud shading and Phong shading both fit very well into GLSL. Flat shading is, of course, easiest, where you pass the desired color as one single vector. No interpolation is needed so the rendering will be the fastest imaginable. We saw that already in the first example in section 3.7.2.

7.10.1 Gouraud shading in OpenGL

For Gouraud shading, we should interpolate shades between vertices. To do that, we need to pass the shade from the vertex shader as an *out* variable, received by the fragment shader as an *in* variable by the same name (exColor below).

A variable passed from the vertex shader to the fragment shader this way is interpolated, by default in a perspective correct way (see chapter 15). This interpolation is exactly what Gouraud shading is about, interpolation from vertex to vertex. We refer to this as an *interpolated* variable or *varying* variable.

Let us make a slight variation on it with a hard-coded directional light source. We need an array of normal vectors, and pass it to the shader programs as usual.

```
GLfloat normals[] = {-0.7f, 0.0f, 0.7f,
                0.0f, 1.0f, 0.0f,
                0.58f, -0.58f, 0.58f };
    glBindBuffer(GL_ARRAY_BUFFER, colorBufferObjID);
    glBufferData(GL_ARRAY_BUFFER, 9*sizeof(GLfloat), normals,
                GL_STATIC_DRAW);
    glVertexAttribPointer(glGetAttribLocation(program, "inNormal"), 3,
                GL_FLOAT, GL_FALSE, 0, 0);
    glEnableVertexAttribArray(glGetAttribLocation(program, "inNormal"));
```

In my vertex shader, I add a hard-coded directional light source, declare the normal vectors array and calculate a light level. Real programs include material parameters, specular shading and more.

```
#version 150

in  vec3 inPosition;
in  vec3 inNormal;
out vec3 exColor;

void main(void)
{
    const vec3 light = vec3(0.58, 0.58, 0.58);
    float shade;
```

```
    shade = dot(normalize(inNormal), light);
    exColor = vec3(shade);
    gl_Position = vec4(inPosition, 1.0);
}
```

The fragment shader just puts the interpolated shade into the output.

```
#version 150

in  vec3 exColor;
out vec4 outColor;

void main(void)
{
    outColor = vec4(exColor,1.0);
}
```

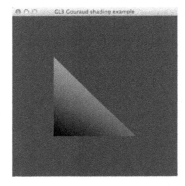

FIGURE 54. Gouraud shaded polygon.

The result is the smoothly shaded polygon in Figure 54. However, note that all values are between the vertex shades. There can be no extreme points between them. For that we need Phong shading.

7.10.2 Phong shading in OpenGL

When making a Phong shader of the example above, the main program uses the same data, the change is in the shaders. The whole change is to move the light calculation (the dot product) to the fragment shader, and interpolate normal vectors instead of shades. Thus, the exColor variable disappears and is replaced by exNormal.

Vertex shader:

```
#version 150

in  vec3 inPosition;
in  vec3 inNormal;
out vec3 exNormal;

void main(void)
```

Light models and shading

```
{
    exNormal = inNormal;
    gl_Position = vec4(inPosition, 1.0);
}
```

Fragment shader:

```
#version 150

out vec4 outColor;
in vec3 exNormal;

void main(void)
{
    const vec3 light = vec3(0.58, 0.58, 0.58);
    float shade;

    shade = dot(normalize(exNormal), light);
    outColor = vec4(shade, shade, shade, 1.0); // inColor;
}
```

And the result is indeed better, as of Figure 55. Add specular reflections and you get nice reflections as in Figure 52.

FIGURE 55. Phong shaded triangle.

7.11 The normal matrix

For calculating light, we need normal vectors. When we apply rotations (and more) on our models, the normal vectors must also be transformed. See Figure 56.

At first glance, we could be tempted to use the same transformations as for vertices, but that will not work at all.

- Vertices should have the projection transformation applied on them, transforming them to projected coordinates, while normal vectors should be transformed to view coordinates.

- Normal vectors are directional vectors while vertices are positional. Because of that, translations make no sense for normal vectors.

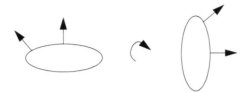

FIGURE 56. Normal vectors must rotate with models

This leads to one simple solution: apply the model-to-world and world-to-model transformations, but *only the rotation part* (3x3 matrix). Since this matrix is the same for many vertices, it makes sense to create it on the CPU. Basically, multiply your model-to-world and world-to-view matrices but zero out the translation part, or pass only the 3x3 rotation part to the shaders.

This will help in many cases, namely as long as there is *no non-uniform scaling*. I have assumed that we only do rotations, although scaling may also be part of the 3x3 submatrix. Uniform scaling will not cause any problems, but non-uniform scaling will demand a very different normal matrix.

As a clarifying example, take the situation shown in Figure 57, where a normal vector to a surface in a model, scaled by the same scaling as the model, turns out not to be a normal vector to the surface any more.

FIGURE 57. Non-uniform scaling applied incorrectly on normal vectors

To solve this problem, we must modify the normal matrix. The solution is to calculate the *inverse transpose* of the rotation/scaling part of the matrix, $(R^{-1})^T$, which transforms normal vectors like: $\mathbf{n}' = (R^{-1})^T \mathbf{n}$.

We should not take that for granted, so let us try to prove it:

Consider a surface with a normal vector $\mathbf{n}$ and a tangent vector (vector in the plane) $\mathbf{x}$. Then $\mathbf{n} \cdot \mathbf{x} = 0$.

A model-to-view matrix M is used to transform vertices. The tangent vector can be defined as the difference of two surface points, $\mathbf{x} = \mathbf{a} - \mathbf{b}$, which will transform linearly with L, that is $\mathbf{x}' = M\mathbf{x} = M(\mathbf{a} - \mathbf{b})$.

The normal vector $\mathbf{n}$ is transformed by a not yet determined matrix N, as $\mathbf{n'} = N\mathbf{n}$. This is a normal vector to the transformed surface if $\mathbf{n'} \bullet \mathbf{x'} = 0$.

We will now prove that $N = (M^{-1})^T$ will produce the appropriate $\mathbf{n'}$. Then

$$N\mathbf{n} \bullet M\mathbf{x} = 0$$

so

$$(M^{-1})^T\mathbf{n} \bullet M\mathbf{x} = 0$$

Now we need to be a bit picky about transposing. A dot product is really a matrix multiplication between one single-row matrix and one single-column matrix. If we consider vectors to be column vectors by default, then the row vector version of $\mathbf{n}$ is $\mathbf{n}^T$. Now we can rewrite the formula to a matrix multiplication (where vectors are intentionally not boldface because they are now 1x3 matrixes):

$$((M^{-1})^T n)^T M x = 0$$

But the transpose of a matrix multiplication is a product of two transposed matrices as $(AB)^T = B^T A^T$, so

$$(n^T M^{-1})(Mx) = 0$$

$$n^T M^{-1} Mx = 0$$

$$n^T (M^{-1} M)x = 0$$

$$n^T x = 0$$

which, in our usual dot product notation is the same as

$$\mathbf{n} \bullet \mathbf{x} = 0$$

which was our initial assumption. Therefore, we conclude that our claim holds.

More intuitively, the inverse transpose will reverse all rotations twice, thereby leaving them unchanged, while scalings are reversed only by the inverse but not the transpose, and will therefore be affected (although we need the proof above to know that it does the right thing).

7.12 Shadows

In the context of light and shading, shadows should be mentioned. The closest we get to shadows in this chapter is that a light source does not contribute to the side of objects that face away from the light source, so we have a limited self-shadowing, However, objects do

---

not cast shadows upon each other. Making such shadows is quite possible. In this book, you will find techniques like ray-tracing, radiosity and light mapping, which all can produce nice shadows, although not in real time.

The real time is mostly left for volume 2, where we will look at several important methods. Here, I will only mention one: planar shadows.

Consider a large, flat surface, a floor. It is so big that we don't need to consider any edges. Over that surface, you place a model. Now we want it to cast a shadow. In this particular case we can make it pretty easy. All you need to do is to draw the object twice, once in its "real" position, and once at floor-level, flattened. You move it to the proper height with a translation, flatten it by a scaling matrix scaling by $(1, 0, 1)$ and finally you draw it without textures, with a dark shade, preferably with some transparency so that the background can shine through a little.

The Figure 58 shows this method applied to the Stanford bunny model.

FIGURE 58. The Stanford bunny model with a planar shadow created by linear transformations

My total model-to-view transformation consists of a camera placement multiplied with a few transform like this:

```
total = camera * T(0, -0.8, 0) * S(1, 0, 1) * Ry(a)
```

The translation places the shadow below the rabbit, and should match the floor position. The scaling flattens the rabbit along the Y axis. Finally, there is a transformation (rotation) matching the movement of the non-flattened rabbit above.

The result in the figure might not look spectacular, but if you do exactly this on a textured floor, maybe with a bit of transparency, you can make pretty useful shadows that will improve the scene considerably. That is, as long as you are on a big flat surface.

You can generalize this method to draw shadows on any flat surface, and with proper perspective, by applying standard transformations (including a projection matrix for perspective) and using the stencil buffer. This, as well as *shadow mapping*, *shadow volumes* and *ambient occlusion*, are subjects for volume 2.

8. Shape representation, curves and surfaces

When building and manipulating 3D scenes, the shape representation is of utmost importance. In this chapter I will discuss not only different ways to represent shapes, but also tools that are useful for controlling animation, in the form of splines.

8.1 Polyhedra models

During the actual rendering of 3D scenes, everything is turned to polygons. Thus, the shortest and fastest path from a shape to screen is from polyhedra, mesh models. Other kinds of shapes are practical at higher levels, so we can consider polyhedra models to be the low-level representation. It is ideal for real-time rendering, but awkward to modify.

A polyhedra model is obviously a set of polygons, triangles or larger. A first question is how that is best stored in memory. Let me first describe a "first try", a format that may at first glance seem suitable. The model consists of polygons, and polygons are built from vertices. Well, that could be stored like this:

```
Vertex = (x, y, z)
Triangle = array of Vertex
3DObject = array of Triangle
```

As an example, the data can look like this:

```
Triangle[1]: (10, 10, 10), (10, 20, 10), (10, 20, 20)
Triangle[2]: (10, 10, 10), 10, 20, 10), (10, 10, 20)
Triangle[3]: ( . . . ), ( . . . ), ( . . . )
. . .
```

This may seem reasonable, but now I claim that this is *not* a good format. Why?

Look at the simple examples in Figure 59.

FIGURE 59. Pyramid and cube - how much data do they need?

The pyramid consists of 4 triangles and 4 vertices. The cube is built from 6 squares (quads) or 12 triangles, with 8 vertices. But with the format above, each vertex is repeated for every polygon it is part of, so the pyramid needs 12 vertices, and the cube as much as 24 or 36!

The problem is that each vertex is multiplied, copies are put into every triangle that touches the vertex. The result is several times more vertices to process than necessary!

If we instead optimize the format a little bit, we can index vertices instead of duplicating them. Then it looks like this:

```
Vertex = (x, y, z)
Vertex table = array of Vertex
Triangle = array of integers
Triangle table = array of Triangles
3DObject = Vertex table + Triangle table
```

The example gets slightly different:

```
Vertex table:
(10, 10, 10)
(10, 20, 10)
(10, 20, 20)
(10, 10, 20)
. . .
Triangle table:
(1, 2, 3)
(1, 2, 4)
. . .
```

Now, all vertices in the object are in one list, where each occurs once. Polygons are efficiently built from indices into the vertex table.

8.2 Loading polyhedra models from disk

There are many disk formats for 3D models. Richer formats include extra information like animation data. Such information may include a skeletal system (skin & bones), or deformation vectors (common for face animation). We ignore such possibilities for now.

A simple format for 3D models is Wavefront OBJ. It is a text based format which in a clear and obvious way has lists for vertices, normals and texture coordinates, followed by a

Shape representation, curves and surfaces

polygon list giving indices to each list for every vertex in the polygon. Here is a trivial example, a textured cube:

```
# cube, example of .obj file
# 8 vertices:
v -2.5 -2.5 10
v -2.5 2.5 10
v 2.5 2.5 10
v 2.5 -2.5 10
v -2.5 -2.5 15
v 2.5 -2.5 15
v 2.5 2.5 15
v -2.5 2.5 15
# 6 normals
vn 0 0 -1
vn 0 0 1
vn 0 -1 0
vn 1 0 0
vn 0 1 0
vn -1 0 0
# 4 texture coordinates
vt 0 0
vt 0 1
vt 1 1
vt 1 0
# 12 triangles:
f 1/1/1 2/2/1 3/3/1
f 3/3/1 4/4/1 1/1/1
f 5/1/2 6/2/2 7/3/2
f 7/3/2 8/4/2 5/1/2
f 1/1/3 4/2/3 6/3/3
f 6/3/3 5/4/3 1/1/3
f 4/1/4 3/2/4 7/3/4
f 7/3/4 6/4/4 4/1/4
f 3/1/5 2/2/5 8/3/5
f 8/3/5 7/4/5 3/1/5
f 2/1/6 1/2/6 5/3/6
f 5/3/6 8/4/6 2/1/6
```

Each row starts with a code that tells what it contains:

v: Vertex, specified as three floats.

vn: Normal vector.

vt: Texture coordinates.

f: Face, that is a polygon.

Making a program that loads such a file and displays it is fairly easy. There are some more features in the format, like material references and Bézier patches, but we skip that for now. A bigger problem is that all models are not quite as simple and symmetrical as this one. There may be many-sided polygons. If you want your model to be triangles only, then you must post-process. A worse problem is that polygons may refer to different normals and texture coordinates for a vertex, which complicates drawing. You may have to dupli-cate vertices to make every vertex have only one normal vector and texture coordinate pair.

The simplest way to deal with .obj is to load it as listed in the file and draw it with OpenGL immediate mode. It is not the most efficient way, but for our purely educational purposes, it is good enough, and you can speed it up with display lists. On the course page, you will find a more advanced loader, which rearranges the data to allow more efficient rendering.

There are countless other 3D formats. Another that is a good first pick is VRML. Although VRML is a very complex format capable of describing entire scenes, its meshes are described straight-forward as plain text, so if you skip everything you don't need, loading a mesh from a VRML is not complicated.

When you want to move to more powerful formats, the choice is likely to depend on what modeling program you use and what features you need.

8.3 Popular standard mesh models

When you have an .obj loader, you can search for models on the web or use some 3D modeling program. (Wings3D and Blender are two free options. You may also try Teddy, see below.) But if you know what you are looking for, things get easier.

There are a few models that are so well known that they can be considered standard. First of all, the quadric surfaces (sphere etc., see page 94) are already defined by the OpenGL libraries, and being simple as they are, they are highly suitable first test models. Another shape that is pre-defined for you is the *Utah Teapot*, in Figure 60.

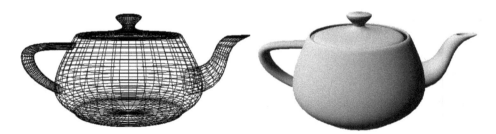

FIGURE 60. The Utah Teapot

The Utah Teapot was created as early as 1975 by Martin Newell, which makes it a very early 3D model for being with this detail. It was created from measurements done on a real teapot.

The Utah Teapot is available in GLUT/FreeGLUT as glutSolidTeapot(). (Not, however, currently in MicroGLUT as of 2017.) That makes it the only shape beyond the quadrics that is available with no extra effort using these libraries.[1]

---

1. In case you don't find teapots amusing, I recommend that you listen to "The Flying Teapot" by the french psychedelic jazz-rock group Gong. Then you might get inspired, maybe for strange retro space creations.

Shape representation, curves and surfaces

With a mesh loader such as an .obj loader, however, there are many others. The most significant one is probably the *Stanford Bunny*, shown in Figure 61. It is available in different resolutions on the web and is widely used in research. In this book, we use a low-resolution version, since that is most suitable for illustrating graphics algorithms.[1]

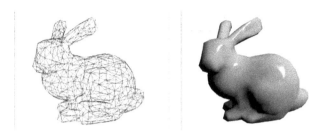

FIGURE 61. The Stanford bunny, low resolution (899 triangles)

You usually find this model in higher resolutions. When your goal is good looks, that is certainly preferrable, but polygons get so small that it is hard to illustrate things like Gouraud shading on it.

The Stanford bunny[2] was created in 1993 or 1994 (sources disagree on the exact year) by scanning a physical plaster model. A Googling on "bunny.obj" should find many downloads. At Stanford [23], it can be downloaded in high resolution as a PLY file, a format closely related to the OBJ format, but you will be better off starting with a low-res version.

One of my favorites, maybe not as widely known as the teapot and the Stanford bunny, but still fairly well-known, is *Teddy*, in Figure 62.

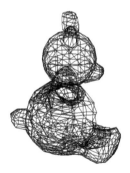 

FIGURE 62. Teddy

1. It should be noted that there is also another, simpler bunny which I often use in my examples. It is even more low-polygon than the most simplified Stanford bunny I can imagine, so each have their use. Unfortunately I have no source for the other bunny so I avoid using that in the book.
2. Speaking on inspirational songs, in this case just sing *"My bunny is over the ocean, by bunny is over the sea..."*

Teddy[1] was provided as example model for the highly intuitive and easy-to-use modeling program by the same name, created by Takeo Igarashi [22]. The modeler does not give you the control of serious 3D modeling packages, but it is very nice for quick drafts, which may be just what you need for creating contents for a student project.

Given a good loader, you may also want to consider other formats, like Quake2 and Quake3 formats and the 3ds format. Writing one yourself is, however, a harder task than dealing with .obj meshes or extracting meshes from VRML.

8.4 Specifying geometry in OpenGL

Without geometry, OpenGL does nothing. In OpenGL, you should specify geometry as arrays that you upload to Vertex Buffer Objects, as we have seen in earlier examples. There are some other ways, like the old, slow but easy "immediate mode", and display list, that you may see in old examples, but I recommend you to avoid them.

We have already seen how to draw a single triangle with VBOs, so let's expand that a little bit, and draw a cube. A cube can be specified like this:

```
GLfloat vertices[8][3] = {{-0.5,-0.5,-0.5},
                          {0.5,-0.5,-0.5},
                          {0.5,0.5,-0.5},
                          {-0.5,0.5,-0.5},
                          {-0.5,-0.5,0.5},
                          {0.5,-0.5,0.5},
                          {0.5,0.5,0.5},
                          {-0.5,0.5,0.5}};
GLfloat normals[8][3] = {{-0.58,-0.58,-0.58},
                         {0.58,-0.58,-0.58},
                         {0.58,0.58,-0.58},
                         {-0.58,0.58,-0.58},
                         {-0.58,-0.58,0.58},
                         {0.58,-0.58,0.58},
                         {0.58,0.58,0.58},
                         {-0.58,0.58,0.58}};
GLubyte cubeIndices[36] = {0,3,2, 0,2,1,
                           2,3,7, 2,7,6,
                           0,4,7, 0,7,3,
                           1,2,6, 1,6,5,
                           4,5,6, 4,6,7,
                           0,1,5, 0,5,4};
```

Load it onto the GPU essentially as before, but with some higher numbers and specific calls for the index array:

```
// Allocate and activate Vertex Array Object
glGenVertexArrays(1, &vertexArrayObjID);
glBindVertexArray(vertexArrayObjID);
// Allocate Vertex Buffer Objects
glGenBuffers(1, &vertexBufferObjID);
glGenBuffers(1, &indexBufferObjID);
glGenBuffers(1, &normalBufferObjID);
```

---

1. Maybe you think I will suggest Lasse Berghagen, but no, I'd rather suggest Elvis Presley. Can you put a chain around Teddy's neck - with the challenge to make it move right - then we have a point.

Shape representation, curves and surfaces

```
// VBO for vertex data
glBindBuffer(GL_ARRAY_BUFFER, vertexBufferObjID);
glBufferData(GL_ARRAY_BUFFER, 8*3*sizeof(GLfloat), vertices, GL_STATIC_DRAW);
glVertexAttribPointer(glGetAttribLocation(program, "inPosition"), 3, GL_FLOAT,
                      GL_FALSE, 0, 0);
glEnableVertexAttribArray(glGetAttribLocation(program, "inPosition"));
glutPrintError("init vertices");

// VBO for vertex data
glBindBuffer(GL_ARRAY_BUFFER, normalBufferObjID);
glBufferData(GL_ARRAY_BUFFER, 8*3*sizeof(GLfloat), normals, GL_STATIC_DRAW);
glVertexAttribPointer(glGetAttribLocation(program, "inNormal"), 3, GL_FLOAT,
                      GL_FALSE, 0,0);
glEnableVertexAttribArray(glGetAttribLocation(program, "inNormal"));
glutPrintError("init normals");

glBindBuffer(GL_ELEMENT_ARRAY_BUFFER, indexBufferObjID);
glBufferData(GL_ELEMENT_ARRAY_BUFFER, 24*sizeof(GLuint), cubeIndices, GL_STATIC_DRAW);
glutPrintError("init index");
```

and draw it like this:

```
glBindVertexArray(vertexArrayObjID);
glDrawElements(GL_TRIANGLES, 36, GL_UNSIGNED_BYTE, NULL);
```

I used the Phong shader from section 7.10, and a rotation and the result (Figure 63) is quite similar to the ray-traced rendering from section 7.8.

FIGURE 63. Simple cube model rendered with OpenGL.

An important difference from our earliler examples that that we now use *glDrawElements*, which uses an index list just as discussed in section 8.1. The size of the arrays is reduced, and performance is improved as a comfortable side effect.

Note that there are 36 indices, 6 sides times 2 triangles 3 vertices, but only 8 vertices in the vertex list. When drawing polyhedra models with thousands of polygons, the reduced number of function calls alone will raise performance significantly. From this point, it is comfortably easy to move to bigger models. As an example, let us render Teddy (as shown above). I use the .obj loader that is available in the on-line lab material. This is also the right time to use a projection matrix (as of chapter 6.6) in a full demo.

We use the following transformation matrices:

```
GLfloat rotationMatrix[] = { 0.7f, 0.0f, -0.7f, 0.0f,
                             0.0f, 1.0f, 0.0f, 0.0f,
                             0.7f, 0.0f, 0.7f, 0.0f,
                             0.0f, 0.0f, 0.0f, 1.0f };
GLfloat translationMatrix[] = { 1.0f, 0.0f, 0.0f, 0.0f,
                                0.0f, 1.0f, 0.0f, 0.0f,
                                0.0f, 0.0f, 1.0f, -2.0f,
                                0.0f, 0.0f, 0.0f, 1.0f };

#define near 1.0
#define far 30.0
#define right 1.0
#define left -1.0
#define top 1.0
#define bottom -1.0
GLfloat projectionMatrix[] =
    { 2.0f*near/(right-left), 0.0f, (right+left)/(right-left), 0.0f,
      0.0f, 2.0f*near/(top-bottom), (top+bottom)/(top-bottom), 0.0f,
      0.0f, 0.0f, -(far + near)/(far - near), -2*far*near/(far - near),
      0.0f, 0.0f, -1.0f, 0.0f };
```

For this demo, we consider the rotation matrix our model-to-world matrix, the translation is the world-to-camera, and then we use a perspective projection matrix directly modelled after chapter 6.8. Naturally, all these matrices should be created by convenient functions.

For loading the .obj, we use the loadobj loader, which loads the obj into a structure like this:

```
typedef struct
{
  GLfloat* vertexArray;
  GLfloat* normalArray;
  GLfloat* texCoordArray;
  GLfloat* colorArray;
  GLuint* indexArray;
  int numVertices;
  int numIndices;
} Model;
```

As you can see, all we need is there, vertices, normals, indices, length of all parts, and some more that we will need later (texture coordinates). Granted that LoadModel loads the model, we load and upload like this:

```
// Upload geometry to the GPU:
m = LoadModel("teddy.obj");

glGenVertexArrays(1, &teddyVertexArrayObjID);
glGenBuffers(1, &teddyVertexBufferObjID);
glGenBuffers(1, &teddyIndexBufferObjID);
glGenBuffers(1, &teddyNormalBufferObjID);

glBindVertexArray(teddyVertexArrayObjID);

// VBO for vertex data
glBindBuffer(GL_ARRAY_BUFFER, teddyVertexBufferObjID);
glBufferData(GL_ARRAY_BUFFER, m->numVertices*3*sizeof(GLfloat), m->vertexArray,
        GL_STATIC_DRAW);
glVertexAttribPointer(glGetAttribLocation(program, "inPosition"), 3, GL_FLOAT,
        GL_FALSE, 0, 0);
```

Shape representation, curves and surfaces

```
glEnableVertexAttribArray(glGetAttribLocation(program, "inPosition"));

// VBO for normal data
glBindBuffer(GL_ARRAY_BUFFER, teddyNormalBufferObjID);
glBufferData(GL_ARRAY_BUFFER, m->numVertices*3*sizeof(GLfloat), m->normalArray,
        GL_STATIC_DRAW);
glVertexAttribPointer(glGetAttribLocation(program, "inNormal"), 3, GL_FLOAT,
        GL_FALSE, 0, 0);
glEnableVertexAttribArray(glGetAttribLocation(program, "inNormal"));

glBindBuffer(GL_ELEMENT_ARRAY_BUFFER, teddyIndexBufferObjID);
glBufferData(GL_ELEMENT_ARRAY_BUFFER, m->numIndices*sizeof(GLuint), m->indexArray,
        GL_STATIC_DRAW);
```

Drawing is just like before, you just have to get the length of the index array.

```
glBindVertexArray(teddyVertexArrayObjID);
glDrawElements(GL_TRIANGLES, m->numIndices, GL_UNSIGNED_INT, 0L);
```

And, of course, we need to upload all matrices:

```
glUniformMatrix4fv(glGetUniformLocation(program, "mdlMatrix"), 1, GL_TRUE,
            rotationMatrix);
glUniformMatrix4fv(glGetUniformLocation(program, "camMatrix"), 1, GL_TRUE,
            translationMatrix);
glUniformMatrix4fv(glGetUniformLocation(program, "projMatrix"), 1, GL_TRUE,
            projectionMatrix);
```

I could make a normal matrix to but I create them in the shader from the others.

The shaders are getting closer to "real" shaders now. Here is the vertex shader:

```
#version 150

in  vec3 inPosition;
in  vec3 inNormal;
out vec3 exNormal;

uniform mat4 mdlMatrix;
uniform mat4 camMatrix;
uniform mat4 projMatrix;

void main(void)
{
    mat3 normalMatrix = mat3(camMatrix * mdlMatrix);
    exNormal = normalMatrix * inNormal;

    gl_Position = projMatrix * camMatrix * mdlMatrix * vec4(inPosition, 1.0);
}
```

Many components of a full-blown vertex shader are in place. We have a model-to-world matrix (mdlMatrix), a world-to-view matrix (camMatrix) and a projection matrix (proj-Matrix). I chose to make the normal matrix by casting camMatrix*mdlMatrix to a vec3, thereby *removing the translation part* (since a 3x3 matrix will not fit the homogeneous coordinate parts of a 4x4 matrix). See section 7.11 on page 81.

The fragment shader is not so exciting in this case, just the simple diffuse Phong shader as of chapter 7.10:

```
#version 150
```

```
out vec4 outColor;
in vec3 exNormal; // Phong

void main(void)
{
    const vec3 light = vec3(0.58, 0.58, 0.58);
    float shade;

    shade = dot(normalize(exNormal), light);
    outColor = vec4(shade, shade, shade, 1.0); // inColor;
}
```

The result (Figure 64) is, of course, similar to what we saw above but included as reference for the code above.

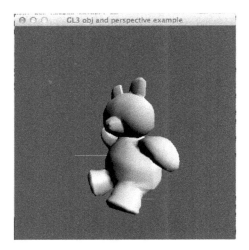

FIGURE 64. Teddy loaded from file, drawn lit, rotated and with perspective

I have deliberately skipped some optimizations. It is questionable if the normal matrix should be constructed in the shader, since it is global for the whole model and we could strip off the translation once and for all on the CPU. An even bigger waste is the multiplication of all matrices in the vertex shader. That operation is also best done once and for all.

8.5 Quadrics

Even though polyhedra models may be the final target for rendering, we often want to work with other shapes that are easier to describe and modify. A highly mathematical option is to use *quadrics*. A quadric is an implicit representation of a surface, where the surface is described by second-degree polynomials. At first glance, this is very nice. Since shapes are described by simple functions, it is easy to calculate intersections with lines, which makes them great for ray-tracing. With only very few parameters, you can describe spheres, ellipsoids, toruses, cones... See Figure 65.

Shape representation, curves and surfaces

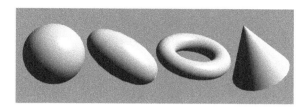

FIGURE 65. Quadrics: sphere, ellipsoid, torus, cone

…but the problem is that the possibilities pretty much end there. It is very hard to find other, useful shapes.

A sphere is described by the following equation:

$$x^2 + y^2 + z^2 = r^2$$

You will often prefer the parametric form, which delivers coordinates as a function of some parameters (radius and two angles), as in Figure 66.

$$x = r \cos \phi \cos \theta$$

$$y = r \cos \phi \sin \theta$$

$$z = r \sin \phi$$

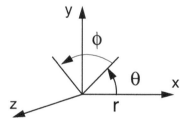

FIGURE 66. Polar coordinates: positions are given as a radius placed on the X axis, rotated around Z by θ, and then rotated around X by ϕ.

where

$$-\pi/2 \leq \phi \leq \pi/2$$

$$-\pi \leq \theta \leq \pi$$

An ellipsoid is slightly more complex to describe. The equation is

$$x^2/r_x{}^2 + y^2/r_y{}^2 + z^2/r_z{}^2 = 1$$

The parametric form is:

$$x = r_x \cos \phi \cos q$$

$$y = r_y \cos \phi \sin q$$

$$z = r_z \sin \phi$$

$$-\pi/2 \leq \phi \leq \pi/2$$

$$-\pi \leq q \leq \pi$$

This is actually a limited form of the ellipsoid, where the main axes of the ellipsoid are parallel to the main axes. It is possible to define rotated ellipsoids, but doing that takes more effort than it is worth.

The torus is, in my opinion, the most amusing quadric, where the concept is taken to a second level. What it does is to rotate a circle around an axis. The equation is:

$$\left(r - \sqrt{\frac{x^2}{r_x^2} + \frac{y^2}{r_y^2}} \right)^2 + \frac{z^2}{r_z^2} = 1$$

The parametric form is more understandable in this case:

$$x = r_x (r + \cos \phi) \cos \theta$$

$$y = r_y (r + \cos \phi) \sin \theta$$

$$z = r_z \sin \phi$$

$$-\pi \leq \phi \leq \pi$$

$$-\pi \leq \theta \leq \pi$$

Quadric surfaces were defined in the old GLU library, and also in GLUT, but these calls are largely obsolete (they were omitted from MicroGlut since they are not shader friendly). Today, I consider it something that can be done in external code. You can also construct the quadrics in your own code. You just sample the functions above properly and store the result in arrays.

Alas, as said above, the possibilities are limited. Except for the limited freedom in design, many quadric surfaces are hard to rotate freely. Trying to find more usable quadrics is not a very meaningful thing to do. You can find twisted, possibly visually interesting shapes, but you are unlikely to find something that you really need. A particularly twisted variant exists, called "superquadrics", which gives slightly more freedom, but the effort is big, the advantage is small and the result marginal.

Shape representation, curves and surfaces

So my advice concerning quadrics is to build them with modelling programs like Wings 3D and import like other models.

8.6 Constructive solid-geometry (CSG)

One attempt to make quadrics more useful is constructive solid geometry, CSG. CSG defines how you can combine overlapping 3D objects with set operations (AND, OR, XOR). Since it is usually based on quadrics, CSG was popular in ray-tracing packages of the past.

All resulting edges of CSG objects are edges of the components (although many edges of the components are hidden or cut away).

However, when trying to model shapes with CSG, you will find that it is not very powerful. The advantage over quadrics is marginal. We need to go further.

8.7 Splines

After my rather pessimistic comments on quadrics and CSG, it is about time I get to interesting methods that I can recommend, and that is where we are now. Splines are extremely useful, versatile tools that can be applied on many problems, modeling being only one of them. It is also quite usable for describing 3D objects which real-time changes.

The original spline was a physical drafting tool which was used by designers to create smooth curves. In computer graphics it is something else. It is a curve built from sections, each described by a polynomial, e.g. a 3rd degree polynomial.

A spline is usually (in practice I would say always) specified by a set of *control points*. These control points may have identical or different meanings, depending on how the spline is defined. There are two distinct classes of splines, *interpolation splines* and *approximation splines*.

For an interpolation spline, all control points lie on the curve, so the spline interpolates the curve from control point to control point. For approximation splines, however, control points do not need to be on the curve. Rather, control points can act as attractors, so the spline pulls toward the control point, but does not necessarily pass through it. With that description, just about any curve and set of points can be an approximation spline. There is, however, a demand that is often fulfilled by approximation splines, namely that the spline should stay within the *convex hull* of the control points.

How can we know that we make a spline that will always stay in the convex hull of the control points? Remember the barycentric coordinates from section 4.10 on page 30! If the demands of barycentric coordinates are fulfilled, then we are within the convex hull! And as we will see soon, there are splines that fulfill the demands, like Bézier curves.

Without control points, it is possible to write a parametric representation for a spline, as a set of functions:

$$x = x(u)$$

$$y = y(u)$$

$$z = z(u)$$

If each of these functions is a polynomial, the section $0 \leq u \leq 1$ would be a typical range that defines a spline. We will, however, rather use forms involving control points.

When you design a curve or a surface with splines, you often design it from several sub-sections. A very important concept for joining such sections is *continuity*. Depending on how a spline is to be used, there are different kinds of continuity criteria that need to be met. There are two classes of continuity, *parametric continuity* and *geometric continuity*.

Parametric continuity describes how the splines behave with respect to the control parameter (in the examples above, u). That is, the curves are continuous from a mathematical perspective. There are three levels of parametric continuity that are meaningful for us:

C^0 = continuous position = the curves meet

C^1 = continuous direction = the curves meet at same angle (first derivative)

C^2 = continuous curvature = the curves meet at same bend (second derivative)

C^0 and C^1 are clearly important for most usages. In design work, C^1 should be good most of the time, while C^0 may be appropriate when you simply want a sharp edge. C^2 is particularly important when using splines for animation paths, where a sharp change in acceleration may be perceived as unnatural. See Figure 67.

FIGURE 67. Two spline sections with C^0, C^1 and C^2 continuity

Geometric continuity, G^0, G^1, G^2, have the same meaning except that they only require the first and second derivative functions to be proportional, not identical. For a shape, G^1 is essential to avoid edges. However, when defining splines for other purposes, like defining movement for animation, parametric continuity is preferable.

Say that we have two spline sections defined as follows, illustrated in Figure 68. As mentioned above, we define each section with a variable in the interval $[0, 1]$, here with the functions p_1 and p_2, controlled by the variables u and v.

$$\mathbf{p_1}(u) = \mathbf{a_1}u^3 + \mathbf{b_1}u^2 + \mathbf{c_1}u + \mathbf{d_1}$$

Shape representation, curves and surfaces

$$\mathbf{p_2}(v) = \mathbf{a_2}v^3 + \mathbf{b_2}v^2 + \mathbf{c_2}v + \mathbf{d_2}$$

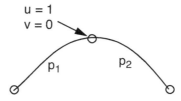

FIGURE 68. Two splines connected in a point

Parametric continuity is fulfilled if the following equations are fulfilled;

$$C^0: \mathbf{p_1}(1) = \mathbf{p_2}(0)$$

$$C^1: \mathbf{p_1}'(1) = \mathbf{p_2}'(0)$$

For two curves in 3D space to fulfill C^1, we thus need 6 equations per vertex, 12 coefficients per section.

For geometric continuity, we add a free variable $k > 0$:

$$G^0: \mathbf{p_1}(1) = \mathbf{p_2}(0)$$

$$G^1: \mathbf{p_1}'(1) = k \cdot \mathbf{p_2}'(0)$$

This essentially gives one less constraint.

From this description, the *natural cubic spline* comes, well, naturally. It is an interpolation spline that was one of the first spline curves to be developed. It provides C^2 continuity. For n sections, we get n+1 control points and 4n coefficients. For C^2 continuity, we get $(n-1)\cdot 4$ boundary conditions, plus two for the end points. This gives two free parameters, which can be determined by zeroing the second derivative for the end points. This gives us a solvable equation system. However, any local change anywhere in the spline will cause global changes. This makes natural splines unsuitable for things like design works, and it was abandoned for splines where each section is defined from local data only.

8.8 Specification by blending functions

Above, I described splines directly by functions. It is of course possible to set up the continuity criteria and solve the resulting equation system. However, in practice it is more convenient to base the spline on control points, and let a set of known functions calculate the spline. In this case, the continuity and type of spline is determined from the chosen set of functions. We say that the control points are blended together by *blending functions*.

As a rough guide to what blending functions must look like, they will have different behavior for interpolation and approximation splines. An interpolation spline must pass through the control points, so at the u value that corresponds to the intersection with the control point, the blending function for that control point must be 1, and all others must have zero crossings for that u. Approximation splines, on the other hand, do not need to have that behavior for control points that need not be hit. This is the case for Bézier curves, where only the end points are guaranteed to lie on the curve.

Another kind of spline that is specified by blending function is the *Hermite spline*. A Hermite spline is specified for two control points plus a slope vector for the endpoints. Thus, it provides G^1 continuity. However, this spline is less popular that Bézier curves and Cardinal splines, which we will focus upon.

8.9 Bézier curves

One of the most popular and elegant splines is the Bézier curve. A Bézier curve is a spline defined over n control points specified with a polynomial of degree n-1. In practice, the cubic spline is most popular, defined by 4 control points per section.

A Bézier curve always passes through the first and last control point, while the others (usually 2) work as attractors. The curve is always within the convex hull of the control points. See Figure 69.

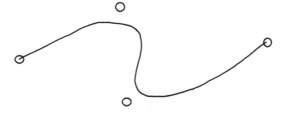

FIGURE 69. The 4 points are blended together using 4 blending functions

The blending functions for a Bézier curve are so-called Bernstein polynomials. In the 4-point case (which we assume from here on) they are defined as follows:

$$BEZ_{0,3} = (1\text{-}u)^3$$

$$BEZ_{1,3} = 3u(1\text{-}u)^2$$

$$BEZ_{2,3} = 3(1\text{-}u)u^2$$

$$BEZ_{3,3} = u^3$$

This set of functions is both mathematically and visually highly symmetrical. See Figure 70.

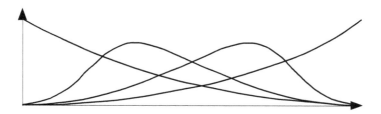

FIGURE 70. Blending functions for a 4-point Bézier curve

Note that the sum of these functions is always 1, for any u. (Verify it yourself.) They are also positive within the range. Compare these blending functions to the definition of barycentric coordinates, section 4.10 on page 30. They fulfill the demands for all $0 \leq u \leq 1$! Thus, any point on the curve segment will be in the convex hull!

Each function is multiplied by one of the control points. Notice how all functions but one go to zero at the ends. This directly means that the endpoints must be at the curve. There are, however, no u for which $BEZ_{1,3}$ and $BEZ_{2,3}$ go to one while the others go to zero, which is why the curve does not pass through the middle points. Figure 71 illustrates how each control point corresponds to one curve.

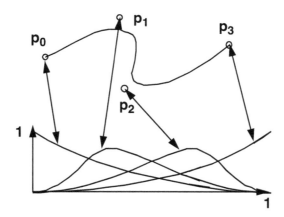

FIGURE 71. The four control points are blended to the spline by the blending functions

Thus, any point $\mathbf{p}(u)$ on the spline can be calculated by the function

$$\mathbf{p}(u) = \mathbf{p_0} \cdot (1-u)^3 + \mathbf{p_1} \cdot 3u(1-u)^2 + \mathbf{p_2} \cdot 3(1-u)u^2 + \mathbf{p_3} \cdot u^3$$

The different meaning of the endpoints and the middle points makes it tempting to consider only the endpoints as true control points, while the others are rather vectors specifying slope and speed.

Let us now have a look at what happens when we connect two Bézier curves. What continuity criteria does such a connection fulfill, and under what circumstances? This is of vital importance to know what the spline can be used for.

The first spline segment is defined by the points $\mathbf{p_0}$, $\mathbf{p_1}$, $\mathbf{p_2}$ and $\mathbf{p_3}$. The second is defined by $\mathbf{p_3}$, $\mathbf{p_4}$, $\mathbf{p_5}$ and $\mathbf{p_6}$. Thus, they are connected in p_3 and the C^0 and G^0 criteria are fulfilled.

Let us write the formula for these two curves.

$$\mathbf{p}(u) = \mathbf{p_0} \cdot (1-u)^3 + \mathbf{p_1} \cdot 3u(1-u)^2 + \mathbf{p_2} \cdot 3(1-u)u^2 + \mathbf{p_3} \cdot u^3$$

$$\mathbf{q}(v) = \mathbf{p_3} \cdot (1-v)^3 + \mathbf{p_4} \cdot 3v(1-v)^2 + \mathbf{p_5} \cdot 3(1-v)v^2 + \mathbf{p_6} \cdot v^3$$

where $v = u-1$.

Let's now calculate the first derivative of these functions. They are essentially identical so doing it with p(u) will do.

$$\mathbf{p'}(u) = \mathbf{p_0} \cdot (-3u^2+6u-3) + \mathbf{p_1} \cdot (9u^2-12u+3) + \mathbf{p_2} \cdot (-9u^2+6u) + \mathbf{p_3} \cdot 3u^2$$

$$\mathbf{p''}(u) = \mathbf{p_0} \cdot (-6u+6) + \mathbf{p_1} \cdot (18u-12) + \mathbf{p_2} \cdot (-18u+6) + \mathbf{p_3} \cdot (6u)$$

C_0 and G_0 are fulfilled, that is, $\mathbf{p}(1) = \mathbf{q}(0)$.

C_1 is fulfilled if $\mathbf{p'}(1) = \mathbf{q'}(0)$.

$$\mathbf{p'}(1) = -3\mathbf{p_2} + 3\mathbf{p_3}$$

$$\mathbf{q'}(0) = -3\mathbf{p_3} + 3\mathbf{p_4}$$

This means that the slope of the curve at the end is given by a line through the endpoint and the next. For C^1,

$$-3\mathbf{p_2} + 3\mathbf{p_3} = -3\mathbf{p_3} + 3\mathbf{p_4}$$

This means that two connected Bézier curves fulfill G^1 if the three points around the connection are in a line, and C^1 if they are on a line and placed on equal distance! This is of great importance. When modeling objects, G^1 is generally desirable, and we see that by adding the constraint with equal distance, it can fulfill C^1 and is thereby also usable for designing animation paths.

Shape representation, curves and surfaces

We can also see that the second derivative at the end depends on three of the points. It is of course possible to arrange these for C^2 continuity, but that is not worthwhile to pursue here.

On the topic of Bézier curves, we should also mention *quadratic* Bézier curves. Such a spline is defined by three control points rather than four, the two end points and a single "attractor" control point between them. If we call the end points $\mathbf{p}_0$ and $\mathbf{p}_2$, and the middle point $\mathbf{p}_1$ (as in Figure 72), the quadratic Bézier curve can be expressed as:

$$\mathbf{p}(u) = (1\text{-}u)^2\mathbf{p}_0 + 2u(1\text{-}u)\mathbf{p}_1 + u^2\mathbf{p}_2$$

FIGURE 72. A quadratic Bézier spline has three control points

As an example of the practical importance of quadratic Bézier curves, they are used in the TrueType font to define curved areas. PostScript, in contrast, uses cubic Béziers.

How did we get these two seemingly unrelated Béziers? The answer appears when looking at Béziers from another point of view, the *de Casteljau algorithm*. This algorithm expresses the evaluation of a Bézier curve as an *interpolation of interpolations*.

For a four-point Bézier, as in Figure 71, de Casteljau makes linear interpolations between each pair of points, finding the points $\mathbf{q}_0$, $\mathbf{q}_1$ and $\mathbf{q}_2$ as of Figure 73. In the figure, u is approximately 1/3.

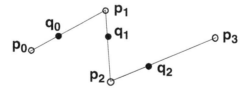

FIGURE 73. The four control points are blended to the spline by the blending functions

With u ranging from 0 to 1 as above, we find these points as

$$\mathbf{q}_0 = \mathbf{p}_0 + (\mathbf{p}_1 - \mathbf{p}_0)u$$

$$\mathbf{q}_1 = \mathbf{p}_1 + (\mathbf{p}_2 - \mathbf{p}_1)u$$

$$\mathbf{q}_2 = \mathbf{p}_2 + (\mathbf{p}_3 - \mathbf{p}_2)u$$

Then we interpolate the same way between points between q_0 and q_1 and q_1 and q_2, as in Figure 73. We now get two points, r_0 and r_1. (Figure 74.)

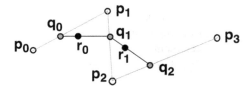

FIGURE 74. A second interpolation results in r_0 and r_1.

A final interpolation between r_0 and r_1 gives us the final point $p(u)$. (Figure 75.)

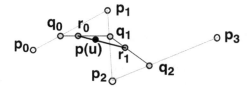

FIGURE 75. A final interpolation to get p(u).

If you rewrite the interpolations, inserting one level into another, we find that

$$p(u) = r_0 + (r_1 - r_0)u = q_0 + (q_1 - q_0)u + (q_1 + (q_2 - q_1)u - q_0 - (q_1 - q_0)u)u$$

$$= q_0(1-u)^2 + q_1 2u(1-u) + q_2 u^2$$

which is a quadratic Bézier! And taking this yet another step yields nothing but the cubic Bézier! So Béziers of different degrees are simply linear interpolations in many levels. I will leave to the reader to figure out how to make a 4th degree Bézier.

8.10 Cardinal splines, Catmull-Rom splines

The Cardinal spline is a class of splines for which we will be most interested in the Catmull-Rom spline [14]. It is an interpolation spline calculated by four control points, but unlike Bézier the four points only define the section between the two middle points (see Figure 76). For making the next section, you add a single point and disregard one at the other end. This is a very desirable behavior. What we get is a spline that is defined only by its control points and that passes through all of them. This makes the Cardinal splines excellent for taking a many-sided polygon as input, from which it creates a smooth curve.

FIGURE 76. For the Cardinal (Catmull-Rom) spline, any set of four control points define a curve between the middle two

In the definition, there is a tension parameter t, which can be varied to adjust the shape somewhat. If t = 1/2, we get the special case of the Catmull-Rom spline. This is not an odd special case but rather the normal, most usable case.

The blending functions of the Catmull-Rom spline do not look as symmetrical and pretty as for the Bézier curve:

$$CAR_{k-1} = -u^3/2 + u^2 - u/2$$

$$CAR_k = 3u^3/2 - 5u^2/2 + 1$$

$$CAR_{k+1} = -3u^3/2 + 2u^2 + u/2$$

$$CAR_{k+2} = u^3/2 - u^2/2$$

Despite the apparent chaos and asymmetry in how the functions are written, they are quite symmetrical when you draw the graphs. See Figure 77.

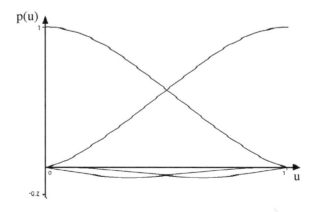

FIGURE 77. Blending functions for Catmull-Rom splines

The blending functions are most conveniently written in matrix form

$$p(u) = \begin{bmatrix} u^3 & u^2 & u & 1 \end{bmatrix} \cdot \begin{bmatrix} -\dfrac{1}{2} & \dfrac{3}{2} & -\dfrac{3}{2} & \dfrac{1}{2} \\[2mm] 1 & -\dfrac{5}{2} & 2 & -\dfrac{1}{2} \\[2mm] -\dfrac{1}{2} & 0 & \dfrac{1}{2} & 0 \\[2mm] 0 & 1 & 0 & 0 \end{bmatrix} \cdot \begin{bmatrix} p_{k-1} \\[1mm] p_k \\[1mm] p_{k+1} \\[1mm] p_{k+2} \end{bmatrix}$$

Thus, the full formula for calculating a point is.

$$\mathbf{p}(u) = \mathbf{p_{k-1}} \cdot CAR_0(u) + \mathbf{p_k} \cdot CAR_1(u) + \mathbf{p_{k+1}} \cdot CAR_2(u) + \mathbf{p_{k+2}} \cdot CAR_3(u)$$

$$= \mathbf{p_{k-1}}(-u^3/2 + u^2 - u/2) + \mathbf{p_k}(3u^3/2 - 5u^2/2 + 1) + \mathbf{p_{k+1}}(-3u^3/2 + 2u^2 + u/2) +$$

$$+ \mathbf{p_{k+2}}(u^3/2 - u^2/2)$$

Note that only two of the functions need to reach 1. The two lower curves are for the outermost control points, who are not part of the segment.

Like we did with Bézier, let us look at what happens at the edge between two spline segments. In this case, it is a matter of adding a single control point at the end. The first segment is between $\mathbf{p_0}$ and $\mathbf{p_1}$ and the second from $\mathbf{p_1}$ to $\mathbf{p_2}$. Thus the first segment is defined by $\mathbf{p_{-1}}$ to $\mathbf{p_2}$:

$$\mathbf{p}(u) = \mathbf{p_{-1}}(-u^3/2+u^2-u/2) + \mathbf{p_0}(3u^3/2-5u^2/2+1) + \mathbf{p_1}(-3u^3/2+2u^2+u/2) + \mathbf{p_2}(u^3/2-u^2/2)$$

$$\mathbf{p}'(u) = \mathbf{p_{-1}}(-3u^2/2 + 2u - 1/2) + \mathbf{p_0}(9u^2/2 - 5u) + \mathbf{p_1}(-9u^2/2 + 4u + 1/2) + \mathbf{p_2}(3u^2/2-u)$$

$$\mathbf{p}''(u) = \mathbf{p_{-1}}(-3u + 2) + \mathbf{p_0}(9u - 5) + \mathbf{p_1}(-9u + 4) + \mathbf{p_2}(3u - 1)$$

$\mathbf{q}(v)$, the function for the next segment, is one step ahead, at $\mathbf{p_0}$ to $\mathbf{p_3}$.

$$\mathbf{q}(v) = \mathbf{p_0}(-v^3/2+v^2-v/2) + \mathbf{p_1}(3v^3/2-5v^2/2+1) + \mathbf{p_2}(-3v^3/2+2v^2+v/2) + \mathbf{p_3}(v^3/2-v^2/2)$$

As expected, $\mathbf{p}(1) = \mathbf{q}(0) = \mathbf{p_{k+1}}$, so C^0 and G^0 are fulfilled.

Now we want to know if and when $\mathbf{p}'(1) = \mathbf{q}'(0)$.

$$\mathbf{p}'(1) = \mathbf{p_{-1}}(-3/2+2-1/2) + \mathbf{p_0}(9/2-5) + \mathbf{p_1}(-9/2+4+1/2) + \mathbf{p_2}(3/2-1) = -\mathbf{p_0}/2 + \mathbf{p_2}/2$$

$$\mathbf{q}'(0) = \mathbf{p_0}(-1/2) + \mathbf{p_1}(0) + \mathbf{p_2}(1/2) + \mathbf{p_3}(0) = -\mathbf{p_0}/2 + \mathbf{p_2}/2$$

Shape representation, curves and surfaces

Exactly the same, in *any case*! The slope at any point is in a line between the two closest neighbors, and the bend as well as speed are continuous, This means that Catmull-Rom splines have C^1 and G^1 continuity, always! This makes it ideal for designing animation paths. However, the Bézier curves may appear easier to fine tune. Both kinds of curves appear in 2D design programs, sometimes both in the same application, but Bézier is clearly the most popular of the two.

8.11 B-splines, NURBSs

The B-spline is a more general variant of the Bézier curve, and the NURBS (Non-Uniform Rational B-Spline) is a more general variant of the B-spline. NURBS has gained considerable popularity in CAD and other 3D modeling programs. It can exactly represent all quadric curves. As modern, popular splines they deserve mentioning, but we choose not to go into any depth here.

8.12 Bézier patches

So far, we have only discussed curves, not surfaces. However, defining a surface with splines turns out to be rather straight-forward. With a 2-dimensional array of control points, say 4x4 control points, you can obviously define splines along any four points that form a row or a column. However, if you take four such splines in one direction, and select a specific u value, you get four points at any point along the curves, and these four points define a spline in the other direction. Thus, this set of 16 points define a surface patch, a Bézier patch, as shown in Figure 78.

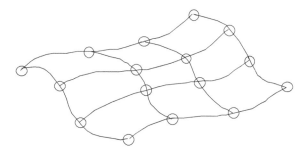

FIGURE 78. Bézier surface patch

The calculation is very straight-forward. You simply multiply the blending functions for each direction. This makes the blending a 2-dimensional sum:

$$p(u, v) = \sum_{j=0}^{3} \sum_{i=0}^{3} BEZ_{j,3}(v) BEZ_{k,3}(u)$$

As shown earlier, you can connect two Bézier curve segments with G^1 continuity by placing the three control points around the connection in a line. The same rule applies to Bézier surfaces. However, the dependency between the two dimensions will complicate things a little bit. Connecting two patches is easy, but consider the center when you connect four patches! You get no less than six spline ends that must match one of the others. See Figure 79.

The center pixel (black) is where all the patches meet. That point, and the eight neighbors around it, must all be in the same plane! This means that those nine points can be specified by the following information:

- The center point, in full 3D freedom

- A normal vector for that point. Since its length has no specific meaning, that gives 2 more degrees of freedom.

- The four corner control points can be moved in the plane. That gives 2 degrees of freedom for each point.

- The four side points are given by these data and need not to be specified at all.

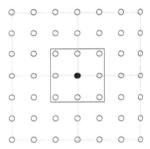

FIGURE 79. Four Bézier patches connected. The nine center control points must be in a plane

Thus, every corner of a Bézier patch can be specified with 13 degrees of freedom.

8.13 Curved PN Triangles

The 16-point Bézier patches as described in section 8.12, is directly derived from 1D Bézier curves, and was supported by OpenGL in older versions. Alas, that support is now deprecated. This brings another kind of Bézier patch into focus, the Curved PN Triangles.

Curved PN Triangles, proposed by Vlachos et al [33], is another kind of Bézier patch, this time based on a triangle rather than a quad. PN means "point-normal" and refers to the triangle being defined as three vertices (points) with normal vectors given for each. With this representation, we can create a curved surface patch with no information whatsoever about neighboring geometry, only the vertices and the normal vectors. This can be applied to just about any model, since all models can be converted to triangles.

Shape representation, curves and surfaces

And if that wasn't enough, PN Triangles are highly suited for implementation using geometry or tesselation shaders, two relatively new, advanced shader types that can create additional geometry. Alas, the implementation does not fit here but is left for volume 2.

A Curved PN Triangle is a shape that is determined as follows. From the three vertices and the normals, a total of ten control points (including the three vertices) are calculated. See Figure 80. Note the 3-dimensional index on each point.

Six of the control points are located along the edges, based on points evenly offset along the edge, then projected to the plane defined by the closest vertex and its normal vector. See Figure 81.

The final point, b111, in the middle of the triangle, is calculated as

$$b_{111} = ((b_{300} + b_{030} + b_{003}) / 3 + (b_{201} + b_{102} + b_{012} + b_{021} + b_{210} + b_{120})/6)/2$$

that is, average of two points: the average of all corners and the average of all edge points.

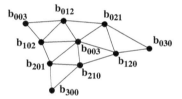

FIGURE 80. Control points used by a curved PN triangle

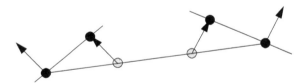

FIGURE 81. Evenly spacing + projecting on plane defined by normal vector

Using these points, we can use barycentric coordinates (see section 4.10) to specify where we want to create a point. We use the symbols u, v, w as barycentric coordinates here, to conform to Vlachos et al [33]. There are three symbols, but $w = 1 - u - v$ so two are enough input. From [33] we have:

$$b(u, v) = \sum_{i + j + k = 3} b_{ijk} \cdot \frac{3!}{i!\,j!\,k!} \cdot u^i v^j w^k$$

$$= b_{300}w^3 + b_{030}u^3 + b_{003}v^3 + b_{111}6uvw$$

$$+ b_{210}3w^2u + b_{120}3wu^2 + b_{210}3w^2v + b_{021}3u^2v + b_{102}3wv^2 + b_{012}3uv^2$$

The exact formula is rather different from the usual Bézier, since the patch is defined from a triangle and needs an inherently 2-dimensional behavior, but the principle is the same: a formula to blend together a set of control points with simple polynomials.

8.14 Evaluating polynomials

When working with splines and surfaces, a possible performance bottleneck is the evaluation of polynomials. This almost sounds unlikely, since a polynomial only requires multiplications, which is an operation that current CPUs are very good at, but when you need to evaluate huge amounts of polynomials, it may have an impact on performance.

We will cover two methods for optimizing the evaluation:

1) Horner's Rule

2) Forward-difference calculations

Horner's Rule is so simple that you almost wonder why you didn't think of it straight away (or maybe you did?). Take a third-degree polynomial:

$$f(u) = a \cdot u^3 + b \cdot u^2 + c \cdot u + d$$

Evaluating this costs 6 multiplications and 3 additions. That is not a terribly expensive computation, but if it is in an inner loop, optimization can make a difference. A simple rewrite will change it significantly:

$$f(u) = ((a \cdot u + b) \cdot u + c) \cdot u + d$$

This costs 3 multiplications and 3 additions! We cut the number of multiplications in half and lost nothing!

Forward-difference calculations can have even higher impact, but it not as generally applicable. It requires that we need to evaluate the same polynomial many times for constant increments of u. In such a case, we can remove all multiplications and replace them by additions!

Let us take that same function again:

$$f(u) = a \cdot u^3 + b \cdot u^2 + c \cdot u + d$$

Take the constant step forward, by Δ.

$$f(u+\Delta) = a \cdot (u+\Delta)^3 + b \cdot (u+\Delta)^2 + c \cdot (u+\Delta) + d =$$

$$= a(u^3 + 3u^2\Delta + 3u\Delta^2 + \Delta^3) + b(u^2 + 2u\Delta + \Delta^2) + cu + d$$

Shape representation, curves and surfaces

Then we can form the difference

$$f(u + \Delta) - f(u) = 3a\Delta \cdot u^2 + (3a\Delta^2 + 2b\Delta)u + a\Delta^3 + b\Delta^2 + c\Delta = g(u)$$

This new function, $g(u)$, is one degree lower than $f(u)$, it is a second (rather than third) degree polynomial! This is the secret behind the method.

Replace all constant expressions as

$$a_g = 3a\Delta$$

$$b_g = 3a\Delta^2 + 2b\Delta$$

$$c_g = a\Delta^3 + b\Delta^2 + c\Delta$$

and we have

$$g(u) = a_g u^2 + b_g u + c_g$$

We repeat the process by forming

$$g(u+\Delta) - g(u) = a_g(2u\Delta + \Delta^2) + b_g\Delta = h(u)$$

Again we define symbols for the constants as

$$a_h = 2\Delta a_g$$

$$b_h = a_g\Delta^2 + b_g\Delta$$

to get

$$h(u) = a_h u + b_h$$

One last time!

$$h(u+\Delta) - h(u) = a_h(u+\Delta) - a_h u = a_h\Delta$$

Finally, we define the constant $a_i = a_h\Delta$

Now we have the functions $f(u)$, $g(u)$ and $h(u)$. For any starting value u_0 we can calculate starting values for all functions, and the constant a_i. After that initialization, we can take a step by Δ like this:

$$f(u+\Delta) = f(u) + g(u)$$

$$g(u+\Delta) = g(u) + h(u)$$

$$h(u+\Delta) = h(u) + a_i$$

Thus, for each step we take, we calculate a new function value with only three additions!

8.15 Drawing and subdividing splines

When drawing a spline, you may draw it as a series of lines, subdividing the spline to a sequence of points on the curve. It is easy to subdivide it in uniform steps, e.g. 10 steps per spline (also giving us the option of using forward-difference calculations), but to create high quality curves, you should subdivide until the distance between the curve and a line between two points is small enough, if the curve is approximated within some tolerance level.

If you start with a spline from u=0 to u=1, a straight-forward approach is to split it in half, recursively. Measure the distance between the midpoint and the line beween the endpoints, and decide whether to continue or not.

Subdividing splines is not only a matter of drawing existing splines, but also a method for improving the quality of low-polygon models. Instead of using the polygons as flat surfaces, you can define splines from the polygons, and subdivide the splines to create models with higher resolution. We say that we make a *tesselation* of the model.

9. Creating natural shapes

While chapter 8 assumed that you are working with models that are manually designed or scanned, this chapter will discuss the topic of procedural methods for generating content, 3D shapes in particular. This will open new possibilities, especially the possibility to create objects that have a natural look, that mimic nature. Fractals form the foundation for these techniques, and at the end we will go somewhat outside that topic. Another fundamental tool for these purposes is noise functions.

9.1 Fractals

I am sure you have heard about fractals before. When you hear the word, you might think about pictures like Figure 82.

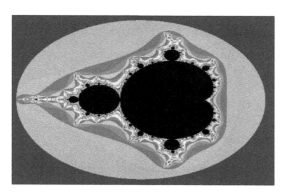

FIGURE 82. Typical fractal image (Mandelbrot set)

What is it, more than a pretty image? We will have a very different approach. This section will make a look into fractals from a very practical perspective: using fractals as a tool in computer graphics. I will ruthlessly skip over all the interesting theory.

Fractals are shapes with:

- self-similarity

- infinite resolution

A fractal function can be used for modeling such shapes. Now, what do we need self-similar shapes with infinite resolution for? Answer: natural objects. Many natural objects have fractal features. Let us look at the classic example: a coastline, in Figure 83.

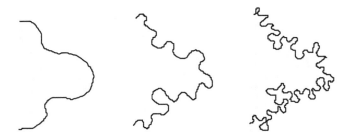

FIGURE 83. The shape and length of a coastline varies with resolution

The length of a coastline (usually Britain's in examples) is not constant, it varies with the resolution with which it is reproduced. At a coarse level, the length of the coast gets close to the convex hull, but the higher the resolution, the closer you look, the more detail will appear and the longer it will get. You will trace it into large bays, into small ones, around rocks, around small stones, around sand particles... when should you stop?

There are many kinds of objects with this behavior, and we can often create models, or the base structure for models, from fractals. But not from fractals like the Mandelbrot. There are several kinds of fractals:

- Geometric, self-similar fractals

- Statistically self-similar fractals (stochastic fractals)

- Self-squaring fractals

There are other ways to classify fractals, these are just the ones we will discuss further.

9.2 Self-similar fractals

Self-similar fractals are highly useful for computer graphics. A geometric, self-similar fractal is described by two objects, the initiator and the generator. This is best explained by example: the Koch curve. See Figure 84. The initiator consists of a number of areas that can be replaced by the generator, scaled to fit. The generator also contains such areas, so this process can be made recursive.

In this case all parts of the initiator and generator can be replaced by scaled-down generators. This is not necessarily the case. A generator or initiator can contain fixed, non-fractal parts.

Creating natural shapes

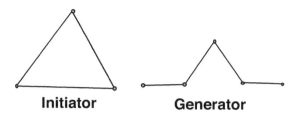

Initiator   **Generator**

FIGURE 84. A self-similar geometric fractal is defined by an initiator and a generator

This can be implemented by a recursive function. The initiator is defined, but passes all parts to next level without drawing anything itself. The recursive function replaces selected parts with the generator, which is scaled to fit the part. The generator itself contains the same replacable part, but at a smaller scale, and that part will be passed on into the next level of recursion. The recursion will stop at desired recursion depth or when sections are small enough (e.g. 1 pixel long). The result for different depth are shown in Figure 85.

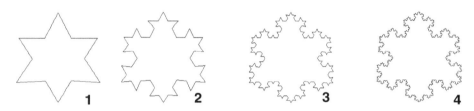

1   **2**   **3**   **4**

FIGURE 85. Resulting Koch curves

Here is pseudo code for drawing the figures above.

```
procedure DrawKoch(p1, p2, depth)
if depth >= maxDepth then
    MoveTo(p1)
    LineTo(p2)
    return
else
    calculate p3, p4, p5 as the three points inside the generator
    DrawKoch(p1, p3, depth+1)
    DrawKoch(p3, p4, depth+1)
    DrawKoch(p4, p5, depth+1)
    DrawKoch(p5, p2, depth+1)

main procedure:
Choose three initiator points, g1, g2, g3
DrawKoch(g1, g2, 0)
DrawKoch(g2, g3, 0)
DrawKoch(g3, g1, 0)
```

This principle can be carried on to 3D. Figure 86 hints at the possibilities.

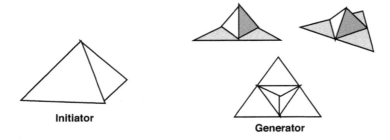

Initiator

Generator

FIGURE 86. Self-similar fractals in 3D

These shapes were not so obviously useful, perhaps, so let's try something different: Generation of plants. Plants are very regular, highly self-similar, but extremely complex, which makes them ideal for this kind of algorithms. A first try may look like Figure 87.

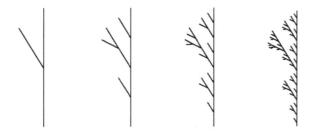

FIGURE 87. Not really a plant

It is somewhat promising, but too self-similar! Plants are not that regular. What we need are *statistically self-similar fractals*, fractals that are not exactly self-similar, but only mostly. We add some random variation in the generator, and the result is striking, Figure 88.

FIGURE 88. Same branch generator as before, with some randomness!

This is much better, it actually reminds of a plant, which the previous one did not. Let's try one more time, with a modified generator. The result is shown in Figure 89.

Creating natural shapes

FIGURE 89. Even better tree

Now we are getting somewhere. With 3D depth in the definition, you can create the structure of a detailed 3D tree with only a few lines of code.

There are also fractals for generating terrains. A popular one is the *random midpoint displacement* method. We start by looking at it in 2D, in Figure 90:

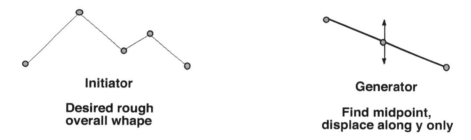

Initiator

Desired rough overall whape

Generator

Find midpoint, displace along y only

FIGURE 90. Hinted random midpoint displacement method

Running this algorithm for a few iterations generate the shape in Figure 91.

FIGURE 91. Random midpoint displacement method after 7 iterations

This is somewhat OK, but we want 3D, not 2D. Or more specifically a 2D array to use in a 3D world.

In 3D, we no longer work on lines, but rather patches, squares. In every iteration, you split a square to four, and make some kind of displacements. The sides, the edge points, have to match the neighbors. See Figure 92.

An algorithm that solves this in an elegant way is the *Diamond-Square algorithm*, where in each step the center point between four points is generated. This makes the space sampled in squares or diamonds, alternating.

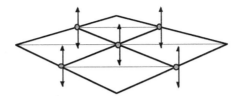

FIGURE 92. Random midpoint displacement in 3D (2D data to use in 3D)

Figure 93 shows the two phases of one iteration. The first phase creates new values (white circles) inside each square of existing ones (black circles). First, we calculate the height of the center by interpolation of the surroundings. This is, in the simplest form, the mean of the four existing neighbors, which is bilinear interpolation. Even better results are calculated with a bigger filter, taking more samples into account. Then a random offset is added, scaled by the length of the side of a square.

The new points will change the grid to a grid of "diamonds", squares standing on the corner. The second iteration, shown to the right, does the same thing, but now from the "diamonds" (black circles), interpolating the center of each, and adding a random offset, now scaled by the size of the diamonds, creating new samples (white circles).

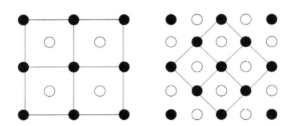

FIGURE 93. The two phases of the Diamond-Square algorithm

This is then iterated to the desired resolution. Thus, the grid will switch between axis aligned squares and "diamonds", hence the name. Notice that the size of the squares change by 1 over the square root of 2 in each phase, so the random offset is scaled down by that factor.

The Diamond Square algorithm has an undeserved reputation for producing an unsatisfactory terrain with noticable artifacts. This is to a considerable degree caused by bad scaling of the offsets. With proper scaling, this method creates very good results with excellent performance. To our knowledge this is the only algorithm that will create a high quality fractal terrain in linear time!

It does have two weaknesses. First, the higher frequencies generated in the later, finer stages, can not affect the samples generated at earlier levels. This makes these samples fixed at zero for the higher frequencies. This is hardly noticable, and a weakness it shares

---

     Creating natural shapes

with some other methods. Second, it is challenging to expand the data later, like making new patches and make them fit existing ones.

One method that solves the first problem is the related Square-Square algorithm, which creates a higher resolution version of the data by upsampling and adding noise. Like before, the amplitude of the noise must be smaller for every iteration, proportional to the distance between the elements. If we illustrate the method similarily to diamond square, we can get an image like Figure 94.

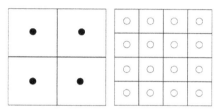

FIGURE 94. The Square-Square algorithm

We will return to terrains with additional methods at the end of the chapter.

9.3 Fractal dimension

The self-similar fractals shown above can be analyzed and characterized by a measure called the *fractal dimension*. This is a value that measures the fractal's space filling behaviour. A process that results in a line will have fractal dimension 1, it fills one dimension. An area-filling fractal will have fractal dimension 2. There are also cases in-between.

The fractal dimension is defined as

$$ns^D = 1$$

from which we get

$$D = \frac{\ln(n)}{\ln\left(\frac{1}{s}\right)}$$

where D is the fractal dimension, n is the number of subparts in the generator, and s is the scale factor from one level to the next.

Example: The Koch curve has 4 parts, so n = 4, and each part is 1/3 of the generator, so s = 1/3. That gives us D = ln 4 / ln 3 ≈ 1.26.

Another example: If you take a line and split it in two, recursively, you get a process just like a fractal. Then n = 2 and s = 1/2, and the fractal dimension then is ln 2 / ln 2 = 1. Plain, 1-dimensional, which describes the result perfectly!

9.4 Self-squaring fractals

Now, for completeness, let us turn to *self-squaring fractals*. These are the usual fractals, the strange but beautiful images that look like nothing you ever seen from Saturnus[1]. These images, like the ones above, are created with extremely simple functions. In this case they are based on simple functions in complex space.

They work like this: You insert complex numbers (points) into a function. Then you apply the function recursively, generating a new point in every recursion, and analyze the behavior. Does the function

- diverge?
- converge?
- have a chaotic behavior?

In case it converges or is chaotic, the question is, does it keep within some limit in a number of iterations? This is the measure you use, a limit, like a circle with radius 10.

Here is an example, the *Julia set*. It is defined by the function

$$z_{k+1} = z_k^2 + \lambda$$

where λ is some complex constant. A simple function, to say the least, but remember that squaring a complex number not only changes the magnitude, but also makes it rotate. By picking a limit and checking if it is still within the limit after different numbers of iterations, and running it for different starting points, we get the image in Figure 95.

This means that if you start outside the outermost area, the function diverges immediately. For different shades, it stays within the limit for a larger number of iterations. Here is pseudo-code for the implementation:

```
for y = miny to maxy
   for x = minx to maxx
      (zr, zi) = scaling of (x,y)

      for i = 0 to maxiterations
         z = z2 + lambda
         if |z| > R then Leave
      Draw pixel (x,y) (different colors for different i)
```

---

1. That is a reference to an old comic strip. Don't worry about it. :)

Creating natural shapes

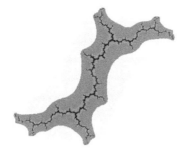

FIGURE 95. Julia set for $\lambda = (0, 1) = 0 + j$

The maximum recursion depth (maxiterations) can be around 15, so this is a fast function. The radius can be small, $R^2 \approx 10$ in the example.

There are several Julia sets depending on the λ value in $z_{k+1} = z_k^2 + \lambda$. With other λ values we can get images like Figure 96.

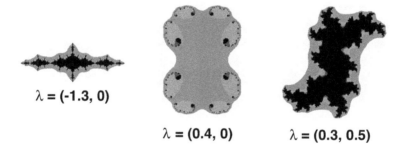

$\lambda = (-1.3, 0)$

$\lambda = (0.4, 0)$ $\lambda = (0.3, 0.5)$

FIGURE 96. Other Julia sets

Let us not also have a look at the *Mandelbrot set*. The Mandelbrot set is the most famous self-squaring fractal, based on the following function:

$$z_{k+1} = z_k^2 + z_0$$

The difference to the Julia set is that the function itself depends on the starting point. Otherwise it works the same, and we get this result in Figure 97.

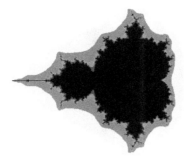

FIGURE 97. The Mandelbrot set

If you zoom in to Julia or Mandelbrot sets, into areas where there is detail, then you can zoom forever and there will still be detail, with the same structure. This is interesting, but is it useful? I am sure you can find some use for it, but it lacks the immediate and obvious use that the geometric fractals have. So my opinion is that self-squaring fractals are

- beautiful

- non-predictable

- of limited usability

- mathematical curiosities

So let us leave them as far as computer graphics go (but not without trying to run one yourself, of course).

9.5 Other procedural methods for generating geometry

I will end this section by returning to the geometrical case, with a quick introduction to alternative ways for procedural geometric modeling that are not strictly fractals.

What I have been talking about most of this chapter is procedural methods for generating shapes. If we skip the infinite self-similarity and change the behavior on different levels, we get a result that is no longer a fractal. It has no unlimited resolution, it is not self-similar, it can be based on a recursive function but it is not really recursive any more.

Figure 98 shows a simple example: a tree with leaves.

This is a very small change on the tree generating function. All I have done is to replace the last iteration with leaf generator.

The term "graftals" has been used for these functions, to show the difference but also the relation to fractals. We leave the mathematical foundations of the fractals to get the tools we need. There are methods for creating not only large structures like a tree, but also to create shapes that are used for surface detail, like fur.

Creating natural shapes

FIGURE 98. A tree with leaves

9.6 Terrains and other shapes from noise functions

In section 9.2, I touched upon the problem of generating terrains. This is an important problem with several good solutions with different characteristics. These include:

- Random heightmap with spatial filtering

- Recursively detailed heightmap with diminishing random offsets

- Random heightmap with filtering in frequency space

- Random gradients (Perlin noise)

A critical component in the generation of natural objects, apart from the self-similarity, is the randomness. In many cases, it is easier to work directly with noise rather than working with fractal functions. An effective, although not as easily scaled, method for creating a terrain is to fill a height map with random numbers, and then apply filtering until it looks nice. In other words, *noise*.

Notice that we intuitively should know that we must filter the data, since straight white noise will not do, and this is certainly correct. But the need for filtering is distressing until you understand why it is there. The frequency content of natural functions, be it shapes or sound or whatever, tends to be high for low frequencies and drop for higher frequencies, approximately by f^{-1}. This is an example of *colored noise*.

Filling a big buffer with noise and then applying spatial filters on it is highly inefficient. You will need very large and well designed filters to get the behavior you want. This is often taken as an argument for ruling out random height map filtering altogether. We will not do that, however, but rather look at other approaches.

A different method for getting this behavior is to generate noise at different resolutions, with lower amplitude at higher resolutions. What we do then is to generate noise in different frequency bands.

Let me apply that technique to terrain generation. I call this the height field approach. In this first step, I stay very close to the fractal methods. In fact, this method is fractal, in that it gives infinite resolution. Self-similarity, however, will be harder to find since it is generated entirely from noise.

We define the terrain by several levels. Terrain level k is an array of resolution 2^k x 2^k. This means that the next level has 4x the resolution. At the lowest level, we have a single height value, a single height field block. What you set it to is irrelevant.

For every iteration, every single height value is split to a new 2x2 block. The heights in the block should be generated by a filter over a small neighborhood. Then add random offset to all values. The offset should be smaller for higher k.

This gives us the behavior we wanted, the magnitude of the frequency components will be inversely proportional to frequency! What I just described is really the Square-Square algorithm from section 9.2.

This will generate very realistic terrains, a resolution pyramid with high detail that we can use when close-up. The computing is incremental so we can wait with computing any data that we don't need yet for a later time. (Managing the resolution pyramid in real-time can be improved using a method called *geomipmapping*, see chapter 13.)

Notice that what we did was to, with some effort, create noise with varying frequency one band at a time. We can do the same thing directly in the frequency plane, by using the Fourier transform. In practice, we use FFT, the Fast Fourier Transform. In this case we can do the same thing in one single step.

Create a 2D image with the maximum resolution you need. This is *frequency space*, it is not an image. You fill frequency space (2D) with random numbers. Then, you filter it by

$$G(f) = F(f) \cdot 1/|f|$$

Since we are in frequency space, this is merely a multiplication of every element.

Then you convert it to a spatial image with FFT. What we get is an image filled with colored noise. The result can be something like Figure 99.

FIGURE 99. Colored noise generated by FFT

Creating natural shapes

Is it a cloud? Is it a terrain? Is it something else? You use it to anything you like. What is important is that it has a very natural feel. As a bonus, the image is even wrap-around, a feature provided by the nature of discrete Fourier transforms.

Finally, let us turn to the option of random gradients. The most famous noise functions are of that variety, *Perlin noise*. The concept of using colored noise for natural shapes was popularized in computer graphics by Ken Perlin [30], who used it in the groundbreaking movie TRON. Thus colored noise is often referred to as *Perlin noise* in computer graphics. Perlin noise is less general than the FFT based noise I described above, in the sense that it covers a limited range of frequency space. Perlin noise is generated in screen space, like the terrain generator I outlined above, but instead of randomizing offsets, it randomizes the *slope* of the function.

Perlin noise defines a set of random gradients in a set of discrete points. Then you can look up function values on the resulting function, calulated by interpolation. The function value in the discrete points is always zero. That gives us a function somewhat like Figure 100.

FIGURE 100. 1D Perlin noise, interpolation between discrete points with random offsets. Based on a figure from Gustavsson [34].

The interpolation between the points is, obviously, of great importance. It must create a continuous function, with continuous derivatives at the very least of the first order. Perlin originally used splines with the blending function $t*t*(3\text{-}2t) = 3t^2 - 2t^3$, which has a first degree derivative of zero in the endpoints. He later changed to $6t^5 - 15t^4 + 10t^3$, which also gives a continous (zero) second derivative.

Perlin noise can be generalized to higher dimensions. The example in Figure 101 was created with Perlin's original code, as available on-line [35].

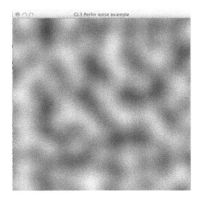 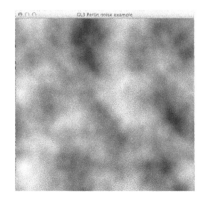

FIGURE 101. 2D Perlin noise, 1 octave (left) and 4 octaves (right)

As Figure 100 and Figure 101 (left) suggest, this gives us a function with very narrow frequency range. In order to get a richer, more varied function, we need to combine several noise functions of different density, "octaves". Using 4 functions at different density, with lower amplitude for higher frequencies (1/f as before, that is, twice the frequency half the amplitude), we get the result shown to the right in Figure 101. As you can see, this results in a fuzziness similar to Figure 99, but the cost is multiple look-ups in the Perlin noise functions, and less precise control over frequency behavior. The closer you want to get to the highly general and flexible FFT solution, the closer you will get in complexity. But for simpler cases, when you really want narrow band noise, Perlin noise has a computational advantage. But do not forget about Diamond Square, above, which produces results similar to the FFT method in linear time. So, Perlin noise is slow, but it has an important advantage: You can easily extend it to new areas with no special processing for edges.

It should be noted that Perlin has developed a newer noise algorithm, "Simplex noise", but for that I refer to the description by Stefan Gustavsson [34].

You can vary these ideas a lot. Make it random, make it noisy. Anything that looks stale and static can be brought to life with some noise. Let the noise go into shapes, into textures, and into movement. Noise is only a problem when there is so much of it that it destroys the signal. Otherwise, it is a good thing!

And this is one of the laws of computer graphics:

Noise is beautiful!

10. Surface detail

Shading is nice, but the objects still look like something between plastic and metal. We want to add surface detail, preferably without needing more polygons. To achieve that, there are a number of surface mapping techniques that map varying kinds of data onto the surface. The most obvious one is texture mapping. With texture mapping, you can make it look like wood or textile, and with bump mapping you can get some very convincing surface variations without actually modeling it in 3D.

Possible mappings include:

- Texture mapping
- Billboards (3D sprites)
- Bump mapping
- Light mapping
- Environment mapping

Let's start with the most important case:

10.1 Texture mapping

Texture mapping is the most important mapping. As such, it is well supported by both software and hardware solutions.

For our purposes in this volume, texture mapping is the task of mapping a 2-dimensional image onto a surface. For a surface triangle, each vertex is not only a point in 3-dimensional space, but it also specifies a point in texture space, a point in the 2-dimensional image. Thus, we are mapping coordinates in the texture image, texture coordinates, to 3D view/world/model coordinates, as shown in Figure 102. These coordinates are usually denoted (s, t).

The actual rendering of the texture upon the surface is done with depth taken into account. The texture data is loaded into VRAM, and the polygon is rendered by the GPU. This process is part of the *scan-line conversion*, and is discussed further in chapter 15.

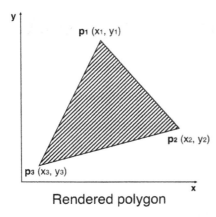 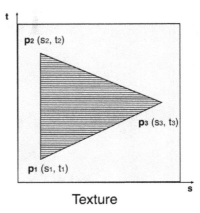

FIGURE 102. Texture mapping

The obvious use for textures is to map surface images, images of the material such as wood, rock etc. However, they are also useful for other purposes. They can hold information about lighting (light mapping), small surface variations (bump mapping), reflectivity variations and more.

To do texture mapping, coordinates in texture space (s,t) must be mapped to world space coordinates. When you examine the problem, two central problems arise:

1) How do you find the texture coordinates (s,t) from (x,y) screen coordinates?

2) How do you render texture mapped polygons efficiently and correctly?

Generally, we pre-generate texture coordinates for every vertex. This pre-generation can be done by hand, but this is unreasonable for anything beyond trivial models. Instead, we can calculate the texture coordinates in some more practical way.

10.2 Texture coordinate generation

Low-level implementation of texture mapping is, just like Z buffering, something that we let a hardware accelerator handle for us. Generating the texture mapping coordinates, however, is something that we have reasons to do ourselves, even if packages like older versions of OpenGL provide some automation for us. The question today is rather whether you want to do it as a preprocessing step or on the fly in a shader.

The problem that we want to solve is how to wrap a texture around a model, usually so that it covers the entire model. This is done as follows: Consider a simple geometrical shape used as intermediate surface around the model. For every vertex in the model, project it onto the surface. This point can then be transformed to a coordinate system from which we extract the texture coordinates (s,t).

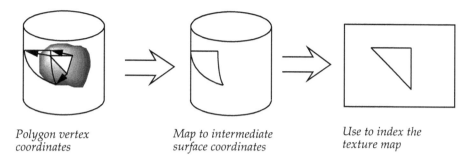

| Polygon vertex coordinates | Map to intermediate surface coordinates | Use to index the texture map |

FIGURE 103. Texture coordinate generation

The most common mappings are linear, cylindrical and spherical. Then the intermediate surfaces are a plane, a cylinder and a sphere. Figure 103 illustrates the case with a cylinder. Which mapping to use depends on the model. Generally, you should pick a mapping where the shape is as close to the model as possible. Cylindrical mapping works well with elongated models. Linear mappings are best on rather flat models.

10.2.1 Linear mapping

$$u = x$$

$$v = y$$

This maps along z. You may want to generalize it to map in any direction. This can be done by a change of basis, or by rotating the model. For example, if we first rotate around x by the angle a, and then map along z as above, we get:

$$u = x$$

$$v = y{\cdot}\cos(a) - z{\cdot}\sin(a)$$

The z component, $y{\cdot}\sin(a) + z{\cdot}\cos(a)$, is discarded. You can derive expressions for any direction you want by multiplying (x, y, z) by rotation matrices and then map (x, y) to texture coordinates.

10.2.2 Cylindrical mapping

You are probably used to seeing cylindrical coordinates defined as

$$x = R{\cdot}\cos(\theta)$$

$$y = R{\cdot}\sin(\theta)$$

$$z = z$$

but for texture mapping, we need the inverse:

Surface detail

$$u = \arctan(y, x)$$

$$v = z$$

See below for the definition of the arctan function.

10.2.3 Spherical mapping

Again, the usual definition is

$$x = R \cdot \cos(\phi)\cos(\theta)$$

$$y = R \cdot \cos(\phi)\sin(\theta)$$

$$z = R \cdot \sin(\phi)$$

but we want the inverse mapping, in order to map the angles onto texture coordinates:

$$u = \arctan(y, x)$$

$$v = \sin^{-1}(z/R)$$

If you are uncomfortable with the definition of spherical coordinates above, you may swap $\cos(\phi)$ and $\sin(\phi)$. That will redefine the angle ϕ to be zero at the zenith, instead of at the equator. Both definitions appear in literature, and I don't find the difference particularly interesting. Use what you prefer.

The function arctan is a function of two variables that is defined like this:

```
arctan(y,x) =
    x > 0: tan⁻¹(y/x)
    x<0: π + tan⁻¹(y/x)
    x = 0, y > 0: π/2
    x = 0, y < 0: -π/2
```

In all the examples above, u, v are intermediate coordinates that have to be normalized to [0..1] to make the texture fit. As an example, the cylindrical coordinates can be normalized like this (with the z range given as $z_{min} \leq z \leq z_{max}$):

$$s = (u + \pi/2)/2\pi$$

$$t = (v - z_{min})/(z_{max} - z_{min})$$

This will map the texture so that it covers the entire model, with no part of the texture appearing in more than one place.

Note that other implementations of 2-argument arctan may output other ranges. The function atan in GLSL comes in a 2-argument version, with output in the range $[-\pi, \pi]$.

Surface detail

The mappings above are not the only possibilities. You may consider mappings like a two-sided mapping, where you put the face onto a model with one half of the texture, and fold it over to put the other half from the other side, that is, a "flattened" cylindrical mapping where it is much easier to create the textures. An extension of that idea is the cube map, where you have no less than six textures, each mapped onto the sixth of the model where the normal vectors are pointing in its way. Cube mapping, however, is primarily a question of environment mapping, chapter 10.10.

10.2.4 Handling discontinuous coordinates

A very practical aspect of wrapping textures onto objects is what happens at the edge of the parameter space, where spherical or cylindrical coordinates make jumps by 2π. If this discontinuity, this jump in cylindrical or spherical coordinates, is not taken into account, polygons at certain locations will have badly placed textures. See Figure 104, a six-sided approximation of a cylinder seen from above.

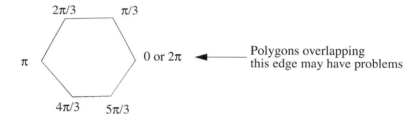

FIGURE 104. Texture mapping may need special considerations at the $0/2\pi$ edge

Let us take a more specific example, with a triangle overlapping the edge. In Figure 105, consider the box to be a cylinder seen from the side. The vertical bar is the $0, 2\pi$ edge.

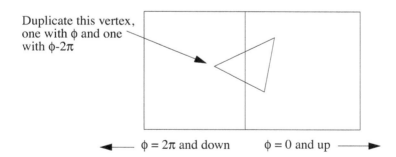

FIGURE 105. Handling texture mapping of problematic polygons by splitting vertices

If the s, t coordinates generated are straight from the definitions above, the triangle will be mapped into s, t space as in the right part of Figure 106 below. This is, however, incorrect. It should be mapped over the edge, as in the left figure. Texture space is really an infinitely repeating, wrap-around space, and the mistake here is that this is not taken into account.

What can you do about that? One option is to duplicate vertices on polygons that overlap the edge, so that the vertex to the right is mapped onto negative u. If you want to be able to render the mesh with calls like glDrawElements, this is necessary. The drawback of that solution is that such meshes are harder to process for other problems, like level-of-detail.

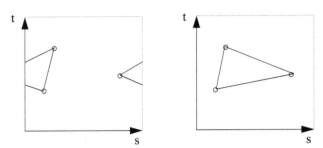

FIGURE 106. Correct (left) and incorrect (right) mapping of the triangle in the previous figure

So in order to hint at an algorithm, here is an outline of how you can do:

Create an array of duplicate vertices, initially only holding markers for unused members.

For every polygon in the mesh, test whether it overlaps the 2π edge by inspecting the positions of its vertices. For most interesting meshes, you can rule out all vertices with $\pi/2 < \theta < 3\pi/2$. When you are in the interval(s) around the edge, test if the vertices in the polygon map to θ on different sides. If that happens, continue with all vertices on a specific side, say the high range, $3\pi/2 < \theta < 2\pi$. Test whether the vertices already have duplicates. If not, create a duplicate in the duplicate array and set its u coordinate to θ-2π (and thereby the s value to the normal value minus 1). See Figure 107.

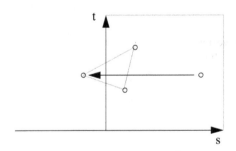

FIGURE 107. Solution to the edge problem: Problem polygons are detected, selected vertices are duplicated and the corresponding texture coordinate is moved down by -1

When all polygons are processed, delete all unused placeholders and keep the needed duplicates.

Strangely, few computer graphics textbooks mention this problem. An exception is professor Buss [3], who comes to conclusions similar to the ones above.

Surface detail

Another solution is to generate texture coordinates in the fragment shader, instead of by vertex, but the increase in computations is considerable. Generation by vertex can be done once and for all, possibly stored back into the model, while doing it in a fragment shader means computing it *for every pixel in every frame*. That kind of computational cost is not to be taken lightly.

10.3 Billboards and impostors

A *billboard* is a textured polygon facing the viewer, closely related to the concepts sprite and impostor. Although texture mapping is a vital part of the concept, it is essentially a case of level-of-detail, so it will be discussed further in chapter 13.8.

10.4 Texture filtering and MIP mapping

This is really a subject that seems more appropriate for chapter 16, but it is intimately related to your setup of texture mapping in OpenGL, so I choose to put it here.

When a texture is accessed, the texture coordinates are usually not exactly on a texel, but somewhere in between. For making the access, you can choose between different filtering options. The two standard options are nearest neighbor (no filtering) or linear filtering.

Generally, linear filtering produces better results than nearest neighbor. For minification, when we are far from the surface, that is certainly the case. However, it is questionable if you really want filtering for magnification, close up, since that causes more conflicts with the visual perception than it removes. (The fact that hardware accelerators routinely provide such filtering doesn't necessarily make it desirable!)

For minification, filtering is often not enough. Severe Moire distorsion can occur. MIP mapping is a method for reducing such aliasing effects in texture mapping, without having to do interpolations or averaging (filtering) in real-time with large filter kernels. It may also be used in conjunction with filtering, for even better results.

The acronym MIP is short for *multum in parvo*, which is latin and means "much in a small space". It is an application of the resolution pyramid concept, which is used a lot in image analysis. We often write "mipmapping" and refer to the image pyramid as a "mipmap" just for comfort, but it really is an acronym.

To do MIP mapping, create a resolution pyramid from the textures used. This is done by sampling down the original texture image with appropriate filtering. Simple averaging of 2x2 pixels to one gives acceptable results. The downsampling is done in several steps, as illustrated by Figure 108. (OpenGL will do this for you. See section 10.5.1.)

When drawing textures, an appropriate resolution is selected depending on distance. This method reduces aliasing effects at high distances for a very low cost in memory (33% more), and a marginal increase of computational burden.

The memory cost for making a resolution pyramid is easily calculated as a sum.

$$\sum_{N}^{i=0}\left(\frac{1}{4}\right)^i \to \frac{1}{3}, N \to \infty$$

The quality of your MIP mapped texture will depend on the filtering used. In magnification, you have the usual choice between linear or nearest-neighbor filtering, but in minification, you can filter not only between texels (bilinear filtering) but also between the mipmap levels (trilinear filtering). See further section 10.5.

FIGURE 108. Resolution pyramid for MIP mapping. Original 128x128 image to the left, followed by three steps of downsampling with low-pass filtering.

MIP mapping does not totally eliminate aliasing. When a polygon is tilted, the texture will vary faster in one direction than another, which will result in different sampling frequencies. MIP mapping can't avoid that problem. There exists variants of MIP mapping that deal with this problem by creating non-square downsamplings, but the memory cost will grow dramatically which often makes it too expensive.

10.5 Texture mapping in OpenGL

Texture mapping is controlled by your fragment shaders. We will now discuss how to get textures from disk into OpenGL, apply them to your models, and how to deal with texture coordinates.

10.5.1 Uploading textures to the GPU

When using texture mapping with OpenGL, you should use "texture objects". You create a new texture object with glGenTextures(), and select it with glBindTexture(). You load textures into VRAM with the call glTexImage2D(). The texture will then be attached to the current texture object.

There are also corresponding calls for 1D and 3D textures, which are both quite useful, but we choose to ignore them here.

Example: If you have a small texture declared as

```
GLubyte texture[4][4][3] =
{
```

```
        { {255,   0,255}, {  0,   0,255}, {  0,   0,255}, {  0,255,255}},
        {  0,   0,255}, {255,   0,255}, {  0,255,255}, {  0,   0,255}},
        {  0,   0,255}, {  0,255,255}, {255,   0,255}, {  0,   0,255}},
        {  0,255,255}, {  0,   0,255}, {  0,   0,255}, {255,   0,255}},
};
```

then you can load it into VRAM and use it by doing

```
glGenTextures(1, texId);
glBindTexture(GL_TEXTURE_2D, texId);
glTexImage2D(GL_TEXTURE_2D,0,3,4,4, GL_RGB,GL_UNSIGNED_BYTE, mini-
tex);
```

Note that I create a texture object, referenced to by texId, selected by glBindTexture. You will need to set the state.

```
glTexParameter(GL_TEXTURE_2D, GL_TEXTURE_WRAP_S, GL_REPEAT);
glTexParameter(GL_TEXTURE_2D, GL_TEXTURE_WRAP_S, GL_REPEAT);
glTexParameter(GL_TEXTURE_2D, GL_TEXTURE_MAG_FILTER, GL_NEAREST);
glTexParameter(GL_TEXTURE_2D, GL_TEXTURE_MIN_FILTER, GL_LINEAR);
```

GL_NEAREST means that when looking up a pixel, OpenGL will simply use the texture element (texel) which is closest to the texture coordinates given. With GL_LINEAR it will interpolate between the four closest texels, which will reduce aliasing considerably.

Finally, you probably want to use mip-mapping. You use glGenerateMipmap to create mipmaps for a texture. With mip-maps, you can no longer specify GL_NEAREST or GL_LINEAR for the minification case. That would turn mip-mapping off again and you would be back at the top-level texture. Instead, you should use GL_LINEAR_MIPMAP_LINEAR. In mip-mapping we not only have a 2D texture, but also a third coordinate, the mipmap level, determined from the density of the texture. GL_LINEAR_MIPMAP_LINEAR specifies that linear filtering should be used both within the texture and between the mipmap levels. It is possible to turn off linear filtering in either direction, using GL_NEAREST_MIPMAP_LINEAR, GL_LINEAR_MIPMAP_NEAREST or even GL_NEAREST_MIPMAP_NEAREST, but I would stick to the higher-quality GL_LINEAR_MIPMAP_LINEAR if at all possible.

10.5.2 Loading textures from image files

But that was a texture which was already in memory. Then we are ignoring one step, loading textures into memory from image files. That has to be done in different ways depending on the image format. OpenGL has no image loading functionality built-in, so we must use external image loading units.

One of the simplest formats you can use is the PPM format. Unfortunately, it is also one of the least capable (no transparency and no compression), and it is rarely supported by image processing programs.

For images with transparency, Targa (.tga) format is a good choice. It is almost as simple as PPM, highly suitable for educational work. Just make sure to get a loader that supports compressed tga's or you will find yourself with images that you can't load.

Portable Network Graphics (PNG) format also supports transparency, and provides better compression than Targa. The library libpng [25] is popular for loading PNG files, but I would rather recommend pnglite [26][27] by Daniel Karling, which is easier to use than libpng. As delivered it lacks demos, but I have provided some myself.

If you have a lot of image data, you will want to save disk space, using JPEG files is an obvious choice. Then the library libJPEG [20] is highly convenient.

On MacOS, MacOSX and MS Windows, QuickTime is an option. It can handle most popular image formats.

10.5.3 Texture coordinates in GLSL

Now, we want to render with the textures that we uploaded. For doing that, we do not only need the texture coordinates, but we also need to get texture data through *texture units*. I will start with the texture coordinates. Passing texture coordinates to your shader is just like other arrays, you need a point in texture space for every vertex.

But you also need to interpolate the texture coordinates between vertices, so the vertex shader should pass the texture coordinates to an out variable, redeclared as in variable in the fragment shader.

You obviously want to look up texture data too, but let's wait with that.

10.5.4 Example: Procedural texture

A procedural texture is a texture that is generated from code instead of stored as an array of texels. A procedural texture can be generated inside a fragment shader, which is exactly what I will do here. What we must do is:

• The vertex shader must pass the texture coordinates to an out variable

• Texture coordinates are used in some creative way, as input to a texture generating function in the fragment shader

This is simpler than you may expect. Of course, I choose a very simple function here, but the result is quite effective. Here is the vertex shader:

```
in vec3 inPosition
uniform mat4 inTransform
in vec3 inTex;
out vec3 texcoord;

void main()
{
    gl_Position = inTransform * vec4(inPosition, 1.0);
    texcoord = inTex;
}
```

This is basically just a "pass-through" shader plus support for texture coordinates, who are simply passed on! The fragment shader is more interesting, but still simple!

```
in vec3 texcoord;
out vec4 outColor;

void main()
{
    float a = sin(texcoord.s*30)/2+0.5;
    float b = sin(texcoord.t*30)/2+0.5;
    outColor = vec4(a, b, 1.0, 0.0);
}
```

So this turns out to be remarkably simple. The fragment value is a function of S and T, in this case simply a sinus function of each, mapped onto the red and the green color channels. Note the sin() function. It is one out of many common mathematical functions. Thus, you do not have to re-implement each and every fundamental mathematical function. Rather, you have a rich toolbox to work from.

And the result from these few lines of code is a quite stunning teapot image, "Ingemar's psychedelic teapot"[1] in Figure 109. It is much more psychedelic in color though.

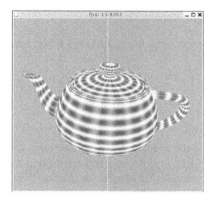

FIGURE 109. Procedural texturing example: Ingemar's psychedelic teapot

10.5.5 Texture units

Procedural textures are fun, but in real life you usually want to use pre-generated textures, textures that are designed for a purpose, textures that are based on photographs or artistic drawings, or calculated in some way that is too complex to do in real-time. In order to use pre-generated texture data, they must be loaded into a *texture object* by the host program,which must then be attached to a *texture unit*, and then you should communicate the texture unit number to the shader.

---

1. This is quite logical, since psychedelic songs often deal with tea and breakfast (as mentioned earlier).

The texture unit number is communicated as a "uniform", that is a variable that can not change within a primitive. It obviously must be a uniform; How can you have different textures in different vertices of the same triangle? Well, actually, I hear some of you arguing that it is very interesting to fade between textures over a triangle. That, however, is a completely different problem, namely multi-texturing. Multi-texturing is both useful and very relevant to shaders, but it is a matter of having several textures in use at once rather than switching between them.

GLSL has a pre-declared type for referencing texture units, called *samplers*.

Example:

```
uniform sampler2D texUnit;
in vec3 texcoord;
out vec4 outColor;

void main()
{
    outColor = texture(texUnit, texcoord[0].st);
}
```

The function texture() makes a texture look-up with the texture (unit) named "texture", which is a variable of the type sampler2D.

Depending of the kind of texture you use, GLSL has a number of types for texture access:

```
sampler1D
sampler2D
sampler3D
samplerCube
sampler1DShadow
sampler2DShadow
```

All these refer to textures by the number of the texture units it is bound to, *not* the texture object itself! They are read-only ("uniform") and are written by and communicated from the host program. The type sampler2D is used for reading from plain 2D textures, which we consider the normal case in the following.

The texture unit is a major source of confusion for beginners. Why do we mess with texture units? It may seem complicated to first load a texture to a texture object, then attach it to a texture unit, and then send the texture unit number to the shader. Why don't we just send the texture object to the shader? See Figure 110.

The reason is that texture access is much more than just reading from a buffer. Texture access needs to perform interpolation (as described in chapter 10.4), and they also perform automatic border checks! In order to do this efficiently, we have hardware that supports it, the *texture units*. They are hardware units on the GPU, and each texture unit can only handle one texture at a time. In the next section, we will look into using more than one at a time.

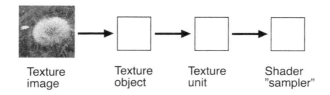

FIGURE 110. Texture access with texture units.

Before going there, let me say more about the automatic border checks. With most other memory access, we need to be careful not to access outside. With texture units, we can not only access *between* data elements (resulting in the specified filtering) but even outside, and the texture units will handle it and save us from errors.

There are two ways to handle borders, clamping and repeating. They are specified by glTexParameter, setting GL_TEXTURE_WRAP to GL_REPEAT or GL_CLAMP_TO EDGE. The effects are illustrated in Figure 111.

FIGURE 111. Texture repeat (middle) and clamp (right)

GL_REPEAT is obviously useful for repeating a texture multiple times, for example for using a small grass texture over a large surface or a brick pattern on a wall. What is less obvious is that GL_CLAMP_TO_EDGE is just as useful, for other situations, especially when multitexturing.

10.5.6 Multi-texturing and texture splatting

In the GPU, there are several texturing units. You are likely to have 16 in modern boards. Texturing units hold one active texture each, and you can draw with them simultaneously. This is highly useful for blending textures into each other (to avoid sharp edges between areas with different texture), for light mapping (see below) and many other effects.

When using multi-texturing, you assign one texture object to each texturing unit in use, switching between texture units with glActiveTexture(). You also will have to specify texture coordinates separately, which unfortunately requires special calls. In immediate mode, you use glMultiTexCoord().

Multi-texturing is performed in the fragment shader, and is marvelously simple. The host program sets up two or more texture references (e.g. sampler2D), and you declare them in the shader. Then you use them in any way you like; you can do just about any kind of calculations involving more than one texture. Figure 112 shows a simple example.

FIGURE 112. Multitextured Utah teapot, mixing two textures in the fragment shader

What you see is two textures mixed by a sin function, mapped onto the Utah teapot.

The biggest problem to do this is to load the textures into the texturing units, using glActiveTexture to select texture unit, and to pass the texture unit number to sampler2D uniforms.

Thus, the critical part of the code in the C program is to bind the textures to the proper texture units:

```
glActiveTexture(GL_TEXTURE0);
glBindTexture(GL_TEXTURE_2D, flower);
glActiveTexture(GL_TEXTURE1);
glBindTexture(GL_TEXTURE_2D, world);
```

and to tell the shader about these texture units:

```
glUniform1i(glGetUniformLocation(shader, "flowerTex"), 0); // unit 0
glUniform1i(glGetUniformLocation(shader, "worldTex"), 1); // unit 1
```

Finally, the shaders are very simple indeed. Vertex shader:

```
in vec3 inPosition
uniform mat4 inTransform
in vec3 inTex;
out vec3 texcoord;
out vec3 pixelPos;

void main()
{
    gl_Position = inTransform * vec4(inPosition, 1.0);
    texcoord = inTex;
    pixelPos = inPosition;
}
```

Fragment shader:

```
uniform sampler2D flowerTex, worldTex;
in vec3 texcoord;
```

```
in vec3 pixelPos;
out vec4 outColor;

void main()
{
    vec4 flower = texture(flowerTex, texcoord.st);
    vec4 world = texture(worldTex, texcoord.st);

    outColor = sin(pixelPos.x*5.0) * flower +
               (1.0 - sin(pixelPos.x*5.0)) * world;
}
```

This can be varied in many ways. Combine with lighting, time variations, you name it.

A special case of multi-texturing is so called *texture splatting*. This means that multi-tex-turing is controlled, specified, by a separate texture, the *splatmap* or *blend map,* which is never rendered, but rather is a "map" over how two or more textures should be blended.

It is possible to mix as much as five textures based on an RGB image in straight-forward ways, by using the primary colors R, G, B, and alpha. You can mix even more with numeric tricks, but the easiest case by far is to mix three, using only RGB. The splatting map texture is read by your fragment shader, and then each texture is weighted by the value of one color from the map. The RGB value should be normalized if you want mixing of the textures really easy and avoid overflow.

For the simple RGB case, making the map is quite easy, just paint with R, G and B in your favourite painting program. Figure 113 shows a sample map, and Figure 114 shows the result when mapping it to a terrain using three textures.

FIGURE 113. An example map for texture splatting.

FIGURE 114. Left: The result of texture splatting. Right: The map mapped to the same terrain.

In code, it can look like this:

```
uniform sampler2D grass, conc, dirt, map;
...
   vec4 m = normalize(texture(map, texCoord));
      outColor = shade * (texture(grass, texCoord) * m.r +
            texture(conc, texCoord) * m.g +
            texture(dirt, texCoord) * m.b);
```

A typical uses of texture splatting is, as hinted by the example, to put in things like roads into a terrain without having to add geometry, but it applies to many other effects as well.

10.6 Skyboxes

Skyboxes and skydomes are two pretty much equivalent ways to give the impression of a sky and other far away surroundings, by putting textures behind everything else. This is much like a backdrop at the theatre. There can be sky, buildings, far away mountains, all adding to the mood but all fake.

A skybox is a textured cube. For this, we need a cube with texture coordinates, and a texture, which may be a single texture or six separate ones, mapped onto the cube. This may look as in Figure 115, which shows the "petomavar" texture, which is available on-line, free for non-commercial purposes.

FIGURE 115. A nice skybox texture, shown as six separate textures and mapped onto a cube.

You may think that the cube should be very big, so it ends up farther away than all other geometry. This is indeed the impression we want, but then we would lose parts of the viewing frustum due to the difference in shape between the skybox and the frustum. When we move around, the shape of the skybox (or skydome) may be visible, and disturbing.

Therefore, we use a different approach without any of these problems:

The skybox does not have to be big. It needs to be big enough not to touch the near plane of the frustum, but that is all. Anything safely between the near and far planes will do, as long as it doesn't obscure anything which is supposed to be "inside it". This is accomplished by drawing the skybox without Z-buffering, that is the Z buffer is temporarily turned off. That is done by:

```
glDisable(GL_DEPTH_TEST);
```

Obviously, you should turn it on again after drawing the skybox:

```
glEnable(GL_DEPTH_TEST);
```

The second trick is to always center the skybox around the camera, that is on origin in view coordinates. Then the skybox object follows the camera. This way you can never move out of it, you never get strange perspectives that reveal that it is a box. You do that by drawing the skybox with a modified world-to-view matrix. You keep the rotation parts but zero out the translation part. Yes, it is that simple.

$$M = \begin{bmatrix} u_x & u_y & u_z & t_x \\ v_x & v_y & v_z & t_y \\ n_x & n_y & n_z & t_z \\ 0 & 0 & 0 & 1 \end{bmatrix} \longleftarrow \text{Zero these!}$$

This is the direct opposite case to view plane oriented billboards (see section 13.8 on page 176). For the skybox, you want the position to follow the camera but the orientation to vary, for the billboard you want the orientation to follow the camera but orientation to be fixed!

Furthermore, you must render the skybox with texture only, *absolutely no lighting*! Whatever the skybox shows should be pre-lit. If you apply a light model to the skybox, it will immediately look like a box. It is, of course, possible to make a complex sky model where dynamic light is handled, but it must be vastly different from the usual light models.

There is one more detail to get right for the skybox: Filtering. You typically have six separate textures, one for each side, positioned so that the edges matches. However, with the wrong filtering, you will end up with visible seams for the edges. Most specifically, if you use GL_REPEAT, you will get an interpolation at the edges from one end of the textures to another, which produces a noticable error. You want to use GL_CLAMP_TO_EDGE.

To summarize, there are four things to get right for a skybox (apart from a nice texture):

- Draw without Z-buffering, will make even a small box seem infinitely large.
- Center the skybox around the camera by zeroing the translation of the world-to-view matrix.
- No light on the skybox, just texture.
- Filter with GL_CLAMP_TO_EDGE to avoid edge artifacts.

The alternative to a skybox is a *skydome*. A skydome will require more geometry, and give few significant advantages. What it can do, that a skybox can not, is to give a decent environment with a large skydome that is *not* centered on the camera, which may make it an alternative for geometry that is not as far away, such as the one in Figure 123 on page 148.

10.7 Light mapping

Light mapping is a family of techniques to pre-generate lighting for parts of a scene where the lighting, or part of the lighting, is static. Take, for example, a building. It is lit mainly by the sun. In reality, the sun moves, so the lighting should be dynamic, but in short term we can get around with static lighting.

Light mapping is a question of performance and quality. Since light mapping is calculated off-line, it can be done with any precision we like, using sophisticated light models. Radiosity is a good candidate for generating light mapping. Some 3D programs have tools for generating light maps.

Once the resulting light has been calculated for a surface, two different approaches are possible:

- Vertex level light mapping. Save only the intensity in each vertex.

- Light map textures. Save an entire image.

With vertex level light mapping, a light value is stored for each vertex, and is applied with an attribute array of vec3's. Thus the polygons are Gouraud shaded, as in Figure 116. The memory cost is very low and the performance is excellent. The quality is pretty good, but models with low polygon count may get too little detail.

FIGURE 116. Vertex level light mapping. A shade is precalculated for each vertex.

With light map textures, quality is significantly higher. The light mapping texture is applied as a modulation of the underlying surface, that is, the surface texture is multiplied by the light map. This can be done by multi-texturing, where two texturing units are used to draw both in one pass, as illustrated in Figure 117.

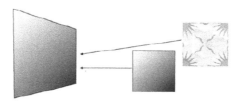

FIGURE 117. Light mapping with light map textures should be applied with multi-texturing

It is clearly unreasonable to keep a full-resolution light map for every surface in any non-trivial scene. Instead, textures are sampled down to very small sizes. With linear interpolation, the quality will still be pretty good. A set of small light map textures is generated, similar to Figure 118, where each new texture is compared to the existing set, and if there is any texture in the set that is sufficiently similar to the new texture, the new texture is discarded and the similar old one is used instead.

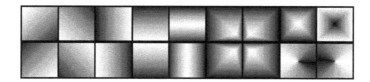

FIGURE 118. For light mapping, a set of small light maps can be used for large scenes.

10.8 Bump mapping

Bump mapping [37], as well as its cousin *normal mapping*, is a technique for adding surface structure rather than patterns. It can simulate bumps and wrinkles in the surface by modifying the normal vector, so that the shading varies with the bumps. Thus, there is no displacement of the texture, and when looking at a surface from the side, it is flat as the polygons it is built from. Only the shading is affected.

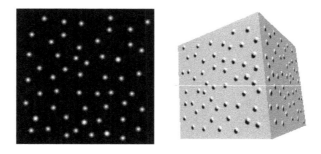

FIGURE 119. A bump map (left) applied to a cube (right)

Figure 119 shows a simple example. Note that the bump map can be combined with a texture for even better results.

Figure 120 illustrates the idea behind bump mapping: The surface is extended by a distance that is given by the bump function. The derivatives of this new surface gives new normal vectors. We don't keep the surface, but we keep the new normal vectors, which will produce a shading that gives the old surface the illusion of the variation of the extended surface.

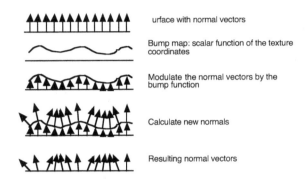

urface with normal vectors

Bump map: scalar function of the texture coordinates

Modulate the normal vectors by the bump function

Calculate new normals

Resulting normal vectors

FIGURE 120. Principle for bump mapping

You may intuitively see that the derivative of the bump function should provide the information we need to modulate the normal vectors to produce this effect. However, in 3D space, the question is in which direction to take that derivative. It must be taken along the texture/bump map coordinate axes, along s and t.

So, if we can calculate the derivatives of the bump map, b_s and b_t, we get two values that tell us how much we would like to "tilt" the normal vector for along s and t, respectively. With the s and t axes denoted $\mathbf{p}_s$ and $\mathbf{p}_t$, it seems reasonable to try

$$\mathbf{n}' = \mathbf{n} + b_t \cdot \mathbf{p}_t + b_s \cdot \mathbf{p}_t$$

which corresponds to the vectors in Figure 121.

FIGURE 121. Bump mapping. The normal vector is modified by components in u and v direction

This will work well if $\mathbf{p}_s$, $\mathbf{p}_t$, $\mathbf{n}$ are orthogonal or very close to orthogonal. If this is not the case, it can be shown that

$$\mathbf{n'} = \mathbf{n} + b_t \cdot (\mathbf{p}_s \times \mathbf{n}) + b_s \cdot (\mathbf{p}_t \times \mathbf{n})$$

where all contributions are orthogonal to $\mathbf{n}$. In either case, we must normalize $\mathbf{n'}$ as a final step.

This is a brief introduction to the concept. In Volume 2, we will return to bump mapping, including its variants and how to implement it in shaders.

10.9 Gloss mapping

Gloss mapping is a technique which is somewhat related to bump mapping in that we don't map image data but rather surface properties onto the surface, texelwise. In gloss mapping, we modulate the *specularity* of the surface with an image, the gloss map. You can control any surface property, but the most rewarding one is probably the specularity value. This technique is particularly suitable for shaders, and one of the easiest ones to try once you have multitexturing in your shader.

10.10 Environment mapping

Environment mapping is a very visually appealing method for rendering reflective surfaces in real time. It is similar to ray-tracing (chapter 17) but only allows one step of reflection (in its basic form), and the reflected ray does not traverse the scene but is mapped onto a bounding box. This bounding box is a virtual shape which is not necessarily drawn as an object. A texture is mapped onto the bounding box, and rendered onto the reflective surface using the (s,t) pair found for every ray. If the texture shows images of the surroundings (or at least something vaguely reminiscent), then the result will look like a reflection of the surroundings.

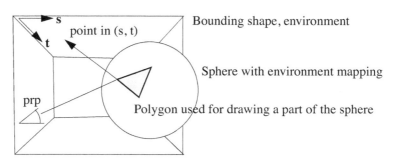

FIGURE 122. Environment mapping

See Figure 122. In real time, this can be solved on vertex basis for a low computational cost. The surface, the sphere in the figure, is in practice rendered using triangles. For each vertex in those triangles, a ray from the camera to the vertex is created. Then its reflection and the intersection between the reflected ray and the bounding shape are calculated. The intersection of the bounding shape is recalculated to a (s, t) pair, which is used for texture mapping the texture associated with the bounding surface.

Mapping at vertex level is somewhat limited. It is also possible to implement it in a fragment shader, but for a much higher cost.

In OpenGL, the recommended environment mapping is called *cube mapping*, where a cube is used as the environment shape. In section 10.6, I discussed skyboxes. If you have a skybox, the skybox and its textures can be used directly as environment map!

OpenGL provides a special kind of texture, the cubemap texture, which is specifically designed for looking up the contents of a texture on a cube map. The lookup is purely based on direction. You don't have to figure out where on each separate side you end up. You just provide a 3-component vector (vec3) and get a texture value back. The vector is directional, has no starting point in space. This is a simplification from the description above.

The cube map consists of six images matching each side of a cubic skybox. You need to supply six separate images, top, bottom, right, left, front and back. Each image is loaded with a target identifier named GL_TEXTURE_CUBE_MAP_POSITIVE_X and similar, six different. This target replaces GL_TEXTURE_2D in glTexImage2D.

Figure 123 shows a cube map, created by Paul Bourke [31]. This is one of the cube maps we use in our student labs. It is free for non-commercial use. Note how every side of the cube has perspective distorsion, so straight lines tend to bend at edges.

FIGURE 123. Example cube map

Let us render this cube map on a shape. I can not list the entire demo code here, so I will only quote the most essential parts. First, we need to load the cube map into OpenGL once it has been read from disk. A bare minimum cube mapping code looks like this:

```
makeCubeMap(void)
{
    glTexImage2D(GL_TEXTURE_CUBE_MAP_POSITIVE_X, 0, 3, 4, 4, 0, GL_RGB, GL_UNSIGNED_BYTE, tex1);
    glTexImage2D(GL_TEXTURE_CUBE_MAP_NEGATIVE_X, 0, 3, 4, 4, 0, GL_RGB, GL_UNSIGNED_BYTE, tex2);
    glTexImage2D(GL_TEXTURE_CUBE_MAP_POSITIVE_Y, 0, 3, 4, 4, 0, GL_RGB, GL_UNSIGNED_BYTE, tex3);
    glTexImage2D(GL_TEXTURE_CUBE_MAP_NEGATIVE_Y, 0, 3, 4, 4, 0, GL_RGB, GL_UNSIGNED_BYTE, tex4);
    glTexImage2D(GL_TEXTURE_CUBE_MAP_POSITIVE_Z, 0, 3, 4, 4, 0, GL_RGB, GL_UNSIGNED_BYTE, tex5);
    glTexImage2D(GL_TEXTURE_CUBE_MAP_NEGATIVE_Z, 0, 3, 4, 4, 0, GL_RGB, GL_UNSIGNED_BYTE, tex6);

    glTexParameteri(GL_TEXTURE_CUBE_MAP, GL_TEXTURE_MIN_FILTER, GL_LINEAR);
    glTexParameteri(GL_TEXTURE_CUBE_MAP, GL_TEXTURE_MAG_FILTER, GL_NEAREST);

    glEnable(GL_TEXTURE_CUBE_MAP);

    glTexParameteri(GL_TEXTURE_CUBE_MAP, GL_TEXTURE_WRAP_S, GL_CLAMP_TO_EDGE);
    glTexParameteri(GL_TEXTURE_CUBE_MAP, GL_TEXTURE_WRAP_T, GL_CLAMP_TO_EDGE);
}
```

As you can see, the magic word is GL_TEXTURE_CUBE_MAP with variations.

The next step is to map it onto a surface. This is performed in the vertex shader, with a mirroring as hinted at in Figure 122. You need to get the viewing direction just like in Phong shading, and mirror over the normal vector. The hard part is to do this in the appropriate coordinate system. If your viewing direction, mirrored environment shape and mirroring model are not in the same coordinate system, you will get an incorrect result.

Transform the vertex to view coordinates.

```
vec3 posInViewCoord = vec3(worldToViewMatrix * modelToWorldMatrix *
vec4(inPosition, 1.0));
```

By normalizing the position, we get a direction from the origin to the vertex in view coordinates.

```
vec3 viewDirectionInViewCoord = normalize(posInViewCoord);
```

If we wanted to do this in world coordinates, we would need to take the difference between the vertex position and the camera position. Using view coordinates, however, we must transform the result back to world coordinates (now without the translation part). Thus, we must take the inverse of the world-to-view transform.

```
vec3 viewDirectionInWorldCoord = inverse(mat3(worldToViewMatrix)) *
viewDirectionInViewCoord;
```

No matter how you do it, what you want is the view direction in world coordinates (that is skybox coordinates).

Using a normal matrix (see section 7.11), transform the normal vector to world coordinates too.

```
vec3 wcNormal = mat3(modelToWorldMatrix) * inNormal;
```

Now we can find the reflected direction, again in world coordinates, by reflecting the view direction over the normal vector.

```
    reflectedView = reflect(viewDirectionInWorldCoord, normalize(wcNor-
mal)); // world coord = model of skybox
```

The reflected view direction is now passed as an interpolated variable to the fragment shader. The work there is simple indeed, you just look up the output color in the cube map texture.

```
    outColor = texture(cubemap, normalize(reflectedView));
```

When the demo is running, the cube map looks like in Figure 124 when rendered on the Utah teapot:

FIGURE 124. Cube map rendered on the Utah teapot

I have written complete demo programs showing how this works, available on-line at my course page. (www.computer-graphics.se)

Now consider also rendering the cube map on a cubic skybox (as described in section 10.6)! Then you have a full (static) environment mapped scene, although with only the skybox mirrored in the environment mapped objects!

Your next problem is to find suitable cube maps. There are many cube maps available that are free for non-commercial use (Google and you will find), but for commercial projects, you will need to generate your own. (Of course you can purchase commercial textures but I would not risk using something that might be recognisable from other products.)

Environment mapping is sometimes considered a "poor man's ray-tracing", and in the case when you map diffuse, pre-rendered room-like textures, it certainly is (don't expect to see yourself mirrored in the surface), but it does not have to be. As long as the scene is not too complex, you may have time to render the scene several times for one frame, and then you can render the present scene to texture and have a real-time environment map! Then you will see yourself in the mirror, and you will see the enemy sneaking up from behind mirrored in the glossy surface of a car! This kind of rendering is, however, a matter for volume 2.

11. Text rendering

Text is one of the most basic and essential problems in graphics. Surprisingly, the OpenGL core does not provide any built-in solution for text. Instead, we need to use add-on third party libraries, or roll our own. Creating a simple solution for 2D text is easy. What makes the situation a bit complicated is that there are so many ways to do it. Here are a few:

- Text support in the system dependent units
- GLUT text
- Pre-rendered strings on textures
- Real-time rendered strings on textures
- Character set textures
- 2D vector fonts
- 3D fonts

An indication of how hard this problem is can be found in "Beginning OpenGL Game Programming" by Astle [28]. The suggested solution for text rendering is an MS Windows only library! That is pretty bad if you, like me, want cross-platform portability. There are, however, portable solutions, and you definitely should aim for them first.

11.1 Text support in the system dependent units

The OS dependent OpenGL units, WGL, AGL etc., have some support for rendering fonts. The obvious drawback of using them is that they are not portable. However, they may be the easiest way to get scalable text into your OpenGL application. In WGL, the call wglUseFontOutlines is exemplarily simple to use.

11.2 GLUT text

GLUT (i.e. FreeGLUT) includes some routines for drawing text and is the first cross-platform option that you come across. They are not very flexible, really, but may help if your needs are modest. In my opinion, they are more suitable for tracing bugs than for displaying text in the final application.

GLUT displays a single character at a time, using glutBitmapCharacter() or glutStroke-Character(). You may prefer the stroke font since it is scalable.

Unfortunately, you do not have a free choice of fonts in GLUT. All you have for stroke fonts are GLUT_STROKE_ROMAN and GLUT_STROKE_MONO_ROMAN. This is certainly a limitation. Figure 125 gives you an idea of what it can do.

FIGURE 125. Text rendering with GLUT has limited font options.

So GLUT text is more of an intermediate solution than something you want as your only font rendering option. We need to look elsewhere.

Note that our MicroGLUT package does not support GLUT fonts, but you are encouraged to use SimpleFont (see below) or more general texture fonts as simple, fast and portable solutions.

11.3 Pre-rendered strings on textures

Sometimes, you need to display static text, text that never changes. In such a case, you can pre-design the text just like you design any piece of pre-rendered graphics. But it is only an image, you can't change anything, and it scales like any image, that is, not so well. Mipmapping will help when scaled to small size, but it will be fuzzy when scaled up.

11.4 Real-time rendered strings on textures

A simple but good-looking solution is to render text using external packages, like True-Type or PostScript. That will give access to all text rendering capabilities of your OS. You need to render to an off-screen image, which is then uploaded to an OpenGL texture.

The drawback of this method is that you need to re-upload the texture every time you make a change to the string. Note, however, that this is usually a minor problem, since text changes slowly. You don't ever wish to fill the entire screen with new text in 50 fps. Thus, this is a perfectly feasible solution, especially when you have good control of the scale of the text, so you render in the same size as it is displayed. Rotations will, however, degrade the result a little bit.

11.5 Character set textures

A solution that has been common in games for many years is to pre-render an entire character set to an image. This is usually done with monospaced fonts, for simplicity. A texture font image can look like in Figure 126.

FIGURE 126. A monospaced font pre-rendered into an image.

When drawing a string, each character is drawn as a rectangle, textured by a small part of the character set texture.

Character set textures are useful as long as you draw them below a certain maximum size, just like with other texture-based methods. Just like with any texture-based method, mipmapping with filtering makes downscaling very good. The method is questionable for general use, but its lack of flexibility may not be a problem in a game.

A special case of texture font is the SimpleFont package, which I wrote a few years ago with the now-obsolete technique bitmap fonts (using the old OpenGL call glBitmap), but which is now converted to a texture font. This package has a single font defined entirely in code, so no external data files are needed. You can find this among my code examples.

FIGURE 127. SimpleFont, a minimal text rendering solution for educational purposes

Figure 127 shows the demo. The SimpleFont API is truly minimal:

```
void sfMakeRasterFont(void);
void sfDrawString(int h, int v, char *s);
void sfSetRasterSize(int h, int v);
```

The first call, sfMakeRasterFont, initializes the single supported font. You draw strings using sfDrawString. The last call, sfSetRasterSize, should be called if the viewport is resized.

You may wish to consider this solution for your student projects. However, when making serious game projects, you should consider more flexible solutions.

11.6 2D outline fonts

When you want to render fully scalable text, you will need to move to fonts described in vector formats, by polygons and splines. Using packages like TrueType or FreeType, or even the built-in functions in Win32, you can get outlines for characters in the selected font as a sequence of splines. The task of working with outlines of fonts is clearly more complicated than working with textures. One solution for this is *FTGL*, which seems to be an acronym for "FreeType Graphics Library" although that is rarely stated in FTGL documents. It is a popular library for vector font rendering in OpenGL. See Figure 128.

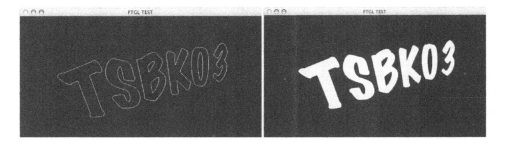

FIGURE 128. Outline 2D fonts with FTGL, border and filled.

FTGL may solve your vector font problems. Under Linux, and using C++, it is probably fairly smooth. However, in other situations FTGL can be trickier to use. The interface is not easy to access from other languages than C++, so for such cases you will need to write additional glue. Furthermore, there is no Mac compatible library in the standard distributions (that is, last time I worked with it).

FTGL has many rendering modes, but I find it to be overkill for texture based fonts. For vector fonts, including 3D fonts, it is of considerable interest.

11.7 3D outline fonts

Once you have a 2D outline font given as a (set of) polygon(s), converting a character polygon to a 3D object is fairly trivial. If you created your outline yourself, this is no problem. With ready-made libraries, it gets harder, but FTGL gives you 3D fonts right out of the box, as you can see in Figure 129.

Text rendering

FIGURE 129. Examples of 3D text from TrueType font using FTGL

11.8 Conclusions on text rendering

So to summarize, if you just want the simplest solution to get text on the screen, you can define a font inline and draw as bitmaps and have decent text with no external files and no external library dependencies. If you want nice, scalable outline fonts, the easiest way to get it is to use system dependent code like WGL, losing portability.

However, for a flexible, cross-platform solution, character set textures and outline fonts are the way to go. Character set textures will give the best performance, preferrable for games and other demanding real-time animations, while outline fonts are more flexible, especially if you want to be able to switch freely between many fonts and make 3D fonts.

For more reading on this topic, there is an article on OpenGL.org, "Survey Of OpenGL Font Technology". [29]

12. Visible surface detection

Visible surface detection (VSD for short) is the problem of making sure that the proper surface, namely the one closest to the camera, is the one that is actually visible. This can be done in several different ways, including some methods that can co-exist. It is partially a matter of drawing right, and partially a matter of drawing fast.

Two methods have hardware support and can be used practically all the time: back-face culling and Z-buffering. However, that is not always sufficient. In this chapter I will describe the following VSD methods:

- Back-face culling

- Z-buffering

- Painter's algorithm

- BSP trees

- The scan-line method

In later chapters (especially chapter 13), I will describe some other VSD-related methods, including ray-casting, octrees, portals and potentially visible set. Ray-casting is the VSD method that is used in ray-tracing. Portals and potentially visible set are high-level methods and are covered in the visibility processing chapter, which deals with the visibility problem on a much larger scale. Finally, octrees will appear mostly dealing with other problems, but there is also an octree-based VSD method, which I choose not to include here.

It is possible to categorize VSD methods in "object-space methods", that is methods that work on the geometric primitives, and "image-space methods", methods that work at the pixel level. Out of the methods we will discuss here, only Z-buffering is purely in image space, while Painter's algorithm as well as its refinement using BSP trees are partially in image and object space. All others are object space methods. In particular, high-level VSD methods are in object space by necessity.

12.1 Back-face culling

Back-face culling is an integrated part of the OpenGL pipeline, and exists in any 3D system. It is a simple operation that removes ≈ 50% of all polygons, all the polygons that are "facing away" from the camera and thereby can't be visible. Removing them at an early stage obviously reduces following computation to half! This operation should be applied on all geometry that are built from closed polyhedra. In most cases this is true.

In OpenGL, back-face culling is enabled by

```
glEnable(GL_CULL_FACE);
```

and you can configure it to cull back or front with

```
glCullFace(GL_BACK);
glCullFace(GL_FRONT);
```

Why would we ever want to cull the *front* faces? That is actually quite valuable, for example when rendering transparent objects.

Now, how does the 3D system know which polygons are facing away? When we have access to the entire polyhedron, it is possible to test that by an inside-outside test (see section 15.7 on page 221) but that is not only too slow, the information needed is not available at all in the OpenGL pipeline, where we work on one polygon at a time.

Instead, we must decide from the polygon itself. By deciding that all polygons must be defined in the same direction, clockwise or counter-clockwise, the problem is solvable. Then there are two other ways to perform back-face culling:

12.1.1 Camera space back-face culling

In camera space, you can calculate the vector from the camera (projection reference point) to the surface point, and take the dot (scalar) product between that vector and the surface normal. The sign of the dot product tells whether the surface can is facing towards the camera or not. See Figure 130.

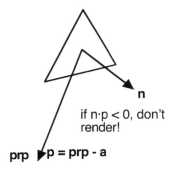

FIGURE 130. Camera space back-face culling

Visible surface detection

What you can *not* do is to take the Z component of the normal vector (in viewing coordinates) and inspect its sign, a common misconception. That will work most of the time but produce visible errors in some cases.

12.1.2 Screen space back-face culling

You can also do the same thing in screen space. In this case, you use the projected coordinates. By taking the cross product of two appropriately chosen vectors in the polygon, you will get a resulting vector that only has a z component. Here, you can use the sign of z.

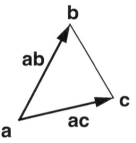

FIGURE 131. Screen space back-face culling – using a polygon projected to screen

See Figure 131. Note that the cross product can be optimized since we know that all points have the same z:

$$ab \times ac = (ab.y \cdot ac.z - ab.z \cdot ac.y, \ ab.z \cdot ac.x - ab.x \cdot ac.z, \ ab.x \cdot ac.y - ab.y \cdot ac.x) =$$

$$= (0, 0, ab.x \cdot ac.y - ab.y \cdot ac.x)$$

since $ab.z = ac.z = 0$.

So, which one is best? This depends on who performs it, and how. Calculations are similar, a few subtractions and one dot or cross product, respectively. If we have a system where the projection is performed separately from the model-world-view transformation, then the camera space method would make sense. The screen space method is done after projecting the points to screen, which costs calculations that are wasted on polygons that are not visible anyway. But, if the projection transformation is done at the same time as the modelview transformation, which is the case in the OpenGL pipeline, then screen space is what we should use. In other words, you should let OpenGL take care of it most of the time.

12.2 Z-buffering, the depth buffer method

While back-face culling has more impact on speed than on looks, Z-buffering has no influence on speed at all, but will solve most VSD problems in an easy way.

The principle for the Z-buffer method is to store a depth (Z) value for each pixel in the image. Every time a pixel is to be drawn, its Z value is compared to the value in the corresponding position in the depth buffer, and if the distance is lower than the one stored, the pixel may be drawn, and the Z value is written to the depth buffer.

The depth buffer is an entire extra image buffer, with the same size as the frame (image) buffer, but with only a single scalar for each pixel.

We usually refer to the "Z-buffer", but the real name is "depth buffer". The Z comes from the simple fact that we look along Z, so the depth buffer consequently holds Z values.

As rough pseudo-code, the algorithm works like this:

```
initialize Z-buffer to infinite distance
initialize the image buffer to background
for each polygon (in any order)
    for each pixel (x,y) in the polygon
        calculate z value
        if z closer than the current z-buffer value Z(x,y)
            write pixel to image (x,y)
            write z to z-buffer Z(x,y)
```

In this pseudo-code, there is one missing piece of information: What does "closer" mean? The answer can be found in the section on projection transformations, page 55. The "calculated" z value is a function of z^{-1}, not z, so the same range goes into the Z buffer. This is actually a desirable thing, since it gives the Z buffer higher precision near the camera, where any errors are the most visible.

Errors may indeed occur. An important aspect of Z buffering is the resolution of the Z buffer. If the resolution is low, which was common in the past, then surfaces located near each other could get the same Z value, and artifacts would be visible.

It is also important for performance. In chapter 15.13, we will present a proof showing why having values that are linear with z^{-1} are necessary for efficient implementations.

12.3 Z-buffering in OpenGL

In OpenGL, Z-buffering is enabled with

```
glEnable(GL_DEPTH_TEST);
```

When you allocate your frame buffer, you will need to specify that a Z-buffer is allocated. This will look different depending on what platform you work on. In GLUT, it is done by adding the flag GLUT_DEPTH to glutInitDisplayMode.

At the start of every frame, you need to clear the Z-buffer, that is set its contents to maximum distance. You do that with

```
glClear(GL_DEPTH_BUFFER_BIT);
```

Usually you clear the frame buffer and the depth buffer at the same time, using

Visible surface detection

```
glClear(GL_COLOR_BUFFER_BIT | GL_DEPTH_BUFFER_BIT);
```

OpenGL supports a configuration of how the Z-buffer test is carried out, which is highly valuable in some situations. By the call glDepthFunc, you can specify under what condition drawing is allowed. The default is GL_LESS, which means that a distance lower than the one stored will pass. Other options, like GL_LEQUAL, are useful in more advanced cases, multi-pass drawing, where you draw several times on the same surface. That, however, belongs to the next course so let's discuss that there.

It is also possible to make the Z buffer read-only, so drawing tests against it but without being allowed to change it. This is done with glDepthMask().

12.4 Painter's algorithm, the depth-sorting method

With back-face culling and Z-buffering in hardware, most VSD problems are solved for us in a highly efficient way. Why would we need more? There are two reasons:

- Z-buffering does not support transparency
- We need high-level algorithms to boost performance

An algorithm that handles transparency very well is Painter's algorithm, or the Depth-sorting method. It is one of the simplest and oldest of the VSD algorithms. Its name refers to how an oil painter can create a painting by painting the background first, and then paint close details over the distant objects. Similarly, the principle of Painter's algorithm is to render distant objects first, and nearby last, back-to-front. This may at first glance seem wonderfully easy to do; just sort all objects by their distance to the camera, and start drawing! Alas, things are not that simple. How do you sort 3D objects? They do not have one Z value but many.

A popular example to show the problems with this approach is an image like Figure 132. Three objects overlap each other, and since their Z values vary from end to end there is no sorting order that will solve this.

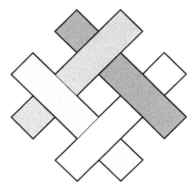

FIGURE 132. An set of objects that can not be sorted

Thus, making an implementation of Painter's algorithm that works in most cases is pretty easy, while making one that draws correctly all the time is awkward.

A complete depth-sorting can be done with a sequence of tests:

```
0. Z interval overlap
1. Bounding rectangle overlap in xy plane
2-3. Tests using surface normal
   2. Surface completely behind
   3. Surface completely in front
4. Polygon-level check of projected polygon
```

Test 0: Z interval overlap, simply tests whether the polygons have any Z overlap at all. If they don't, they can be sorted, like the right ones in Figure 133.

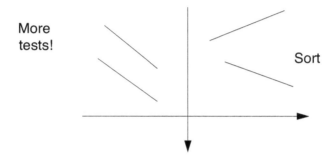

FIGURE 133. Z overlap test

If that did not help, the next test checks whether or not the polygons' bounding rectangles in projected coordinates overlap. (Figure 134.)

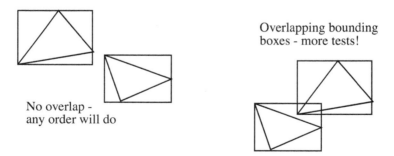

FIGURE 134. Bounding boxed tests

2-3, the surface normal tests, test whether the points in each polygon are completely in front of or behind the other. This must be tested both ways. In Figure 135, the polygon B is completely behind A, while A is neither behind or in front of B.

Visible surface detection

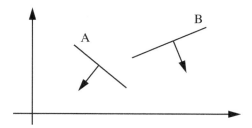

FIGURE 135. Surface normal tests

If neither of these tests succeed, test number 4 checks for overlap on polygon level. If even this test suggests an overlap, either of the polygons must be split into two. If you go this far, you should turn to BSP trees (see below) that will solve the problem in a more efficient way.

However, let us not discard the straight Painter's algorithm just yet. There are some "cheap" versions of Painter's algorithm that can be useful.

In certain special cases you can sort on distance to center only. This is particularly true for billboards (see section 10.3 on page 133). Since billboards are extremely likely to use transparency, this is both simple and useful.

Also, a simplified Painter's algorithm that only uses the surface normal test will handle most cases at a fairly low cost.

But for a good, general solution of Painter's algorithm, the tool we need is a BSP tree.

12.5 BSP trees

BSP trees (binary space-partitioning trees) is a very useful tool that appears in several contexts. One usage is for refining the Painter's algorithm. Painter's algorithm, although straight-forward in principle, has to go through much trouble to determine the sorting order of polygons, and only after many tests can it decide to split a polygon. BSP trees, however, make much simpler tests, and doesn't hesitate to split polygons the way Painter's algorithm does. It also produces a tree structure that speeds up the real-time sorting tremendously for static scenes.

There are two parts of the BSP tree algorithm, building the tree and drawing the scene using the tree. Expressed in pseudo-code style, these two algorithms can be written as follows:

12.5.1 Building the BSP tree

Building a BSP tree is done with a recursive algorithm:

```
procedure BuildBSP(polygon list)
Pick one polygon as "splitting plane"
```

For all other polygons, determine what side their corners fall on.
All on front (positive) side: Put polygon in front list.
All on back (negative) side: Put in back list.
Some front, some back: Split polygon in two, put one in each list.
BuildBSP(front list)
BuildBSP(back list)

12.5.2 Drawing the BSP tree

Drawing is also done recursively:

```
DrawBSP
if n · prp > -D then
    DrawBSP(backBranch)
    DrawPolygon(pol)
    DrawBSP(frontBranch)
else
    DrawBSP(frontBranch)
    DrawPolygon(pol)
    DrawBSP(backBranch)
```

The problem of building a BSP tree includes some sub-problems, like determining on which side of a plane a point is located, and how to split a polygon. They are detailed in section 4.7 on page 28 and section 4.9 on page 29.

12.6 BSP tree example

I find the example in Figure 136 quite enlightening.

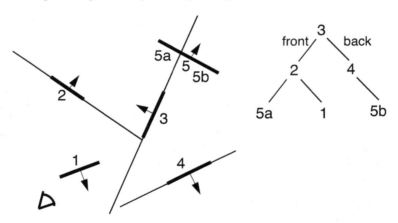

FIGURE 136. BSP tree example (Adapted from Foley, van Dam [24].)

In the figure, a few randomly placed polygons are shown as lines, each with a normal vector to show what side is front. When building the BSP tree, viewing direction does not matter. One of the polygons is chosen, either randomly or with some strategy like picking one in the center. In the example number 3 is chosen. The entire scene is split by the plane defined by this polygon, which places polygon 1 and 2 in the front, 4 in the back, and polygon 5 must be split in two, 5a in the front and 5b in the back. On these two piles, the same thing is repeated recursively until no leaf node contains more than one polygon. The splitting polygon belongs to the node for which it splits its local volume in two. Thus, every node contains a polygon.

When using the BSP tree for drawing (that is for doing Painter's algorithm) the tree is traversed from the top. For each node, check if the front side is facing the camera or not, then traverse the side facing away, then draw the polygon in the node, and finally traverse the side facing the camera. In the example, we start at the top, find that polygon 3 is facing the camera, and thus the back side (4 and 5b) are handled first. Polygon 4, however, faces away, so its front side (empty) goes first, doing nothing, and then polygon 4 is the first polygon that is getting drawn. Continue recursively with the rest of the scene.

12.7 Drawing with transparency

Transparency is a subject that I had a hard time figuring out where to put. Is it a light/shading problem? Yes, I think so, but pretty trivial in that context. Is it a surface detail problem? Hardly. Is it a VSD problem? Yes, I think so, because VSD is what makes it challenging. We will have to rethink the VSD problems to support transparency.

Color can be specified either as a straight RGB triplet, or as RGBA, where A is the alpha channel, specifying transparency. Drawing with transparency may seem trivial at first glance, but there are many options, many possibilities to consider.

The alpha value is a value between 0 and 1. Note that there may exist an alpha value both in the source and the destination. Which one should be used, and how? The default is to blend using the source alpha, like this:

$$\text{dest}_{new} = \text{source} \cdot \alpha + \text{dest}_{old} \cdot (1-\alpha)$$

Simple, seems reasonable, or even obvious. Is that the only way to blend? Actually, no. There are situations when you need a different blending, for example in video systems where the resulting alpha value will be used to make *another* blending, where graphics is mixed with live video. But in less exotic situations, the formula above will do fine most of the time.

In OpenGL, alpha blending is activated with

```
glEnable(GL_BLEND);
```

and the blending function is specified by glBlendFunc(). The default blending function, as above, is specified with the parameters GL_SRC_ALPHA and GL_ONE_MINUS_SRC_ALPHA. Many other options are available, listed in the "red book" (The OpenGL Programming Guide).

There is also an "alpha test" specified by GLAlphaFunc. This is a less important test, which you can use to avoid frame buffer operations for fragments with alpha values under a certain treshold. I mention it primarily to avoid confusion between "alpha" and "blend".

A related option is to test alpha in your fragment shader and use the discard() call to discard the fragment altogether. This is a lower quality solution but it removes the need for sorting.

So we have some freedom, but the principle is simple enough, just blend in the source with the destination. But this will lead to more challenging problems.

What makes transparency challenging is the VSD tests. If you fill a scene with transparent objects, using Z-buffering for VSD, you will get lots of anomalies, depending on drawing order. When opaque objects are drawn, in any order, only the object closest to the screen should be visible in any given pixel the final result, and Z-buffering will handle that nicely. With transparency, objects should be blended into each other. If a front object is drawing before an object behind it, the Z buffer will get the closer object's distance, and the object in the back will not be drawn at all! See Figure 137.

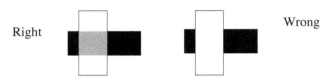

FIGURE 137. A dark object behind a semi-transparent white object, with a result depending on drawing order

The solution here is to use Painter's algorithm in some form, to draw objects back to front. If we are doing this on object level rather than polygon level, the problem can be simplified somewhat. This is particularly true for billboards, and billboards are objects that almost always will need transparency!

With transparency, even a single model may look strange. If you use back-face culling as usual, it will look as if it only has the front side. If you turn off back-face culling, the back will sometimes be drawn, and sometimes not, depending on the drawing order of the faces!

The solution here is to use back-face culling creatively. If you first cull front faces,

```
glCullFace(GL_FRONT);
```

draw, and then cull back-faces,

```
glCullFace(GL_BACK);
```

and draw again, you will draw the object with both back and front, in the proper order! For non-convex objects, there will still be some problems, though.

Note that both a color value as well as a texture may have alpha values that are active at the same time if they use a format with transparency, like RGBA format. However, you have little interest in creating such a situation, except for effects like fading objects in and out.

Visible surface detection

13. Large worlds

When working on small scenes, when most of the scene is visible all the time, the scene has few objects and the objects are not extremely detailed, then performance is not an issue with modern GPUs. You may not even have to consider the performance hit from immediate mode specification of geometry.

However, you will sooner or later want to handle larger scenes, larger worlds. A modern computer game has big levels, often with amazingly high detail. Gamers have grown to expect this, especially from expensive retail titles. Although there will always be a market for small, fun toy games, they belong to the class of free or low-cost shareware games.

With large worlds, you will need to optimize your game code on a higher level. You can not expect the GPU to perform well if you feed it hundreds of times more geometry than is actually needed. Brute force will only take you to a certain limit. You will also need structures to organize your scene, if not for performance, then for keeping it manageable from the programming and design point of view. This chapter is about various high-level methods that will help you with these problems. Visibility processing is the main subject, but the chapter will also deal with the level-of-detail concept and hierarchical modeling.

13.1 Visibility processing: Visible surface detection in large and complex environments

The problem of visible surface detection is really two problems. One is to produce a correct result, where each pixel is assigned a value that comes from the proper surface(s). This problem is nicely solved by Z-buffering or BSP trees as described above, or even by ray-casting, since we have said nothing about performance.

But performance is the other issue. How can we get rid of all polygons that can not be of interest for rendering? How can we do that with sufficiently little processing?

This is no small issue, but one that is not very obvious until you try to manage a large world. I once did some work on a kind of driving simulator. When I started out, I just sent all my polygons to the API. The API didn't suggest anything else, and all its demos ran nice and fast. When I expanded my world a bit, the program slowed down badly. This was not a problem of too many visible polygons. I had a limited far Z plane, which kept the rendering to decent amounts. No, the problem was that too many polygons had to be processed before they were found to fall outside the scene.

I solved this with a space subdivision method, where each polygon was found as part of a multi-level grid. When passing polygons to the API, I first found out what grid cells fell inside the viewing frustum. All other polygons were collectively discarded, without applying any operations on them. My animation promptly speeded up to usable speed.

Notice that this important feature is not covered by the 3D engine above. I would add that as a first step, a high-level filter that removes many polygons with collective tests.

13.2 Types of visibility processing algorithms

Visibility processing can be done with different goals and results, depending on the kind of environment and whether performance or precision is in focus. There are three categories that they can be divided into:

Exact algorithms: Such algorithms will finds all visible or partially visible polygons, and no hidden polygons. The drawback of such algorithms is that they tend to be too computationally expensive.

Approximative algorithms: Such algorithms find most visible polygons, and excludes most invisible ones. They do not guarantee perfect results, there can be some artifacts, but the advantage should be speed.

Conservative algorithms: Such algorithms find all visible polygons but include some invisible ones. This results in no artifacts, but has a certain potential to have lower performance than "approximative" algorithms.

In real-time rendering, exact algorithms only appear in special situations, when the geometry allows it, while we otherwise expect approximative or conservative algorithms.

13.3 Frustum culling

The most fundamental principle for visibility processing is to exclude geometry that will not be drawn, and doing that with collective tests that take away large parts of the geometry with few tests. Doing that with respect to the frustum is probably the most fundamental problem on this subject.

The frustum (chapter 6.7) is a 6-sided closed convex polyhedron, enclosed by a top, bottom, right, left, near and far plane. In view coordinates, the top, bottom, right and left planes all intersect the origin, since that is usually the PRP, the camera position.

Finding the plane equations for these planes is very simple. Our goal here is to use the frustum to perform *frustum culling*, the early removal of geometry outside the frustum. However, you don't want to carry out frustum culling in view coordinates. If you do, then you must transform a lot of data from model and world coordinates in order to carry out the tests. It is better to transform the frustum planes.

You already have the world-to-view transformation in your system. Let us call it M. What you need to do it to transform the frustum to the world coordinates using M^{-1}. If you transform it as its positions only, you can form the normal vectors in world coordinates. You can also transform the normal vectors using a normal matrix version of M (chapter 7.11).

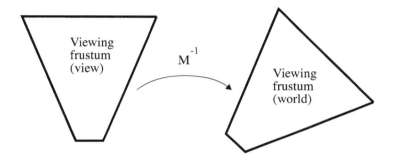

FIGURE 138. Frustum transformation to world coordinates.

We perform this transformation in order to make the frustum culling efficient. This is an example of an operation that obviously must be done by the CPU. In case you thought that you don't need vector operations, matrix multiplications and transformations in your OpenGL program since OpenGL does it for you, think again. OpenGL can do much in its pipeline, but as soon as you need to do non-trivial things, you need a nice little vector/matrix package. Making that is not hard, do it as an exercise. You can find plenty of them on the web, but it is easier to roll your own.

The transformation above is done for all six frustum planes. You should seriouslty consider skipping the near plane. It makes little difference. Nothing should be in that little volume anyway. Depending on your scene, you may also choose to skip other planes, e.g. top and bottom. Now, let us see what we should we do with those planes, performing the culling.

A simple but very important case is frustum culling of *single objects*. A single polyhedron model can consist of thousands of polygons. Thus, it is very important to test objects against the frustum using a bounding shape, preferably a sphere.

The test is similar to the camera-plane test in the collision detection part. Given the bounding sphere to an object, by its center **c** and radius r, as in Figure 139, it is very easy to test whether it is inside any of the frustum planes. Suppose the normal vector of the frustum plane points into the frustum. Find a point on the sphere by moving along the normal vector of a plane, $\mathbf{p} = \mathbf{c} + \mathbf{n} \cdot r$. Test if this point is inside or outside the plane by using the plane equation. If this test fails for any of the frustum planes, that is the sphere is on the outside of the plane, the object does not intersect the frustum and can be skipped.

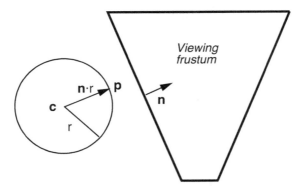

FIGURE 139. Sphere-frustum test used for bounding spheres of objects

This principle can be extended to object hierarchies, to optimize even further. Figure 140 shows an example.

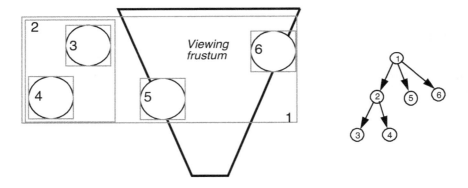

FIGURE 140. Frustum culling of objects and object hierarchies.

This kind of hierarhy is known as a Bounding Volume Hierarchy (BVH). In the figure, a number of objects that are related to each other in some way (e.g. movable parts attached to the same object, animals in the same herd, nearby plants in a forest...) and likely to be close have enclosing boxes that can be tested before the objects. This optimization may help in complex scenes. However, the most important thing is to test the individual objects themselves.

Unless the hierarchy is taken to extreme ends, frustum culling of objects is conservative, since some parts of the objects may be outside the frustum and still processed.

A somewhat different case is that of a scene based on a grid, like a terrain. This is particularly easy and straight-forward since the data is organized. Find the intersection between the grid and the frustum. This is a simple polygon. (Figure 141) You can then search the polygon with algorithms similar to polygon-fill or triangle-fill algorithms.

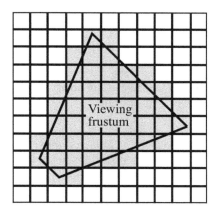

FIGURE 141. Frustum culling in a grid is particularly simple.

To make it even easier, you can calculate the axis aligned bounding box of the frustum, and search its contents by a straight for-loop. It will search up to ≈50% too many grid spaces, but that is a cheap price to pay for all that you cut away!

Testing the grid by the exact frustum will give us an exact culling, while the simplified solution with the bounding box is a conservative algorithm.

13.4 Frustum culling using BSP trees

BSP trees can be used for frustum culling, in a way that is similar to how they are used for visible surface detection. Consider a scene that is stored as a huge BSP tree, illustrated by Figure 142.

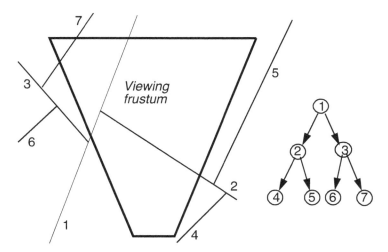

FIGURE 142. Clipping using a BSP tree

First, notice that if any node in the tree defines a plane that does not intersect with the view frustum, all polygons on one side are outside the viewing frustum, and you can discard them all by just ignoring that branch!

This alone will take away much of the scene. Furthermore, even if planes do intersect the viewing frustum, the combined planes above any node define a convex volume. This volume can be tested against the viewing frustum.

In Figure 142 above, the top node (1) cuts the viewing frustum, so both sides must be checked further. (2) and (3) do too, but (3) combined with (1) defines a volume that falls outside, so we can skip (6) and all its sub-nodes. Likewise, (4) and (5) both are outside the viewing frustum, so one side of their sub-trees can be skipped.

A common form of BSP tree for this and similar problems is the *kD-tree*, where space is always divided in axis-aligned planes. That makes calculations easier.

This will efficiently eliminate all polygons outside the viewing frustum, but we may also be able to, or even desperately need, to take away large number of polygons that are inside the viewing frustum but will be hidden. For example, consider an indoors scene, a maze of narrow passages. There may be many nearby passages within the viewing frustum, but they will be totally obscured by walls.

There are several methods for solving this, and I will mention two: Portals and PVS.

13.5 Portals

Portals is an intuitive and efficient method for splitting the world into rooms. These rooms are connected through "portals", and only if the portal is visible, the neighboring room needs to be considered for rendering. The principle is illustrated in Figure 143. The old game Dark Forces uses 2D portals, while the somewhat newer Tomb Raider does the same thing in 3D.

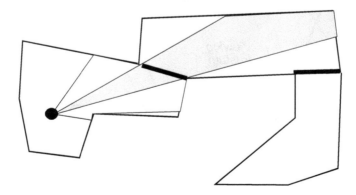

FIGURE 143. Example of Portals. The thick "walls" are portals, openings into the next room.

Tha portal approach is good, but has some drawbacks. It works best in indoor environments. In outdoor environments, we may process sequences of portals to no effect, wasting performance. This problem can be seen in some scenes in the Tomb Raider games, when played on the old computers they were designed for.

A problem with portals is the design. Cells must be designed explicitly by the scene designer. Portal polygons must be matched between different polyhedra, forming these cells. This may call for special tools. There are also interesting advantages. If the portal includes a transformation matrix, portals may implement mirrors, or even "magical" portals that leads to another place. The game Portal uses such additions.

The implementation of portals is very much a question of working with the frustum. Each room (cell) uses different frustums. When a portal is found to fall inside the frustum, a new frustum must be calculated, the intersection between the current one and the portal, so that the next room is analyzed using this smaller frustum.

The optimal frustum needs an arbitrary number of sides, which can be hard to calculate. In practice, the problem can be simplified by always using four sides, just like the initial frustum. Calculate a bounding box of the portal in the viewing plane. This gives four new sides. For each pair of sides (left, right, top, bottom), use the innermost side.

Portals is an exact method, as long as objects within the cells are not considered. It also depends on cell design, so there are cases where it rather is conservative.

13.6 Potentially Visible Set

In Quake, they use PVS, Potentially Visible Set. The point here is to pre-calculate, for each subsection of the world, which polygons that can possibly be visible. The pre-calculation may take long time, but once it is done you can look up the parts of the scene that you need to process, and skip the rest.

The scene is split into cells using a BSP tree (again!) For each cell, a PVS is calculated, possibly for a few different locations within the cell in order to minimize errors.

A possible method for generate the PVS is to use an image-space method, as illustrated by Figure 144. Then, for the point being analyzed, the PRP of our virtual camera is placed in the point and the scene is rendered in all possible directions, to six images. Thus we get a cube of viewing planes surrounding the point. The rendering is done without textures, shading, anti-aliasing etc. Instead it is flat-shaded, with one unique color for each polygon in the scene. Z-buffering should be activated, in order to get proper low-level VSD.

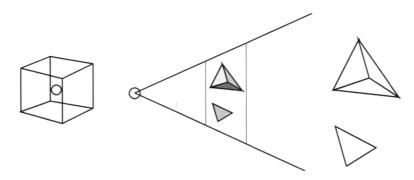

FIGURE 144. Image-space generation of PVS

By inspecting the colors appearing in the resulting images, we can find out what polygons were in the image after rendering.

This method is an approximate method. Its advantage over portals is in the flexibility and design. You don't have to decide where the portals are placed, it is automatic.

13.7 Level of detail

In all of this chapter up to now, the big problem has been how to manage large worlds by avoiding to process large sets of data when calculating visibility. The problem of limiting the amount of data to process also exists in a smaller scale; a 3D model may be defined by far too many polygons than are needed to render it in some specific situation.

When your graphics program simply can't cope with pushing polygons through the pipeline fast enough, you should look into optimization methods. These include using display lists and vertex buffer objects. That way, you may pre-upload geometry to the GPU and speed things up quite a bit.

But if your models are too many and with 1000 times more polygons than the resolution needs (e.g when drawing a forest) this may not be enough. The next remedy is level of detail, to vary the detail level of models depending on the size in which they are drawn.

Level of detail [8] applies to all kinds of geometry. The general idea is to keep the size of polygons approximately constant in regard of the number of pixels they each cover. When polygons are smaller than a pixel, they are clearly too many. At a very large distance, level-of-detail systems may choose to switch to billboards (see chapter 13.8) or systems of a small number of impostors, in some cases even rendering several objects on a single billboard. This is particularly true concerning rendering of forests and other vegetation.

We focus upon two specific problems: single objects (closed polyhedra) and terrains.

Level of detail for objects is based on *mesh decimation*, the simplification of a mesh to a lower resolution, or *tesselation*, the generation of an adjustable detail level from a spline representation. A mesh can be either pre-generated in several detail levels, or progressive. With pre-generated resolutions, the risk for noticeable "popping", changes in the geometry when changing resolution, is high. Using progressive meshes you try to avoid this by making gradual changes depending on distance.

Reducing the detail of a mesh can be done in several different ways.

- Edge collapsing
- Insertion of new vertices, removal of neighbors
- Vertex removal
- Vertex removal with re-triangulation

Edge collapsing and vertex removal, illustrated in Figure 145 and Figure 146, are quite similar, and the simplest methods. The other two require re-triangulation. Re-triangulation is desirable since it avoids very elongated triangles, but it is hard to combine with progressive level of detail.

FIGURE 145. Edge collapsing

In edge collapsing, a suitable edge is selected. The two vertices are removed and replaced by one in between. Two triangles are removed. Note that all vertex attributes, light level, texture coordinates etc., must be interpolated for the new vertex.

FIGURE 146. Vertex removal

Vertex removal is quite similar, but only moves one of the two vertices onto the other. As a pre-generation method it is much simpler, since no re-calculation of vertex attributes is needed. The drawback is, as showed in the figure, that triangles can get undesirable shapes and neighboring triangles are unnecessarily different in size.

For progressive meshes, both are good and fairly simple.

The simplification will inevitably result in a reduction in volume. Edge collapsing can compensate for this, while vertex removal can not.

An important problem is to find suitable vertices/polygons to simplify. The selection must be done according to some error metric, and the edge/vertex that can be removed with the smallest error is the one to remove. A simple error measure could be to measure the Euclidean distance between a vertex and the closest point in the surface that results without it. This is a geometric error measure. Other measures may be the area of the polygons being removed, or the screen-space error, in the case when the most likely viewing angle is known. A well-known paper on this subject is that of Garland & Heckbert. [39]

At run-time, the level of detail should obviously be selected with regard to the distance to the camera, so that the sizes of all polygons are roughly the same at all times, but it may also be tuned to the performance, reducing the detail when too many objects are in view, or when running on low performance hardware.

13.8 Billboards and impostors

Billboarding is level-of-detail taken to its extreme, where the model is replaced by a single polygon, typically textured with transparency. As mentioned above, this can be the extreme end of a level-of-detail system, for the most distant objects. For low-polygon situations (older games, platforms with low performance, small objects or low-budget productions) objects may be replaced by billboards altogether. This is particularly true for particle systems.

13.8.1 Billboards

A billboard is, in computer graphics, a polygon that always faces the camera, as in Figure 147, typically with a texture on it, almost certain to have transparency so that it shows a picture of something that is much more complex than the polygon. This is the simplest case of using simplified geometry that replaces complex geometry.

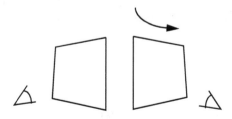

FIGURE 147. A billboard is a single polygon always facing the viewer.

The particular case with a single polygon corresponds exactly to the so-called "sprites" that were used in all early 3D games like Wolfenstein 3D, Doom, Dark Forces and Marathon. The computers had no chance to animate an entire body, so instead a pre-generated image was slapped onto the screen. The hardest problems the graphics engine had to support was proper visible surface detection (so walls overlapped the sprite appropriately) and scaling of the sprite. Animation was achieved by changing the image/texture used. So a storm trooper in Dark Forces supported 4 directions with a few frames for each, one for standing still and two or three for walking, plus a few frames for attacking. One of the most embarrassing defects was that bodies on the floor generally only got a single frame, which made them seem to rotate when the player rotated.

Old news? Who cares about Doom-style sprites? You should, it is far from gone. It has just moved to other problems. Entire characters are made from meshes today (at least when close), but many other objects are best done with billboards or impostors. If you want to draw clouds, or a nice explosion, or a forest, then billboards are marvellous tools.

13.8.2 Implementing billboards

There are a few different variants of billboards, depending on how they face the camera.

- Face the camera in full 3D
- Rotate towards the camera around the Y axis (axial billboard)
- Face the viewing plane, make the billboard orthogonal to the Z axis (view plane oriented)
- The combination of the latter two, a view plane oriented axial billboard

See Figure 148. The viewpoint oriented billboards are really facing the viewer. On the other hand, view plane oriented billboards are all in the same plane, which has advantages, especially when sorting. See chapter 13.8.3.

FIGURE 148. View plane (left) and viewpoint (right) oriented billboards.

We first make an important assumption: We assume that the billboard is defined as a polygon in the XY plane, so its surface normal is parallel to the Z axis. It will also be pointing in positive Z, that is reverse to the (default) viewing direction.

You may think that figuring out how to rotate the objects to face the camera would be a complicated problem. It is not necessarily so. The simplest method is to have the billboards face not the camera but the viewing plane, so that all billboards are parallel to each other as well as to the viewing plane. If the billboards face the viewing plane, they are *view plane oriented*. This is a very effective simplification.

Consider the transformation chain. You make one transformation from model coordinates to world coordinates, and one from world to view. The camera has some orientation, the objects have others, and these rotations are multiplied together. Given the position of an object and the camera, you can find a rotation transform that makes the object "look at" the camera. This is essentially the same problem as with viewing, similar to the "look at" function for the camera.

But the problem actually is much simpler. After all transformations are done, the resulting matrix contains a rotation and a translation:

$$R \cdot T = \begin{bmatrix} u_x & u_y & u_z & t_x \\ v_x & v_y & v_z & t_y \\ n_x & n_y & n_z & t_z \\ 0 & 0 & 0 & 1 \end{bmatrix}$$

Note that the vector direction (u, v, n) in the matrix depends on what we are doing. The horizontal vectors in the rotation part are the new axes expressed in the old system. The vertical vectors are the old axes expressed in the new system. Since you usually want to think in world coordinates, the direction is different when working with camera direction and object direction.

But you only want the translation part. Originally, you translated the object to a place in the world, and it was rotated and translated until it reached view coordinates. All you want to do now is to reset the rotation and keep the translation. And you can do that by writing an identity matrix into the rotation part of the matrix!

$$R \cdot T = \begin{bmatrix} 1 & 0 & 0 & t_x \\ 0 & 1 & 0 & t_y \\ 0 & 0 & 1 & t_z \\ 0 & 0 & 0 & 1 \end{bmatrix}$$

What you have now is a billboard that was view plane oriented from the start, and since we do not rotate it at all, only translate it, it is still view plane oriented!

The *axial billboard,* one that rotates around the Y axis, is most suitable to objects that are more or less rotation symmetric, like trees. If you want an axial billboard, then you can find the rotation by a vector. As before, you can choose to make the billboard face the camera or align it with the viewing plane. For the former case, form a vector from the object to the camera, zero its Y component, and normalize it. Do the same with the normal vector of the billboard. By dot and cross products you can find cos and sin and build a rotation matrix. If the billboard is aligned with the Z axis (which it should, as mentioned above) then the cos and sin are simply the X and Z components of the vector.

Let us make an example, in Figure 149. The billboard is, again, in the XY plane with the normal vector in positive Z. Now we want the camera to be placed along the X axis. How can we make the billboard "look at" the camera (or rather, its projection onto the XZ plane)?

FIGURE 149. Axial billboard example, before rotation (middle) and after (right): The billboard is defined with its normal vector n looking along Z, viewer in the d direction.

The vector **n** is the normal vector. Now, form the vector **d**, a unit vector directed towards the camera. These two vectors form the angle ϕ, around which we want to rotate.

How do we know if we are rotating in the right direction? It is very easy to confuse directions, to mess up the order of the axes (and I will not be surprised if I make a few errors in this book) but the rules are not really that hard. What comes first, X or Z? Z, of course. "Wait", I hear you say, "X is first and Z is last". Yes, but that makes Z the axis immediate *before* X, since it is a wrap-around system. Thus, the sin and cos you are used to do in X and Y will work the same for Z and X! (But don't take my word for it, by all means double-check my conclusions.)

So let us calculate sin and cos for the angle!

$$\cos\phi = \mathbf{n} \cdot \mathbf{d}$$

$$\sin\phi = (\mathbf{n} \times \mathbf{d})_y$$

(where I just invented a shortcut for extracting the Y component of a vector) and we can insert that into the rotation matrix for rotation around Y!

Since n is always $(0, 0, 1)$, the dot and vector products degrade to simply grabbing the X and Z components of **d**!

Doing this for view plane oriented billboards (but only rotating around Y) is as easy. Then you don't form a vector towards the camera, but take the camera direction instead.

A third method is to set the X and Z vectors, and then make the matrix orthonormal without changing the Y component. But doesn't that seem like a detour?

There is one case that I have not discussed, and that is the full 3D billboard, which is neither view plane aligned or axial billboard. It is the most complex case, but the solution is similar to the look-at routine in chapter 6.4.

Consider the case in the figure above. The vector **d** is a normalized forward vector. (Don't be confused by it pointing along X in the figure, that is before rotation) The vector **n** can be used as preliminary side vector, and we will create the up vector by a cross product.

$$u = \frac{d \times n}{|d \times n|}$$

$$n' = u \times d$$

We get a transformation like this:

$$R = \begin{bmatrix} n'_x & u_x & d_x & 0 \\ n'_y & u_y & d_y & 0 \\ n'_z & u_z & d_z & 0 \\ 0 & 0 & 0 & 1 \end{bmatrix}$$

Wait a minute, why did we get column vectors? In chapter 6, we got horizontal vectors! That is because in this case, we express the vectors in world coordinates, which means that the rotation is describing the model coordinate axis in world coordinates, so the *old* coordinate system is expressed in the *new* one.

13.8.3 Billboards and transparency

A very important detail when working with billboards is to take transparency into account. Billboards are almost always implemented with transparent textures. The problem of handling transparency often includes depth-sorting (see the VSD section, page 165). In that case, the view plane oriented approach will simplify even this step, since all billboards will be parallel. Thus, making the billboards parallel to the view plane rather than strictly facing the viewer is not to be considered a cheap shortcut, but rather a desirable method.

It should also be noted that for some cases it may be acceptable to solve the transparency problems by using the discard() function in GLSL, discarding fragments with low alpha.

13.8.4 World oriented billboard

There are cases where billboards are put into games without any rotation, a *world oriented billboard*. This typically happens when the user is only expected to see the objects from one direction. The terra-cotta warriors in Tomb Raider 2 is an example, arranged as in Figure 150. The front row of warriors are full meshes, but the ones in the back are billboards. You are not supposed to be able to get in behind the first row, but this turns out to be possible (with some skill and patience) and then you see that the warriors are not only flat, but also invisible from the back-side.

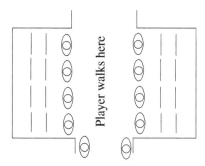

FIGURE 150. Schematic map over half of the terra-cotta warrior scene in Tomb Raider 2 (drawn from memory).

Too cheap solution, or smart? Since players could see the scene from the wrong side, it seems it was a bit too cheap. Otherwise, it is always smart to simplify when there is any need at all. If they had realized that you could get past the first row, they would certainly have used the better multi-face billboards.

13.8.5 Multi-face billboards

A variant of billboards is the case where you use a not one but a small number of polygons to replace many. A billboard of a tree is fine as long as you run around on the ground some distance from it, but if you fly over it with an aircraft, and look down, then the tress will either lay down under you (if they are strictly facing the camera) or turn flat (for axial billboards), which is obviously unacceptable. A solution is to leave the camera-facing approach and make a tree out of a few polygons, which is not affected by the camera placement at all. It can look pretty good from all directions, given good textures.

A tree can thus be built from three flat surface, which may be broken down to several polygons, as in Figure 151, in order to handle the drawing order properly.

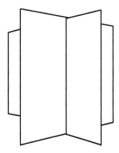

FIGURE 151. A multi-face billboard, with polygons in two or three different planes, does not need any rotation.

There are many examples where you find this kind of objects. For example, the Tomb Raider games use them for many small objects. Look closely at the tea that the servant serves you in Lara's home. If you look from above, the cups turn into crosses. That is because they don't include any horizontal polygon (in the XZ plane).

13.8.6 Impostors

An interesting variant of billboards is the *impostor*. That is a billboard, for which the texture is generated on-line, possibly for every frame. This sounds wasteful until you consider the case where you render to texture once but can reuse the result for many objects.

There is much to win with this approach. When developing, you probably have the full 3D model anyway, but by rendering it to texture on-line, you can save the administrative work of storing it in the static game data. You can also dynamically adapt the views as needed, while you trash views that are not needed any more.

Note that you can not only render to single-polygon impostors, but also render to multi-polygon billboards, thereby generating impostors that will look good from many views without changes, as long as the distance is big.

However, since rendering to texture is a matter for volume 2, I will drop this subject for now.

13.8.7 Particle systems

A particularly important case where billboards should be used is when making particle systems. In a particle system, the particles are typically so small that there is no reason to consider polyhedra models for them. Particle systems as such are treated in chapter 14.7.

13.9 Level of detail for terrains: geomipmapping

A similar subject is to render terrains with varying level of detail. This is sometimes called *geometrical mip-mapping* or *geomipmapping* [15]. Unlike the objects discussed above, a terrain exists close and far from the camera at the same time, so different parts of the terrain needs to be rendered with different detail.

In geomipmapping, a rectangular grid (heightmap) is provided at full resolution. From that, a resolution pyramid is generated, and at any distance, a suitable resolution is used.

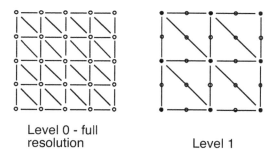

Level 0 - full
resolution

Level 1

FIGURE 152. A terrain grid at two different resolutions

This is illustrated in Figure 152. This would be simple enough if it wasn't for the areas where two areas with different resolution meet, and that when the camera moves, some parts will have to be rendered with a different resolution than the previous frame. This will cause two errors: Cracks and popping.

Popping can only be eliminated by a progressive, gradual change near edges, which is sometimes referred to as geomorphing. Cracks must be solved by modifying the geometry near edges.

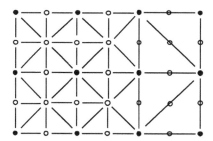

FIGURE 153. A possible way to patch the edge between areas of different resolution

Figure 153 also hints a simple, recursive algorithm for geomipmapping. Each square with nine heightmap samples is one cell, which is generated at a specific resolution. For each side (with two triangles), if the cell can have a lower resolution neighbor at that side, that neighbor is tested, and if the resolution indeed is different, the two triangles are merged to one by skipping the middle edge vertex.

Let us go a bit deeper into this algorithm. Let me stress that this is not a complete, optimal geomipmapping algorithm, but a simplified one that still works pretty well. It starts at the top level, with a single patch, one single square built from 3x3 vertices. It calculates a measure based on the size and geometry of the square, and the distance to the camera from either the center or the closest corner.

This measure is compared to some limit. If the test succeeds, then the patch is small enough, far enough from the camera, and is drawn. If it fails, then the algorithm is called recursively for the four sub-patches formed by each corner, including data of higher resolution.

When a patch is to be drawn, each of its four sides (two triangles each) must be tested against the neighbors. Two of the sides have neighbors that are guaranteed to be at the same level or higher, since they are part of the same super-patch from the previous level. The other two sides, however, must be tested against neighbor super-patches. If these neighbors are drawn at the coarser level, the edge fix from above must be applied. see Figure 154.

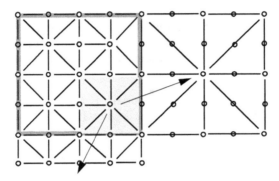

FIGURE 154. When the shaded square is drawn, the algorithm must test the two closest neighbors of its parent square (gray frame)

The algorithm gets more complicated if we want to filter the height map between the levels. Without filtering, you get a sampling of the heightmap, which leads to aliasing. In this case, aliasing will cause extreme peaks to vary in a noticeable way. Then the vertices must be taken from the appropriate level, which means that the test above not only decides on whether to draw one or two triangles at the edge, but the finer level must take any vertices on the edge from the coarser level. In the figure above, the three vertices at the right side of the framed square are taken from the coarse level, while the vertices left of them are from the finer level.

Ideally, geomipmapping should decide resolution from screen-space errors, but in practice that may not be the simplest solution. For our simple algorithm, a possible way to approximate screen-space errors is to measure the height difference between the vertices projected into the camera direction. If the variation is large, a subdivision is needed, and if it is small, it is likely to be less needed.

In geomipmapping, as in any time-critical problem, everything that can be precomputed should be. The geometry should be downsampled beforehand. Error measures can be precomputed, or partially pre-computed. Some calculations for progressive level-of-detail (geomorphing) may be pre-computed, e.g. pre-computing a few discrete morphing steps.

Finally, it is advisable to work with square distances when possible, to avoid square root calculation when possible.

Let me end this section by saying that the level-of-detail problem is a complex and very important subject, important enough to justify entire books on it alone. In the last years, it has moved from research field to an integral part of the computer graphics industry.

13.10 Hierarchical modeling

During most of the course, it may have seemed that a 3D program should be written with a lot of hard-coded geometry calls in the display function. Let me stress that I claim nothing of the kind. In this section, I will explore the problem of finding formal, systematical ways to describe a scene, and thereby finding a standard form for a 3D program.

Some objects are naturally described as hierarchies:

- Windmills
- Bicycles
- Humanoids

Their spatial relationship is described by transformations. In our labs, we have an assignment including a windmill. The top-level code may have looked something like in Figure 155.

```
m = (global placement)
DrawBody();
m = m *Translate(...);
m = m *Rotate(0,0,1, angle);
DrawWings();
m = m * Rotate(0,0,1, 90);
DrawWings();
```

FIGURE 155. Lab-style windmill, code and simplified result

This object, with both shapes and transformations, can be represented as a graph, like Figure 156.

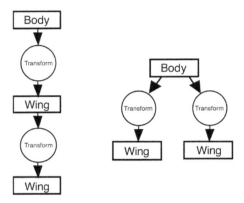

FIGURE 156. Hierarchical representations of the windmill

A more interesting example may be to model a human body, as in Figure 157.

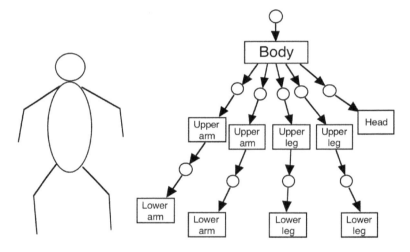

FIGURE 157. Hierarchical representation of a human body

This, however, is an example that really only is good for animating robots, not humans. The human body is not built from rigid bodies alone, so a serious body animation must use other methods (namely skin&bones).

13.11 3D object data representation

When viewing models like this, it becomes more and more evident that 3D objects should not be built from hard-coded calls, like DrawWings() above, but from a data structure from which we can handle any kind of 3D object. Such a data structure may look something like this:

```
struct GraphicsEntity
    {
        Point3D position;
        Rotation3D rotation;
        Mesh3D mesh;
        ...

        GraphicsEntity *child;
        GraphicsEntity *next;
    }
```

Note that this structure includes not only arbitrary 3D and arbitrary transformations, but also pointers to other objects, which may be children of this node (child) or children of the same parent as the current node (next).

We don't only build objects hierarchically. With a structure like the one above, it also becomes natural to represent the scene dynamically, so each object is linked to a part of the scene, and these links can change as the scenery changes. For example, in Figure 158, when a person is in a room, the room object has a pointer to the person object. There may be a house object with pointers to each room, and a world outside that has a list of pointers to houses and other objects in the world. When the human leaves the room, and the house, and gets into a car, the car will point to the human, and if the human drives the car through a window into the house, the house-room structure is updated to point to the car.

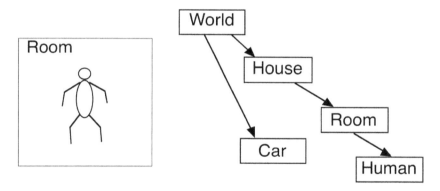

FIGURE 158. A world represented by links between data structures (objects)

This is an example where we see that a hierarchical representation of a scene seems fairly reasonable, and that leads us to the final and main point of this chapter:

13.12 The scene graph

The scene graph is a concept used to standardize this kind of hierarchical structures to a method of representing the entire scene. The scene graph describes the entire scene with one single tree. To do this, it may contain not only shape and transformation nodes, but several other kinds of nodes.

Figure 159 is an example of a Java 3D scene graph. As you can see, many of the concepts that we have dealt with in the course can be identified in the scene graph.

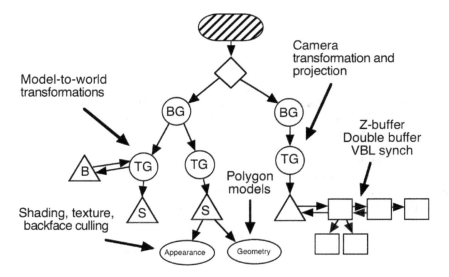

FIGURE 159. A Java 3D scene graph.

A scene graph can solve even more problems than illustrated above, by introducing new kinds of nodes. Additional kinds of nodes may include:

- Bounding shape nodes. Used for frustum culling
- Level-of-detail nodes. Select one branch depending on distance

There are several scene graph systems available, including Java 3D, VRML, Open Scene Graph and Vega Prime. For many problems, the scene graph can be a useful model.

13.13 Discussion on scene graphs and other ways to structure a scene

Given the scene graph as a model for how to handle the world as a graph, as a tree, by all means use it. Just one thing: Just because you have a hammer, don't view the whole world as made of nails. There are many scenes that fit this model nicely, but at least as many that do not. Use what solves the problem best, don't reduce yourself to mechanically doing things "the" way - no matter what it is.

14. Animation

Animation is what you get when you present a sequence of still images and flip between them fast enough to make the viewer perceive motion. In computer graphics, animation is a matter of two things: Presenting the sequence of images, and moving objects in the scene in a way that will produce the desired sequence of images.

An important part of this subject is how to detect and handle collisions between moving objects, between moving and still objects, and between the camera and other objects. These subjects are covered in the later parts of this chapter.

14.1 Double buffering

In most real-time animations, you use double buffering. Double buffering means that at least two image buffers as large as the output area (e.g. the screen) exist. One of these is displayed on the screen while the other is being drawn, to be shown as the next frame.

These two buffers are generally both be in VRAM, in the video memory on the video board, so that you can flip between them just by setting a pointer in the video board (page flipping). Another option is to have one buffer on-screen, and the other off-screen (may be in VRAM or standard RAM), and copy (blit) from the off-screen buffer to the on-screen buffer when you want to display the next frame. This is slower but perfectly possible.

We can safely assume that any modern system (including portable ones) have VRAM enough for two full-screen images. The ability to switch between buffers is less obvious, and note that you often want animations on parts of the screen, not the whole screen.

The case where you have one buffer on-screen and one or more off-screen is sometimes called "single-buffered". What that means is that we have a single buffer in VRAM. To me, double-buffering is what eliminates flicker, no matter where the extra buffer is stored. Be aware of the possible confusion. See Figure 160.

No matter what case you have, the output image should be changed at the appropriate moment. When you use old-fashioned cathode ray tubes (CRT), you have an update beam moving from top to bottom. You should change the output image at the time when the

---

update is at the bottom of the screen. This can be done using "VBL synch", the vertical blanking synchronization interrupt, an interrupt sent to the processor when the update beam moves back to the top.

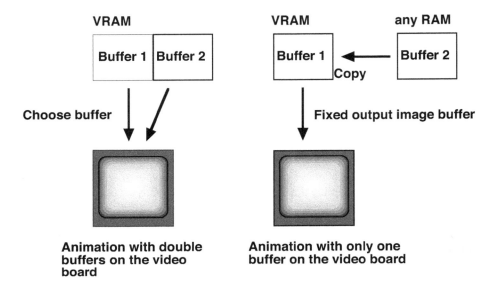

FIGURE 160. Two different cases of double buffering

If VBL synching is not used, artifacts known as *tearing* will occur, illustrated by Figure 161. When the update beam passes over a moving object at the time when the buffers are switched, the upper part of the object will be displayed in the old position, and the lower part in the new position.

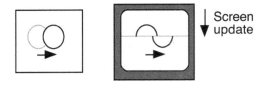

FIGURE 161. Tearing

14.2 Double buffering in OpenGL

OpenGL does not support double buffering in the core (GL) library, but the system dependent libraries do, including GLUT and SDL. Setting up double buffering in GLUT is very easy (as with most other similar APIs). When allocating the display mode in GLUT, you can specify that a double buffer should be allocated. That is done by adding the constant GLUT_DOUBLE to glutInitDisplayMode. Thus, the call may look as

```
glutInitDisplayMode(GLUT_RGBA | GLUT_DEPTH | GLUT_DOUBLE);
```

This line will allocate a color buffer with alpha channel, a Z-buffer and double buffers.

When a frame has been drawn, instead of calling glFlush() to make sure everything is drawn, you call glutSwapBuffers().

If you use other packages than GLUT, there are other calls for both allocation and swapping buffers, but it will be highly similar.

14.3 2D animation: blitters and sprites

2D animations are often built using separate, often fairly small objects over some background that is usually static or scrolling. These moving objects are called sprites. In the past, animation using sprites, *sprite animation*, was an important and not trivial problem, which was used in most 2D games. A central component in such a system was the *blitter*.

The term blitter comes from the acronym BLT, which stands for *block transfer*. What the operation BLT, the blitter, does is to move a block of pixels, typically a rectangular area of an image, from one place to another. This may seem trivial, but it is not. There are many features that a blitter needs, including scaling, clipping at edges, overlapping source and destination, masking, blending... A full-fledged software blitter was a hard task to write.

Nowadays, however, the GPUs do the work for us and we have all the blitting capability we can ever dream of, complete with all features. OpenGL has some pure blitter calls (glDrawPixels/glBitmap) but in general you should use textures, since they are guaranteed to have priority and thereby have high performance.

Another important option for 2D animation is high-level authoring tools like Director and Flash. On-line Flash games have almost entirely taken over the market for simpler 2D games, more recently challenged by WebGL or even plain JavaScript.

14.4 Pseudo-3D effects in 2D animation

Even in 2D, you have some ways to incorporate certain 3D-like effects. Even if we are not working with a full 3D model, these effects can be quite good. Although full 3D is no problem today, pseudo-3D can be useful on certain platforms (e.g. when using multimedia tools unsuitable for 3D) or simply because full 3D isn't appropriate for the animation wanted. Each of these methods use different *depth cues*.

14.4.1 Scale

When using scaled sprites, drawing sprites with a stretching blitter, the goal is usually to display the sprites at different distance. The background should preferably also have appropriate perspective, to support the 3D effect. A classic example is the old arcade game Zaxxon, but the technique is in frequent use ever since. See Figure 162.

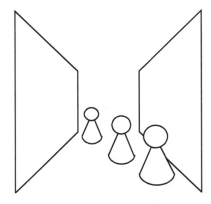

FIGURE 162. Scaled sprites give depth information

14.4.2 Parallax scroll

Another option is parallax scroll, where different parts of the animation move (usually sideways) in different speeds depending on the distance. You can use grass and bushes near the "camera", and mountains in the background. The most classic example is probably Moon Patrol (mimicked in Figure 163). This effect is not as frequently used in games as scaled sprites, but you will often find it in movies.

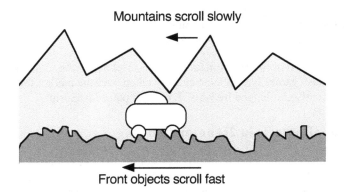

FIGURE 163. In parallax scrolling, the movement gives very strong depth cues

14.4.3 Shadows

The shadow of an object is a very important depth cue, both for pseudo-3D as well as full 3D. The full 3D case is a matter for volume 2 and we will return to them there. In 2D, however, simple shadows are not too hard to add. Even without scaling, we get a strong impression of depth, as shown in Figure 164.

Animation

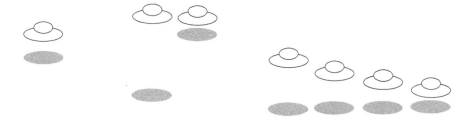

FIGURE 164. Shadows give much 3D information

With these pseudo-3D effects, we get as close to 3D that we can without actually using 3D. But let us now go back to the full 3D world.

14.5 Modeling movement

Above, we touched upon the question of how objects should move in animation. This is obviously the central point in animation, moving things around, and this section is about how we can decide how to move the objects in a scene.

There are several options:

- Procedural animation
- Physics-based animation
- Pre-programmed animation paths

Procedural animation is what you get when you write a program that calculates how the objects should move. In the simplest case, a procedural animation can simply drive a time-dependent rotation transformation like one that makes a moon rotate around a planet.

Physics-based animation is really a kind of procedural animation, but where the paths are decided from formulae that to some extent follow the laws of physics. Such animations include things like bouncing balls. An important aspect of physics-based animation is that it can be given the capability to interact properly with unexpected events, such as player movement. Physics-based animation with a decent system for collision detection and handling will solve many problems, but making one that is truly reliable is an even bigger problem.

The third option that I want to mention is *pre-programmed paths*. If you want an object that flies or drives along a predefined track, but that track is too complex to make a procedural animation, then a path defined by a spline is a good idea. I would particularly suggest Catmull-Rom splines, where you can place a range of points into the scene, and the generated path will pass though all of them in the order you desire. If you take even steps on the controlling parameter (we used u in the blending functions in chapter 8), then the animation speed will be nice and continuous, and you can control the speed by varying the distance between the control points.

14.6 Character animation

Animating human bodies, as well as human faces, are hard problems. They are hard since we are so teriffic at spotting any difference from reality. These topics include key-frame animation, forward and inverse kinematics, skinning, face animation parameters etc. We will go deeper into these topics in Volume 2, especially on skinning.

14.7 Particle systems and instancing

Particle systems have been mentioned (section 13.8.7 on page 182) as a typical application for billboards. That is, billboards are often use to draw the particles in a particle system. An equally important problem is how to move the particles.

A particle system is an entity in a graphics system where a fairly large amount of point-shaped objects, particles, are handled. Typically, all the particles in a specific particle system have similar behavior. Quite often, only the initial values (position and speed) vary.

A particle can be represented by a small data structure with fields for position and speed. Fields for acceleration, mass, physical size (radius) and look etc may also be included. (See further below.)

On these particles, the simplest laws of physics are applied:

$$acceleration = gravity + forces/mass$$

$$speed = speed + acceleration \cdot \Delta t$$

$$position = position + speed \cdot \Delta t$$

In many cases, gravity is the only force that applies, in which case the particle will move in a typical missile trajectory parabola.

If these equations are simply updated once for every frame (preferably with some factors for the time step) you get *Euler integration* of the speed and position. This is a rough approximation of the true integral, but usually quite sufficient for particle systems.

The life-span for a particle can be very short. If the particle system simulates a fountain (a very good application for particle systems) the particle is only interesting until it hits the ground or water surface.

Particle systems come in many kinds. We can categorise them in three groups:

- Independent particles
- Dependent, freely moving particles
- Connected particles

The independent particles are by far t he easiest to create. They only need position and velocity, and require no other tests than a test for the termination. These particle systems are suitable for effects like snow, bursts of water (fountains, waterfalls), clouds and smoke.

Dependent particles, particles for which we perform collision tests with no prior knowledge of which particles may be close, are by far the hardest to do, performance wise. A trivial implementation will have very large complexity, $O(N^2)$.

Finally, connected particles are moderately easy to build and easier to manage (lower complexity), but the hardest to make stable. A typical case here is to simulate cloth. Euler intergration is not sufficient here and may make the particle system unstable.

For our purposes, for this book (part 1) we primarily consider independent particles. More advanced particle systems implemented on the GPU are subjects for part 2.

There are multiple ways to use a particle system to create geometry, but the easiest way to draw a particle system is to draw the individual particles as billboards. This is easy for very small particle systems, but when the numbers rise, the number of function calls becomes so large that it becomes the bottleneck. For this we may use a technique called *instancing*.

What instancing does is simple enough: It draws a specific shape several times with a single function call! This is done with the calls glDrawArraysInstanced or glDrawElementsInstanced, variants of the usual calls adding a parameter which specifies how many instances that should be drawn. This would, of course, draw all instances on top of each other if there was no way to handle them separately. This is done using the variable gl_InstanceID in the shaders, primarily in the vertex shader to affect the location of the instance.

As example, here follows the vertex shader from our demo "Billboard instancing" (available in the PFNP demo archive).

```
#version 150

in  vec3 in_Position;
uniform mat4 myMatrix;
uniform float angle;
uniform float slope;
out vec2 texCoord;

void main(void)
{
    mat4 r;
    float a = angle + gl_InstanceID * 0.5;
    float rr = 1.0 - slope * gl_InstanceID * 0.01;
    r[0] = rr*vec4(cos(a), -sin(a), 0, 0);
    r[1] = rr*vec4(sin(a), cos(a), 0, 0);
    r[2] = vec4(0, 0, 1, 0);
    r[3] = vec4(0, 0, 0, 1);
    texCoord.s = in_Position.x+0.5;
    texCoord.t = in_Position.y+0.5;
    gl_Position = r * myMatrix *  vec4(in_Position, 1.0);
```

}

The important part here is, of course, the use of `gl_InstanceID` to place the instances in different places. The uniforms angle and slope are used to fine tune the result, which may look like Figure 165.

FIGURE 165. Demo of instancing of billboards.

This simple program lends itself to considerable creativity, but also has its problems. If we want the particles to move around with some noise added for variation, how can we do that? How do we get some more data into the shaders? How about a texture with noise?

It should be noted that instancing is at its best for simple models like a billboard. For more complex models, the number if function calls may no longer be the bottleneck, and then instancing is not as significant.

14.8 Collision detection

One of the most vital problems in animation, and thereby in most real-time applications and even many off-line ones, is collision detection.

Several years ago I predicted that collision detection would be the area where we would see the next major break-throughs. Today, physics engines (where collision detection is a very big part) are big products that get much attention, GPUs are used to accelerate them, and for a while there were dedicated physics acceleration boards.

Collision detection and handling include several problems:

- Detecting a momentary collision, at a specific point in time, discrete time
- Detecting collisions that occur between frames, in continuous time
- Separating objects so that they don't overlap
- Changing velocities as response to the collision
- Applying appropriate forces to create a response that is strictly physically based
- Applying forces from hard and soft constraints

- Calculating the exact time of collision and applying forces at that time rather than at constant time steps

I could make the list a lot longer by breaking down the subject into smaller parts. In this chapter, I will only deal with the most important concepts and relatively simple practical solutions, avoiding the later parts of the list. In part 2, we will return to these problems with more elaborate methods. For a deeper analysis of the subject, see [4].

14.9 Collision detection based on the Separating Axis Theorem (SAT)

A particularly simple and straight-forward collision detection scheme can be designed based on the famous Separating Axis Theorem (SAT). Like most collision detection algorithms, it is limited to *convex shapes* only. It is usable for both 2D and 3D collision detection. The theorem states that

Two convex objects do not overlap if and only if there exists a line (called axis) onto which the two objects' projections do not overlap.

The projection of an object onto such an axis (see Figure 166) is done by the dot product. If you take the dot product of all vertices in a polyhedron and a vector, the projection is the range of values resulting from the operation.

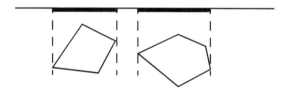

FIGURE 166. Two shapes projected onto an axis (top)

This really means that for every pair of convex objects, if they don't overlap, there exists a separating *plane*, a plane that can fit between them. But this is not quite enough. In most cases (all except the case where two objects are in contact face-to-face) there exists an *infinite* number of planes. A theorem that implies that we need to search an infinite number of planes for one that separates the objects is not helpful.

However, for polyhedra models we can limit ourself to a limited number of planes; the faces of each model! Each face defines a plane, and its normal is a possible separating axis. Furthermore, we don't have to test for overlapping intervals, we just have to test in *one* direction for each plane. Thus, if you find any face in any of the models, for which all vertices of the other are on the outside, you can stop. If all such tests fail, the conclusion is that you have a collision.

You must test both ways between the two shapes. For two shapes A and B, you need to test the faces of A against vertices in B, and faces of B against vertices in A. You can't just take all sides of one model and test for the other. As you can see in Figure 167, there are cases when such an approach fails.

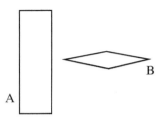

FIGURE 167. A situation where no plane in one object (B) is usable as separating plane

Here follows the collision testing algorithm:

```
for all faces in A
    let a be a vertex in A
    hit = false
    for all vertices b in B
        diff = n • a - n • b
        if diff > 0 then
            hit = true
    if not hit then (we found a separating plane)
        return false

for all faces in B
(same algorithm with A and B reversed)

return true (no separating plane was found)
```

Thus, we test with the dot product whether a vertex is on the "inside" side or the "outside" side. We do not need to test for both ends of the projection. Such a test would not only require more comparisons, but we would also need to, for each plane, find the extreme end of the same model, a totally unnecessary effort.

Any time we get through the test of an object without finding a single vertex on the "inside", we have found a separating plane and we are done!

In 2D, this will produce good results. In 3D, there is one more case to consider, like the one illustrated in Figure 168 (two cubes almost meeting at two edges). To handle this, we need to add the following test:

```
for each edge ae in A
    for each edge be in B
        n = ae x be
        if n is not a zero vector
            make a SAT test with n like above
```

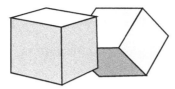

FIGURE 168. A case when the SAT-based method outlined above fails for the 3D case: Two cubes meeting edge to edge.

Thus, for the 3D case we have the following set of potential separating axes (normals to separating planes):

• All faces of A

• All faces of B

• Cross products of every possible pair of edges, one from each model

With this extension, the method clearly gets too computationally heavy for complex models, and it wasn't cheap before. However, what I described is not an optimized method. There are simple approaches to speed it up. First, the broad phase-narrow phase approach (section 14.11) fits perfectly, eliminating many simple cases in a broad phase. Another method is based on the fact that most objects move slowly, so collision detection between them is usually done in positions close to where it was performed the previous time. Thus, if you can remember a separating plane from one frame to another, you can start with that plane next time, and it will most likely be the right plane to test again.

14.10 Sphere-polyhedra collisions

Collision detection is greatly simplified in two specific cases: Sphere-sphere and sphere-polyhedra. The latter case may not be as obvious as the former.

A special case of this is to detect collisions between the camera and a scene with polyhedra objects. If your animation is in first person 3D perspective, you will want to handle camera-to-polygon collision detection. We may here consider the camera to be spherical! Even though your camera isn't visible in the animation, it must have a size and shape. A sphere-shaped camera is practical, with a radius less than the distance to the near Z clipping plane. This simplification may also apply to other cases, including the case where a model is represented by a number of spheres for collision purposes. But let us start by considering the camera-polyhedra case.

This is a much simpler case than checking objects built from polygons against each other. It is similar to the SAT-based approach in section 14.9 but highly simplified.

Detecting collisions between the camera and spheres is trivial, and many objects should be nicely represented by spheres, at least for camera collisions. A somewhat more interesting case is to detect collisions between the camera and polyhedra. In particular, large polyhedra, like walls and large furniture, can not be represented by spheres.

So consider a sphere, the camera with a center **c** and radius r. We want to test if it collides with a mesh. We do that one polygon at a time.

First we can test if the sphere is close to the plane that the polygon defines. With the surface normal **n**, pointing outwards, and a polygon vertex **a**, this is a quick test:

$$\mathbf{n} \bullet (\mathbf{c} - r\mathbf{\cdot n}) > \mathbf{n} \bullet \mathbf{a}$$

which simplifies to

$$r < \mathbf{n} \bullet \mathbf{c} - \mathbf{n} \bullet \mathbf{a}$$

If this test indicates a distance larger than r, that is, if the center of the sphere is so far out that the entire sphere is on the outside, we are done with this particular polygon with no hit. If it is a hit, we may want to calculate the point where the line c + μ·**n** intersects the plane and check if it is inside the polygon, as described in chapter 4, in order to find the point of impact.

If it is in the polygon, then we have a collision and we are done. However, there is still one case of uncertainty: The camera can be close to a corner or edge but its center can be outside the polygon! So we have two cases to consider: Corners and edges.

It is possible to make exact checks for both corners and edges. However, if we accept approximations, this problem turns out to be much easier, to the extent that we can skip the polygon intersection test above!

We simply check each plane, and any time we detect that the sphere is outside one plane, we stop the test. If there is no plane that the sphere is outside, we conclude that there is a collision. This gives a usable approximation for many cases. See Figure 169.

FIGURE 169. Sphere-corner test using planes only. Left: Correct hit. Middle: False hit. Right: Correct miss.

As it turns out, only sharp corners will cause any significant errors. For the 90° case above, the false hits are very close to the corner/edge and may not be offensive.

Note that we will still have to pick the best plane to use for collision handling, based on the speed and position of the objects. If you pick an arbitrary plane, the result may not work as expected.

14.11 Simplifying polyhedra-polyhedra collisions

When working with collisions between polyhedra, the computational complexity easily explodes. Many applications simplify the collision detection to only check for collisions between bounding spheres of the objects, which has the same drawbacks as the unwanted collisions between 2D sprites, as outlined above.

14.11.1 Broad phase-narrow phase

For detailed collision detection, the complexity is much higher. A common optimization is to divide the check into two phases. The first is the broad phase, where fast checks are made between rough approximations of the objects. Only when a hit is detected in the broad phase, the second phase, the narrow phase, is entered. There, an exact check is performed.

According to Watt [27], this phase also includes checks based on global organization of the scene (chapter 13). I would rather consider this a three-phase method, split into the following phases:

- Global phase (scene subdivision)

- Broad phase (enclosing simplified shapes)

- Narrow phase (detailed polygon-level test)

It should be mentioned that the literature disagrees on the meaning of the term "broad phase" and "narrow phase". Here, we use the meanings defined by Watt [27]. Others, like Ericsson [4], use the term "broad phase" for the global organization of large scenes (chapter 13), and "narrow phase" for the simple bounding shapes. Whatever we call the phases, there are really three phases, one *global* phase, one *simplified bounding shape* phase, and one *detailed* phase. Watt merges the first two into one, Ericsson merges the last two, but they are better viewed as three.

This section is mainly concerned with the broad phase. The narrow phase may be solved as described in section 14.9, and we will return to the global phase in section 14.14.

14.11.2 The broad phase

In the broad phase, a relatively simple bounding shape is used for making a quick, rough test. It is common to use bounding spheres or axis-aligned bounding boxes (AABB). An AABB is a six-sided box where all sides are aligned to one of the axes. That makes the collision text between two AABB's a simple task, just six comparisons.

An alternative method is to use OBB's, oriented bounding boxes. An OBB does not have to be aligned with any axes, but should be placed for the best possible fit with the object. This will lead to much fewer false hits, and thereby fewer cases where we unnecessarily go into the narrow phase. See Figure 4.11.

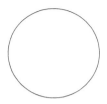 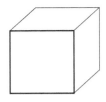 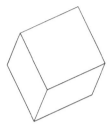

FIGURE 170. The three basic shapes for collision detection: sphere, AABB and OBB

There are even more elaborate methods for the broad phase, where closer approximations to the object is used, for a higher cost in the broad phase but subsequently lower cost in the narrow phase. We will return to them shortly.

Which method to choose is not self-evident. It depends on the application, on the shapes used. The effectiveness of two-phase methods can be measured with this formula:

$$T = N_v C_v + N_p C_p$$

T is the total computation cost, the time to compute collision detection.

N_v is the number of bounding volume pair tests

C_v is the cost for a bounding volume pair test

N_p is the number primitive pair tests

C_p is the cost for a primitive pair test

N_v and C_p are given by the application, by the number of objects and the detail of each object. They do affect performance, but also the quality of the result.

The broad phase method should be selected to balance C_v and N_p. A simple test will lower C_v, but raise N_p as the number of false hits raise. A more detailed broad phase test will reduce N_p, but raise C_v.

Consequently, an animation with few but detailed objects should use a detailed broad phase algorithm, but an animation with many simple objects should use a simple broad phase algorithm. Only after such balancing has been taken into account should we reduce number of objects or object detail.

Apart from spheres, AABBs and OBBs, the broad phase may also utilize other shapes. These include:

- Capsules
- Convex hull

- kDOPs

- A combination of multiple shapes

The *capsule* is a popular shape in the game industry. A capsule is the combination of two spheres and a cylinder, as in Figure 171. Although the shape is relatively complex, the fit to many models is a lot better, and the storage requirements are modest.

FIGURE 171. A capsule is built from two spheres and a cylinder

The *convex hull* of a shape is the minimal convex shape that encloses the shape. Since collision detection is generally based on convex shapes, this is a fairly obvious shape to use. However, the complexity of the convex hull is highly dependent of the enclosed shape, and therefore the convex hull tends to be too complex for the broad phase. It may, however, be a good solution for the narrow phase.

Another option for enclosing shape is to use *k-DOPs* [16], that is, discrete oriented polytopes with k sides. "Discrete oriented" refers to limitations to planes that have normal vectors where all components are in the set $\{-1, 0, 1\}$. Figure 172 shows how these shapes can look.

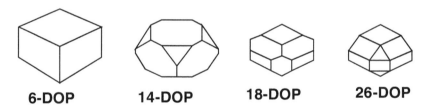

FIGURE 172. The four possible kinds of k-DOPs

Whether k-DOPs is an advantage over AABBs etc or not can be argued, but there are results showing that at least 14-DOPs and 18-DOPs can outperform AABBs (6-DOPs) in some situations. We also note that the algorithm suggested in [16] not only uses k-DOPs but also decomposes them hierarchically for further optimizations.

Finally, the broad phase may use several shapes, either several of the same or different ones. Then it is possible to choose different shapes depending on what fits different parts of the total shape. This solution will handle non-convex shapes nicely. Moreover, it can be optimized by hierarcical approaches, which is the topic of the next section.

14.11.3 Single phase algorithms

It should be mentioned that there are also single phase algorithms, typically hierarchical, where there is no distinction between a broad and narrow phase. An example is illustrated in Figure 173. The object in the example is broken down into a resolution hierarchy of bounding spheres, with a single bounding sphere at the top. With such a structure, it is possible to make the collision detection adaptive to available processing time and perform collision detection to the level that available time permits.

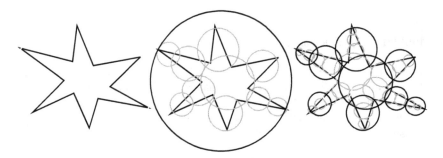

FIGURE 173. An example of a hierarchical collision detection system

14.11.4 The narrow phase

In the narrow phase, tests should be done on polyhedra level. The SAT-based method described in section 14.9 is a straight-forward solution. There are many other approaches, including highly optimized ones. We will cover this some more in Volume 2.

14.12 Objects passing through each other

In both 2D and 3D animations, you can miss collisions completely, resulting in objects passing straight through each other. This happens if velocities are too high or the collision tests are not carried out often enough. One proposed solution is to make sweep representations of moving objects, so that they are converted to elongated forms that represent the volume they move through during the time interval in question.

FIGURE 174. If the movement per cycle is too big, objects run a risk of passing through each other

In the simple example in Figure 174, the rectangle used for collision tests can be expanded by the length of the speed vector. In 3D, the problem obviously becomes harder, and is most easily handled when using OBB's.

14.13 Collisions between a fast-moving camera and polyhedra

The problem above also applies to the camera. If you allow very large velocities for the camera, it may be important to detect collisions with respect to the velocity.

Detecting the problem for a camera and an infinite plane is simple and straight-forward. See Figure 175.

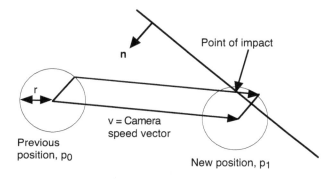

FIGURE 175. Collision camera to (infinite) plane

The collision detection is made by checking if the speed vector from a specific position near the camera's previous location intersects with a plane. This vector should be placed at the edge of the camera sphere, offset from the camera center by the normal vector of the plane multiplied with the camera radius.

So, if $\mathbf{p_0}$ is the previous position, and we want to check if the camera can move to $\mathbf{p_1}$, we do like this:

Speed vector: $\mathbf{v} = \mathbf{p_1} - \mathbf{p_0}$.

Offset starting point: $\mathbf{p_0}' = \mathbf{p_0} - r \cdot \mathbf{n}$

Check if the polygon and the line segment from $\mathbf{p_0}'$ to $\mathbf{p_0}' + \mathbf{v}$ intersect!

This gives you a very elegant collision detection and handling for the camera, but one things is missing. If the camera moves near an edge or a corner, the test is not sufficient. The camera may, as shown in Figure 176, move inside the polygon without having detected a collision. This is not acceptable, so we must add tests for this.

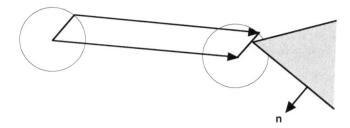

n

FIGURE 176. A case where the speed vector doesn't intersect any polygon, but we should still detect a collision!

Note, however, that if we can find a very rough indication of a potential problem, that is enough, because then we can make thorough tests when absolutely needed. So let us look at a rough but usable way to solve the problem.

One solution is to expand all polygons by r when doing these tests, by expanding them physically or modify the limits for the polygon hit test. If we only get an indication of a potential problem, we can move the sphere to the position in question and make one or more purely positional tests. That should be easier than doing full-scale detailed tests on the movement path.

Another option is to check the distance between in the closest point between the edge and the movement path of the center. Then, the problem is finding the closest point between two lines. Calculating that is fairly simple. You define a plane to which both lines are parallel (using the cross product) and then project a line between a point on either line onto the normal vector of the plane. The projection gives you the distance, which is all we needed.

14.14 Large world handling in collision detection

Collision detection, just like VSD, is a problem where tests have to be made on extensive numbers of objects. Although tests based on bounding shapes needs fewer objects than the number of polygons, the problem needs many-to-many tests which grows by the square of the number of objects. In order to make the problem scale better, some kind of sorting or subdivision is needed. This may be defined as part of the broad phase [27].

The simplest way to speed up collision handling is to apply *linear sorting*. All the objects are organized in a linear list, and the list is sorted by one coordinate, for example by X.

The sorting does not need to be global on every frame. A single check with list neighbors for every frame will perform a bubble sort (preferably bi-directional bubble sort, so called *cocktail sort*) which will keep the list sorted or almost sorted for a minimal cost per frame. Although the sorting algorithm as such is slow, the cost per frame is the important thing here.

The collision detection now only needs to be done a few steps into the list for every object. The limit can be decided from the maximum size of all objects being tested. This reduces the complexity by one dimension, which is clearly significant.

See Figure 177. The gray sphere needs to be tested against the two objects within the indicated distance, but when the search reaches the objects at the top and bottom of the figure, it is out of range and we may stop testing for that object.

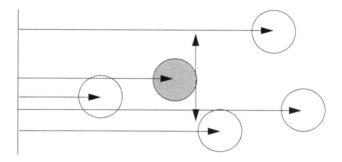

FIGURE 177. Collision detection accelerated by linear sorting

Even better performance can be achieved by 2D or 3D subdivision of the scene, by BSP trees, quad trees or octrees. This is particularly interesting if you have such a subdivision done already, for other problems.

14.15 Collision handling

Once a collision is detected, something appropriate should be done. Typically, the colliding objects should be separated, and their velocities should be modified so that they bounce off each other depending on weight and elasticity.

When collision detection is limited to spheres, AABB's or OBB's, the collision handling is equally straight-forward. Due to the complexity of a general collision handling, you often must resort to some kind of simplified solution.

You may sometimes meet the defensive claim that collision handling is application dependent, and that you can't say much about it because of that. That is an excuse for not dealing with a hard problem. Collision handling is a hard problem, maybe even harder than collision detection.Rather, we make an introduction of the basic principles (somewhat reused from [5]) and leave the harder topics for volume 2. (See also [4].)

Once a collision is found, a number of tasks may be applied:

- Separate
- Change velocities
- Deform

- Maintain constraints

Full (narrow-phase) tests are hard to resolve. There is a risk that objects are interlocked, so that they attach themselves to each other. And even worse, in such situations the resulting attempts by the system to make them separate might add energy that result in very dramatic effects that are totally unintentional.

What I will focus upon here is collision handling for particles, which is usable for particle systems as well as simplified handling of spherical objects. It can also be used as a rough approximation for other objects, although mainly for rather compact ones.

Let us look at a simple case, simple particle-surface collision, in Figure 178. The mass of the particle is much less than the surface, so we can consider the surface to have infinite mass. The particle has an incoming speed vector, and you have a point of impact calculated. At the point of impact, you get the surface normal. By splitting the incoming speed vector into one component parallel to the surface and one parallel to the surface normal, you can create an outgoing speed vector from the components. The component parallel to the surface should be retained or shortened by some factor (to simulate friction). The component parallel to the normal vector should be scaled depending on the elasticity of the objects. For an elastic collision, keep the full normal component (although reversed). For a plastic collision, ignore it completely. And tune it for any degree of semi-elastic collisions.

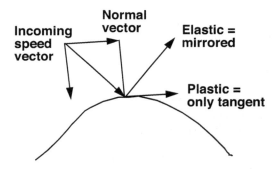

FIGURE 178. Simple particle-surface collision handling

This was an extremely simplified example, where I completely ignored the laws of physics. I only did my best to find a method that resembles the results we would want. This is quite enough for many cases, like particle systems and simpler games. The same method also works for particles colliding with each other, as long as they have the same weight. The only difference is that they should swap the normal component with each other.

The next example, in Figure 178, is slightly more ambitious. Two objects (spheres) collide head-on. They may have different mass and different speed. This gives us a 1-dimensional collision.

FIGURE 179. 1-dimensional collision

When resolving a collision, we must always preserve momentum:

$$m_1v_1 + m_2v_2 = m_1v_{1a} + m_2v_{2a}$$

For a plastic collision, the objects will have the same speed after the collision, which gives us

$$m_1v_1 + m_2v_2 = m_1v_a + m_2v_a = (m_1 + m_2)v_a$$

$$v_a = \frac{m_1 \cdot v_1 + m_2 \cdot v_2}{m_1 + m_2}$$

For the case when the two objects have the same mass, this simplifies to

$$v_a = \frac{v_1 + v_2}{2}$$

which is what we should expect.

Elastic collisions also preserve kinetic energy:

$$m_1v_1^2 + m_2v_2^2 = m_1v_{1a}^2 + m_2v_{2a}^2$$

Combine this with the momentum equation to eliminate v_{2a}, use

$$(v_1^2 - v_{1a}^2) = (v_1 + v_{1a})(v_1 - v_{1a})$$

to be able to eliminate the $(v_1 - v_{1a})$ factor, and you get

$$v_{1a} = \frac{2 \cdot m_2 \cdot v_2 + (m_1 - m_2) \cdot v_1}{m_1 + m_2}$$

$$v_{2a} = \frac{2 \cdot m_1 \cdot v_1 + (m_1 - m_2) \cdot v_2}{m_1 + m_2}$$

If the objects have the same weight, this simplifies to

$$v_{1a} = v_2$$

$$v_{2a} = v_1$$

and we have proven why the famous metal ball desktop toy, Newton's cradle (Figure 180) works as it does.

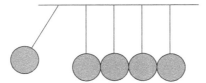

FIGURE 180. Newton's cradle, an example where elastic collisions work as in the formulae above

To handle more complex collisions, where you want to deal with off-center collisions that will cause rotation, we will have to go further. However, that is a matter for the game programming course. What you have now is enough for particle systems and simpler game situations. This is not as much toy-level as it may seem. By connecting particles with simple bonds (springs) you can get pretty good handling with realistic rotations even without any rigid body mechanics.

Collision handling topics that I have so far ignored include:

- deformations caused by collisions
- applying forces to avoid overlap
- stacking, piling objects on top of each other
- support for rotation, rigid body mechanics
- better numerical methods for stability

Alas, those interesting topics are beyond the scope of volume 1!

15. Low-level graphics algorithms

In this chapter, we will look into some of the low-level algorithms that form what I consider "classic" computer graphics. It is not so common to need these algorithms today (although it happens more often than you might think) but as a matter of fact, anyone who has taken a course in Computer Graphics should know Bresenham's algorithm.

15.1 Line-drawing algorithms

As suggested in the first chapters, drawing lines is fundamental, the second thing to do once you are able to draw pixels. We can usually take line-drawing algorithms for granted.

But in this section, we will not take them for granted, but have a look at how they are implemented. There are two kinds of line-drawing algorithms that we will look into, the *DDA algorithm* and *Bresenham's line-drawing algorithm*.

Up to now, we have generally defined lines by two points on the line, $\mathbf{P_s}$, $\mathbf{P_e}$, (where s and e denotes start and end) or the equivalent, a point and a direction, $\mathbf{P} = \mathbf{P_s} + \mu\mathbf{v}$, where $\mathbf{v} = \mathbf{P_e} - \mathbf{P_s}$. I will now reformulate that a bit.

We still work with two points, $\mathbf{P_s} = (x_s, y_s)$ and $\mathbf{P_e} = (x_e, y_e)$. The problem is to draw a discrete line, that is find a connected range of discrete pixels between the two points, which follows a mathematical line as closely as possible.

When I say connected, it requires an explanation. Two pixels are connected if they are neighbors. The type of connectivity is defined by defining the neighborhood. In the Carthesian grid, you may use either a 4-pixel neighborhood or an 8-pixel one. We say that the curve is 4-connected or 8-connected. The most common choice is 8-connected curves. See Figure 181.

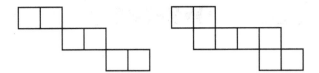

FIGURE 181. 8-connected (left) and 4-connected (right) shape

It should be stressed that a *digital line* is not exactly the same as a line. It is a discretization, a sampling, of a mathematical line, by finding the discrete pixels closest to the mathematical line. This discrete sampling will, by its nature, display aliasing. Digital lines aligned with the X or Y axis, or a diagonal, will look nice and straight, but other digital lines will have different degrees of the "stair-case effect", as in Figure 182. In some cases, like the right line in the figure below, it does not seem very satisfactory as a line when viewed close-up like this. But this is what we want, at least for now.

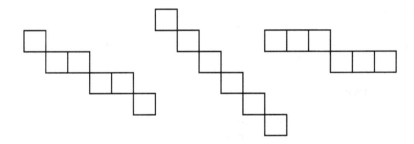

FIGURE 182. Sample digital lines

We will start in P_s and work our way to P_e. Then we can also express the line as the *line equation*:

$$y = mx + b$$

where.

$$m = \frac{y_e - y_s}{x_e - x_s}$$

and

$$b = y_s - mx_s$$

This means that if you take a step ∂x in x along the line, you will take a step $\partial y = m \cdot \partial x$ in the y direction. Now we are ready to make an algorithm out of this!

15.2 The DDA line-drawing algorithm

The DDA algorithm, where DDA stands for Digital Differential Algorithm, is a very simple line-drawing algorithm, based on the ∂x and ∂y steps just mentioned.

Assume that $-1 < m < 1$, that is, the line has a slope of less than 45 degrees. Also assume that $x_e > x_s$. This limits our solution to only a quarter of all possible lines, but it can be easily generalized.

Start in $\mathbf{P_s}$, by assigning the starting pixel $\mathbf{P_0} = (x_s, y_s)$ to $\mathbf{P_s}$. Note that although I said *pixel*, implying that starting and end positions are integers, the y values must allow floating-point coordinates for intermediate values. It is possible to allow for non-integer endpoints, but if we do, the start gets a bit more complicated. See chapter 15.10.

We now generate a sequence of $\mathbf{P_k} = (x_k, y_k)$. It is generated by the following simple algorithm:

```
x_{k+1} = x_k + 1
y_{k+1} = y_k + m
```

Closer to actual code, we can write it:

```
y = ys
m = (ye - ys) / (xe - xs)
for (x = xs; x <= xe; x++)
{
    plotPixel(x, round(y))
    y = y + m
}
```

Concerning the missing directions above, you can add all the cases where $x_e < x_s$ simply by swapping the points, or stepping with the sign of $x_e - x_s$. rather than 1. The cases when m is outside the given range is handled by an equivalent algorithm, where x is swapped with y and m is replaced by m^{-1}.

One more thing: There are cases when you want to use the algorithm above for any m, namely when filling polygons rather that drawing lines. In such a case, the connectivity does not matter since we want to find pixel spans rather than connected pixels. More about that in the discussion on scan conversion.

That was easy! So, is there anything wrong with the DDA algorithm? Not really, not on modern hardware. However, if we need to implement a line drawing algorithm at all today, it is very likely that we work with some special hardware, often small, mobile devices with very low processing power. Such devices often have very limited floating-point capability. Then the floating-point additions above may slow down the algorithm prohibitively. That is the time when you need *Bresenham's Line Drawing Algorithm*.

15.3 Bresenham's line-drawing algorithm

If I had to pick a single low-level algorithm that must be included in any serious computer graphics course, *Bresenham's line-drawing algorithm* [13] is the obvious choice. If you have passed a computer graphics course, *of course* you know Bresenham's. This algorithm is the simplest of a family of curve generation algorithms where all operations are made with additions and comparisons. Other variants include circles, ellipses, actually *any* curve that can be expressed by a polynomial.

We use the same start and end points as before, $\mathbf{P_s}$ and $\mathbf{P_e}$, but this time we assume that both have integer coordinates. We define;

$$\Delta x = x_e - x_s$$

$$\Delta y = y_e - y_s$$

Thus

$$m = \Delta y \, / \, \Delta x$$

We also assume that the line is in the first octant:

$$\Delta x > 0$$

$$\Delta y > 0$$

$$0 < m < 1$$

Like with the DDA algorithm, other cases can be found by small adjustments of what the result we will get for the first octant.

The generated points (x_k, y_k) will be at integer positions. Let us now look at the situation when we are at an arbitrary pixel on the digital line. The previous pixel that was found is p_k. How can we then find p_{k+1}?

Since we generate an 8-connected line in the first quadrant, there are only two possible locations for the next pixel, either one step to the right, at (x_k+1, y_k), or one step diagonally, at (x_k+1, y_k+1).

The actual line at x coordinate x_k+1 can be found from the line equation as

$$y = m(x_k+1) + b$$

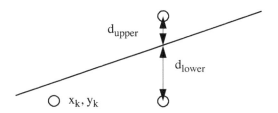

FIGURE 183. d_{upper} and d_{lower} are the distances from the candidate pixels to the line

We can now calculate the distance from the line to the candidate pixels, as in Figure 183.

$$d_{lower} = y - y_k = m(x_k + 1) + b - y_k$$

$$d_{upper} = (y_k + 1) - y = y_k + 1 - m(x_k + 1) - b$$

If $d_{upper} > d_{lower}$, then d_{lower} is closest and should be chosen, otherwise we should choose d_{upper}. This seems good enough if m and b were integers, which they usually are not. But we can rewrite a bit and make this a lot better. Form the difference

$$d_{lower} - d_{upper} = 2m(x_k + 1) - 2 y_k + 2b - 1$$

This is a single value from which we can decide which pixel to pick only by inspecting its sign! Now replace m by $\Delta y / \Delta x$ and multiply by Δx. What we get now is our final *decision variable*:

$$p_k = \Delta x(d_{lower} - d_{upper}) = 2\Delta y \cdot x_k - 2\Delta x \cdot y_k + 2\Delta y + \Delta x \cdot (2b-1)$$

Thus, if you know the decision variable p_k for any iteration k, you know if you should make the move $y_{k+1} = y_k$ or $y_{k+1} = y_k + 1$. (x_{k+1} is always $x_k + 1$.) Negative p_k, choose d_{lower}, make a horizontal move. Positive p_k, choose d_{upper}, diagonal move! The formula is fairly nice, all parameters are integer... except b. But I choose not to care for the moment.

Note that the last terms are constants. We set $c = 2\Delta y + \Delta x \cdot (2b-1)$.

Now comes the magic. Do you remember the forward-difference calculations that appeared in section 8.14 on page 110? There we showed that any polynomial decision variable can be incrementally updated in constant steps using only additions! Since this is a linear function, we can make that simplification in a single step! So let us express p_{k+1} as an increment from p_k!

$$p_k = 2\Delta y \cdot x_k - 2\Delta x \cdot y_k + c$$

$$p_{k+1} = 2\Delta y \cdot x_{k+1} - 2\Delta x \cdot y_{k+1} + c$$

$$p_{k+1} - p_k = 2\Delta y \cdot (x_{k+1} - x_k) - 2\Delta x \cdot (y_{k+1} - y_k)$$

Since $x_{k+1} = x_k + 1$,

$$p_{k+1} - p_k = 2\Delta y - 2\Delta x \cdot (y_{k+1} - y_k)$$

The value $y_{k+1} - y_k$ will depend on the step taken:

Lower candidate: $y_k = y_{k+1} \Rightarrow p_{k+1} - p_k = 2\Delta y$

Upper candidate: $y_k + 1 = y_{k+1} \Rightarrow p_{k+1} - p_k = 2\Delta y - 2\Delta x$

Thus, for any p_k, inspect the sign of p_k, calculate p_{k+1} by a simple addition and increment x_k, y_k to $x_{k+1}\ y_{k+1}$!

One detail remains: the starting value of p_k, that is p_0. Insert x_s, y_s into the p_k formula:

$$p_0 = 2\Delta y \cdot x_s - 2\Delta x \cdot y_s + 2\Delta y + \Delta x \cdot (2b-1)$$

If you go back to the definition of b, it was $y = mx + b$, insert x_s, y_s and replace m by $\Delta y / \Delta x$ and we get $\Delta x \cdot b = \Delta x \cdot y_s - \Delta y \cdot x_s$.

$$p_0 = 2\Delta y \cdot x_s - 2\Delta x \cdot y_s + 2\Delta y + 2(\Delta x \cdot y_s - \Delta y \cdot x_s) - \Delta x = 2\Delta y - \Delta x$$

So the total algorithm is:

```
Calculate the starting value:
    p0 = 2Δy - Δx
Run algorithm (iteration k) while xₖ < xₑ:
    xₖ₊₁ = xₖ + 1
    if pₖ > 0 then
        pₖ₊₁ = pₖ + 2Δy - 2Δx
        Yₖ₊₁ = Yₖ + 1
    else
        pₖ₊₁ = pₖ + 2Δy
        Yₖ₊₁ = Yₖ
```

Here follows an example, illustrated in Figure 184. We plot a line from 10, 10 to 20, 14.

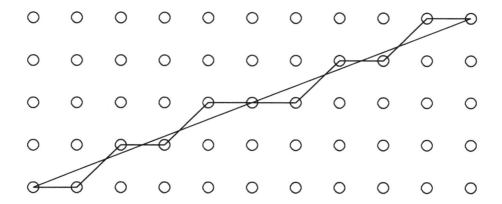

FIGURE 184. Example of line drawing with Bresenham's algorithm

The exact starting coordinates do not matter. The difference is more important. The variables are initialized and updated as follows and the result is listed in Table 2:

$$\Delta x = 10 \qquad \Delta y = 4$$

$$p_0 = 2\Delta y - \Delta x = 8 - 10 = -2$$

$$\text{Horizontal: } p_{k+1} - p_k = 2\Delta y = 8$$

$$\text{Vertical: } p_{k+1} - p_k = 2\Delta y - 2\Delta x = -12$$

TABLE 2. Example of Bresenham's line drawing algorithm

k	x_k	y_k	p_k	Move
0	10	10	-2	⇨
1	11	10	6	⬈
2	12	11	-6	⇨
3	13	11	2	⬈
4	14	12	-10	⇨
5	15	12	-2	⇨
6	16	12	6	⬈
7	17	13	-6	⇨
8	18	13	2	⬈
9	19	14	-10	⇨
10	20	14	-2	-

Notice that the generated curve is symmetrical, which is a good sign. Incorrectly designed algorithms often result in asymmetries. However, slight asymmetries are normal, and occurs when the line passes exactly between two pixels. Then the choice is arbitrary and the algorithm must simply decide a preference when p_k is zero.

15.4 Generating other curves with the midpoint algorithm

The principle behind Bresenham's line-drawing algorithm can be generalized to a method that can be applied to any curve that can be described by polynomial functions. like circles and ellipses. Instead of calculating the distance to the curve, the method samples a function which passes zero at the curve, to see on which side of the curve that particular point is located. This turns out to be a very general method.

However, picking discrete pixels along a curve is not important enough today to justify a detailed description beyond lines. For a thorough description of the midpoint algorithm, I recommend "Computer graphics with OpenGL" by Hearn&Baker [6].

15.5 Curve attributes

The curve generation algorithms describe how to find a connected sequence of pixels along a curve, as close to the curve as possible. Drawing those pixels only gives us a thin curve. This is often not what we want. There are many attributes that we may want:

- Arbitrary width
- Dashed curves
- Patterned drawing
- A choice of end-point shapes (end caps) and corner shapes

Out of these, I choose to concentrate on arbitrary width. To produce a curve of a specified width, there are two major methods: Double curves and using a pen shape. With a pen shape, a shape follows the curve. The union of the shape placed at all curve positions is filled. See Figure 185.

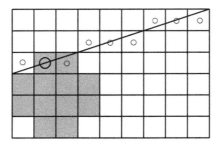

FIGURE 185. Drawing wide curves using a pen shape

This method has the advantage that it provides an easy way to specify endpoint shape as part of the process, but a drawback is that the width of the curve is not constant, and pro-

---

Low-level graphics algorithms

ducing the union of many instances of the shape is not straight-forward, especially not for other curves than lines.

A more efficient method is to use double curves, illustrated by Figure 186.

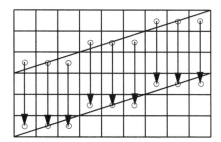

FIGURE 186. Drawing wide curves using two parallel curves

It may be tempting to believe that this can be done by drawing one curve and simply painting a number of pixels to the side, but that is merely a special case of the pen shape method. For lines, that works well, but for a shape like the circle, you should rather generate two circles, simultaneously, and for every iteration fill the pixels between them.

15.6 Pixel geometry

A pixel is always specified by a point (x, y), but a pixel is not a point! A pixel is a rectangular area in continuous space. This leads to an important question: Where is the point in the pixel, the *hotspot* of the pixel? There are two candidates, in the center or in the corner (typically top-left in screen coordinates, Y axis downwards, or bottom-left if the Y axis is upwards). We may use any definition, and both are usable, but the choice will affect the exact placement and size of drawn figures. For example, how long is a line from 1 to 5? With point-in-center, the answer is 5, while with point-in-corner, the answer is 4!

For example, consider the rectangle $(0,0)(4,0)(4,3)(0,3)$: Where is it located? See Figure 187. Point-in-corner is to the left, point-in-center to the right.

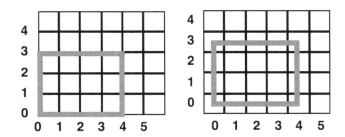

FIGURE 187. The polygon's position varies with the pixel definition

This means that the rectangle will be drawn differently in these two cases, as in Figure 188.

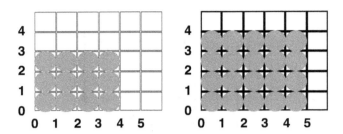

FIGURE 188. Depending on the pixel definition, we may get different interpretation of the same rectangle

This matter is particularly important when rendering polygons. Without a proper definition, we will get errors, seemingly random visible "gaps" between polygons! So, which pixels illustrated in Figure 189 are in the triangle?

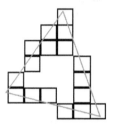

FIGURE 189. Which pixels are in the triangle?

If we know where the pixel's point, its hotspot, is located, this is solvable. See Figure 190. This problem was obvious in many early software renderers, where this was not properly accounted for. Numerical problems due to low-precision math made the matter worse.

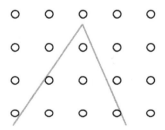

FIGURE 190. Pixels are mapped to points according to the pixel definition, which gives clear decisions

Low-level graphics algorithms

Polygon rendering must be done with sub-pixel precision. If the pixel point, according to the pixel definition, is inside, it should be included. See further the polygon rendering section.

15.7 Inside-outside tests

The question that this section wishes to answer is simple: Given a point, how do you know if it is inside a given closed polygon? The problem at hand may be picking, to determine if a mouse click is inside a polygon or not (e.g. for dragging an object in a vector drawing program) or the question may be a question of defining how a polygon filling algorithm should work. These questions are obviously not without importance.

There are two methods for determining the answer, and the answer is not always the same. The two methods are the *odd-even test* and the *non-zero winding number test*.

For both methods, we form a line from the tested point to infinity, and find all branches in the polygon that intersects the line. Since it does not matter which line we choose, you can make the line horizontal so that the intersection tests are particularly simple to make. See Figure 191.

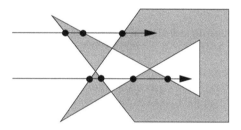

FIGURE 191. The odd-even test: Count the number of intersections

The odd-even test simply counts the number of intersections. If the number is odd, the point is inside, and if it is even, it is outside. It is a very simple rule that usually gives the expected result.

The non-zero winding number test is somewhat more elaborate. It makes a count, where the direction of the intersected branch is important. If the line is horizontal, we may count branches going upwards with +1 and branches going downwards by -1, What sign that goes up or down does not matter, swap them if you like, because what matters is when the sum is zero. If the sum is non-zero, the point is in the polygon, but if it is zero, it is outside. In Figure 192, the winding numbers have been added.

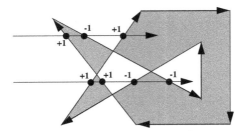

FIGURE 192. The zero winding number test: Count intersections as +1 or -1

Now, what difference does it make which one we choose? Quite a bit, actually! Figure 192 was somewhat incorrectly filled. We correct it in Figure 193.

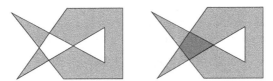

FIGURE 193. Polygons filled according to the odd-even and non-zero winding number rule, respectively. Note the dark area, which is where the rules are different.

In my opinion, the non-zero winding number is the rule that gets this right. In Figure 193, a polygon has two long "legs" that cross each other. The intersection of these two parts should certainly be filled, but the odd-even rule shoots a hole instead.

These definitions have some importance even in 3D. You can determine if a point is inside or outside a closed polyhedron with similar tests.

15.8 Polygon filling

Efficiently filling a polygon is another matter. This must be done in a way that allows us to fill many pixels at a time, and without checking the whole polygon over and over again. The scan-line polygon fill algorithm does this in a very optimized way.

The algorithm uses two primary components: a *sorted edge table* and an *active edge list*. The edge table is an array of linked lists, where each entry corresponds to a row in the image (possibly limited to the number of rows that the polygon spans). The active edge list is a linked list of (references to) edges.

The sorted edge table is created first. For all sides of the polygon, the lowest Y value determines where to put it into the edge table. Thus, we can process the edge table row by row, finding the sides that starts at that Y value.

The active edge list is initially empty. All scanlines are processed in order. When a new scanline is processed, the edge list is updated as follows. If there are any edges present in the edge list that have ended at the previous scanline, they are removed. All remaining edges have their X values updated, to the intersection with the current scanline.

Then, the corresponding entry in the edge list is inspected. Any edges present at that entry are inserted into the active edge list. The edge list is then sorted by X value.

Now we have a simple list telling us exactly what pixels to fill and which ones not to fill. Using the odd-even rule, we should fill between the first and second, the third and fourth, etc. Figure 194 shows an example.

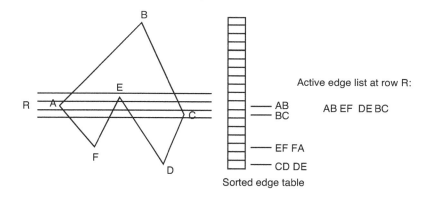

FIGURE 194. Scan-line polygon fill

In the figure above, the row marked R is being processed. The edge AF has been discarded from the active edge list, while AB has been added. Two spans will be filled, from AB to EF and from DE to BC.

There is one potential problem here, where a scan-line intersects a vertex, as in Figure 195. This conflict is most likely to appear when using integers. When using floating-point math, the algorithm designer is more likely to think in sub-pixel numbers, but when you simply have a row number, how do you count polygon branches that end at the scanline that you are working on? See the figure below.

If we only detect if a side reaches the row, we may get erroneous crossing count or winding number for the right and left case in the figure above. The algorithm must take some specific action to avoid such problems. There are at least three different effective remedies:

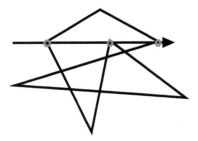

FIGURE 195. How do you count edges for a scan-line that passes through vertices?

1) Do specific checks for vertices, and detect vertices where the two edges are on different sides. Then the two edges count as one!

2) Pre-processing: For vertices with the edges on different sides, shorten one with one scan-line.

3) Use the pixel definition properly and the problem will disappear.

Out of these, (1) is probably the most straight-forward, while (3) is most computationally effective and well-defined. I can see no reason to use the clumsy method (2), but it has been suggested in the literature.

15.9 Flood fill

Flood fill is a common operation in painting programs such as Photoshop. This operation may seem simple to perform by a recursive function like this (pseudo code):

```
procedure FloodFill(x,y,fill,target)
    current := GetPixel(x,y)
    if (current = target) then
       SetPixel(x,y,fill)
       FloodFill(x+1, y, fill, target)
       FloodFill(x-1, y, fill, target)
       FloodFill(x, y+1, fill, target)
       FloodFill(x, y-1, fill, target)

procedure StartFloodFill(x, y, fill)
    target := GetPixel(x, y)
    if (fill <> target) then
       FloodFill(x, y, fill, target)
```

This algorithm, however, will create a recursion depth that is ridiculous, a recursion depth that is proportional to or even equal to the number of pixels to fill.

A more efficient method is to do a breadth-first search. Then the recursion is replaced by a loop processing a list, which is many times less memory- and processor-demanding.

Low-level graphics algorithms

Another method is presented here, to process the images by local horizontal spans. Every found fill-able span is filled, while references to fill-able intervals in the row above and below are put on a stack. Expressed in a kind of pseudo code:

```
get the pixel value of the starting pixel.
push the starting pixel onto the stack.
while the stack is not empty, do
    pull ("pop") the top pixel of the stack.
    for all fillable pixels in the span (pixels equal to the starting
pixel)
        fill the pixel
        for the neighbor above or below
            if the pixel is fillable and is a start of an interval
                put the pixel (reference) on the stack.
```

Thus, the first iteration of the algorithm will start at an arbitrary pixel (white square in the pixel below), fill one span (light grey) and find spans (X) in the row above and below. All the pixels marked with X are put on the stack, and will be starting point for following iterations. Figure 196 shows an example.

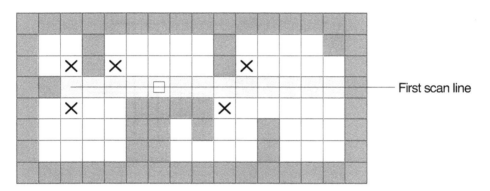

First scan line

FIGURE 196. Flood fill

In some books, a similar operation implements "boundary fill". That operation is hardly used in modern applications. Modern applications rather use even more sophisticated flood fill variants. Among the features that are often added to the routine above are:

- filling with a tolerance value, so that the interior does not have to be an exact color, but vary to a limited degree

- generating a region rather than filling (magic wand tool), or filling into another buffer (CalcMask in QuickDraw)

- smoothing of edges, a kind of anti-aliasing, where pixels at the border of the filled area are blended between original color and the fill color

15.10 Polygon rendering (scan conversion, rasterization)

Earlier in this chapter, we learned how to fill any polygon with a solid color. In that case, it was a general polygon, which didn't even have to be convex. When rendering in 3D, however, renderers are often limited to convex polygons with a limited number of corners. This is no general rule, though. For example, the old software rendering library 3DGM supported and even encouraged the use of many-sided polygons.

Here, I will concentrate on how to render triangles. Simply filling a triangle with a color is simple. The complexity increases when you fill it with something interesting. (Just like life itself, I guess.)

But let's start with the mere filling of a triangle:

Flat shading reduces the problem to scan conversion, which is the problem of finding all pixel coordinates that correspond to a given polygon, as in Figure 197.

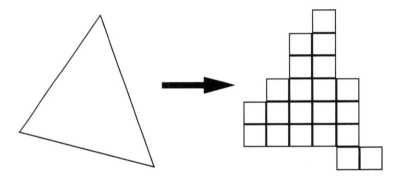

FIGURE 197. Scan conversion: From polygon to fragment (pixel) coordinates

I will work with floating-point here. It is not only fast, it allows us to work in sub-pixel resolution, which is important once we start rendering with textures. In 2D you may be able to specify coordinates as integers, but after 3D transformations, vertices are specified as floating-point values anyway, which rarely hit integer values.

Consider a triangle a, b, c. Sort the three points so that a is the top one and c the bottom one. Now we want to render it row by row from the top, as shown in Figure 198.

Low-level graphics algorithms

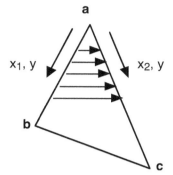

FIGURE 198. Move along the sides

We follow two edges at a time, specified by (x_1, y) and (x_2, y). For every row we go down, x_1 and x_2 change their x value by a constant value. This is just a DDA algorithm, making a linear interpolation from a to b and from a to c. See Figure 199.

Calculate the values to update x_1 and x_2:

$$d_{x1} = (x_b - x_a) / (y_b - y_a)$$

$$d_{x2} = (x_c - x_a) / (y_c - y_a)$$

Start by moving from the non-integer values to the first row:

$$y = \text{Trunc}(y_a + 1)$$

$$x_1 = x_a + d_{x1} \cdot (y - y_a)$$

$$x_2 = x_a + d_{x2} \cdot (y - y_a)$$

Note that the y calculation only holds for positive y_a! For negative y_a, use $y = \text{Trunc}(y_a)$. What we need to do is to move from y_a to the next higher integer (i.e. the roof function).

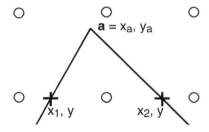

FIGURE 199. Moving from the vertex to the first row

Also, note that the calculations are affected by our pixel definition, that is, where the pixel hot-spots (white circles in the figure) are located in the pixel. What I describe here uses a *point-in-corner* definition.

Now we can render the polygon like this:

```
while y < yb do
    RenderRow(y, x1, x2)
    x1 := x1 + dx1
    x2 := x2 + dx2
    y := y + 1
```

When you reach b, switch to render bc instead of ab, and continue while $y < y_c$.

The subroutine RenderRow is simple in the flat-shading case. Just go from x_1 to x_2, and fill all pixels. Note, however, that x_1 is not necessarily lower than x_2, so you need to sort them, so you get $x_{min} = \min (x_1, x_2)$ and $x_{max} = \max(x_1, x_2)$. As with y, you must start from the roof of x_{min} and increase by 1 as long as $x < x_{max}$. Furthermore, x_1 and x_2 are floating-point, so we should fill all pixels between them, from $\text{trunc}(x_{min} + 1)$ to $\text{trunc}(x_{max})$.

When you switch to Gouraud shading, things get slightly more complicated. Now, you can't just interpolate x_1 and x_2, but you must also interpolate intensity values. You calculate intensities for each vertex, I_a, I_b and I_c. You calculate differentials dI_1 and dI_2 for each side, for interpolating intensity values I_1 and I_2. In RenderRow, a similar interpolation of intensities must be done along the row.

In Phong shading, we go yet another step. Now we don't interpolate intensities, but we interpolate surface normals. A surface normal is calculated for (or provided by) each vertex: N_a, N_b, N_c. These are interpolated along each side, and along each row. The interpolated vector may not be a unit vector, so you will need to normalize the vector when calculating the intensity value.

15.11 Rendering in two phases

The polygon rendering method described above does scan conversion and rendering at the same time, so the calculation of fragment values are done inside the loop that calculates the pixel intervals of each row. This is not a bad thing, it is efficient, but once we render more than flat shades, a lot of variables need to be kept track of, intensities for Gouraud shading, normal vectors for Phong shading, Z value for the Z buffer and texture coordinates.

In order to structure the problem, it can be separated into two phases, one that calculates the pixel intervals, the pixels spans, and stores them into a span buffer, and another phase that processes each span.

The span buffer is a one-dimensional array with two integer values for each pixel row that the triangle touches. See Figure 200.

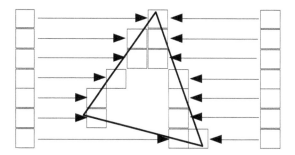

FIGURE 200. Filling the span buffer

Writing the edges of the span-buffer is primarily a question of following each edge with a DDA line drawing algorithm. The only problem is to pick either the start or end value for each edge.

15.12 Screen-linear surface functions

When we render a surface with other than flat shading, we have one or several sets of data that are given at each vertex and should be interpolated over the surface. Let us consider Gouraud shading, where an intensity value (or rather three or four, RGB or RGBA) is interpolated between the vertices. This can be done by linear interpolation.

The intensity values can be viewed as a function over the screen surface, $i(x, y)$. If we use linear interpolation, this is a first-order linear function. That means that it can be expressed on the form $i(x, y) = ax + by + c$.

This means that its differentials are constant over the entire surface, $di/dx = a$ and $di/dy = b$. The horizontal differential, di/dx, is the value with which we should increment the intensity along a span.

This function can be found in several ways. First, each vertex gives one equation, which is a solvable equation system. Second, the dx and dy values can be calculated by finding two points on the same row and same column, respectively. See Figure 201.

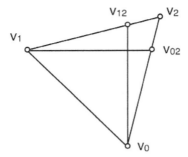

FIGURE 201. dx and dy can be calculated by interpolating the intermediate points v02 and v12 and their intensity values.

Both these methods need checks for special cases, where horizontal or vertical edges can cause division by zero. As a third alternative, you can consider the function to be a plane in the 3D space (x, y, i)! This makes the calculations particularly elegant, with no special cases more than when the three points are on a line.

Let us take an example, in Figure 202.

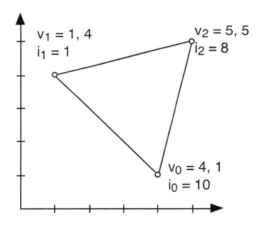

FIGURE 202. Polygon rendering example

Single phase rendering:

Start at

$$x_{left} = x_{right} = x_0 = 4$$

$$i_{left} = i_{right} = i_0 = 7$$

$$y = y_0 = 1$$

Step along the v_0-v_1 and v_0-v_2 edges using these differentials:

$$d_y = 1$$

$$dx_{left} = (x_1-x_0)/(y_1-y_0) = (1-4)/(4-1) = -1$$

$$dx_{right} = (x_2-x_0)/(y_1-y_0) = (5-4)/(5-1) = 1/4$$

$$di_{left} = (i_1-i_0)/(y_1-y_0) = (1-10)/(4-1) = -3$$

$$di_{right} = (i_2-i_0)/(y_1-y_0) = (8-10)/(5-1) = -1/2$$

That's quite a few variables to keep track of.

If we try optimizing this using the i(x,y) function we need to derive it. With an equation system, we get the equations

$$10 = 4a + b + c$$

$$1 = a + 4b + c$$

$$8 = 5a + 5b + c$$

No problem, but the cross product is even easier:

$$v_0 = (x_0, y_0, i_0) = (5, 5, 8)$$

$$v_1 = (x_1, y_1, i_1) = (1, 4, 1)$$

$$v_2 = (x_2, y_2, i_2) = (4, 1, 10)$$

$$N = (v_2 - v_0) \times (v_1 - v_0) = (1, 4, -2) \times (-3, 3, -9) = (-30, 15, 15)$$

$$\Leftrightarrow$$

$$-30x + 15y + 15i + D = 0$$

$$\Leftrightarrow$$

$$i(x, y) = 2x - y - D/15$$

D can be found by inserting a point (x, y, i)

The only thing that can break this calculation is if the factor at i (in this case 15) is zero.

Now, remember why we needed this function. It not only lets us look up the value for any point, it also gives us the differentials d_i/d_x and d_i/d_y that are very important when optimizing the inner loop of the rendering.

So, we have full control over the rendering as long as the surface function is linear. But unfortunately that is not always the case.

15.13 Why the Z-buffer must contain 1/z

One of the most confusing subjects in computer graphics books is how Z-buffering is implemented. It seems simple, just calculate a Z value, compare to a value in the Z buffer, and if the value that is in the buffer is closer, don't draw. But, the important question is how to calculate the Z value. Almost all computer graphics books I have seen skip this problem with at best vague explanations. A shining exception is "Graphics Programming Black Book" by Michael Abrash [10].

We want to render the polygon scan-line by scan-line. Then the problem boils down to this: Given x, y, z for one pixel, what is z for the next pixel?

Well, couldn't you use the plane equation? $Ax + By + Cz + D = 0$? Then, we can calculate z from x and y like this: $z(x,y) = (-Ax - By - D)/C$. Right? In some books, they tell you to do this and that's it. They are not exactly wrong...

But wait a minute! What x, y, z are we talking about? What coordinate system are we discussing? Polygon rendering takes place on the screen. Instead of thinking about x, y, z in some 3D coordinate system, we must start at x_s, y_s in screen coordinates. For any pixel x_s, y_s, what is z, and can you efficiently find z for x_s+1, y_s?

These coordinates are projected, so $x_s = x \cdot f/z$ and $y_s = y \cdot f/z$. Then we can try to calculate z again. Rewrite to get x and y from x_s and y_s:

$$x = x_s \cdot z/f$$

$$y = y_s \cdot z/f$$

and insert in the plane equation:

$$A \cdot x_s \cdot z/f + B \cdot y_s \cdot z/f + C \cdot z + D = 0$$

$$z(x_s, y_s) = -D \cdot f/(A \cdot x_s + B \cdot y_s + C \cdot f)$$

So, we can calculate a z value! Now, given x_s, y_s and $z(x_s, y_s)$, what is $z(x_s + 1, y_s)$? Too bad, you can't find a nice and simple function for that. Whatever you do, you get a division, so you can just as well calculate $z(x_s, y_s)$ by the formula above.

That is, if you must calculate z. Well, of course we must calculate z... right? Wrong! What problem are we solving? We are making a z-buffer. The point with the z buffer is not to have exact z distance values, only to have some values by which we can compare distances! So, we may use some function of z rather than z. As long as the function is monotonic, comparisons will be possible and thereby the z-buffer will work!

So, which function will simplify $z(x_s, y_s)$ and give us incremental steps that are easy to calculate? Answer: 1/z!

$$1/z(x_s, y_s) = -(A \cdot x_s + B \cdot y_s + C \cdot f)/Df$$

$$1/z(x_s + 1, y_s) = -(A \cdot (x_s + 1) + B \cdot y_s + C \cdot f)/Df$$

Then we can incrementally find the next value as:

$$1/z(x_s + 1, y_s) = 1/z(x_s, y_s) - A/Df$$

So, the entire Z-buffered rendering can be done like this: For each vertex, calculate the 1/z value. Since this value (unlike z) varies linearly over the screen, it can be interpolated along each side, and then along every scan-line.

Hey, that wasn't that hard! The whole point is that if you use 1/z for the z-buffer, you get linear variations and can interpolate. But why are all the CG books confusing the students by telling them to insert x, y, z into the plane equation? They also claim that z varies linearly, which it obviously does not.

That is because they work in *normalized device coordinates*, the rather twisted intermediate 3D coordinate system that was described in the 3D transformation chapter (section 6.8 on page 59), which basically is $x_s, y_s, 1/z$. This is the same concept that made the backface culling confusing. The point is that the normalized device coordinates are projected, but the projection operation doesn't trash the z value, but instead provides 1/z as its z value (actually a linear function of it, z" = -(a + b/z)). This is correct and practical, but it may hide the straight-forward functionality of the z buffer.

15.14 Scan-line conversion with texture mapping

In this section, I will continue the discussion from section 15.10 on page 226. In that part, I discussed flat-shaded, Gouraud shaded and Phong shaded polygons (triangles). Rendering a textured polygon is the real challenge.

Let's assume that we have the (u,v) coordinates for every vertex. Somehow, they must be interpolated. This isn't at all as straight-forward as it may seem.

15.14.1 Affine texture mapping

The most obvious solution is to do linear interpolation of the texture coordinates. The algorithm is illustrated by Figure 203.

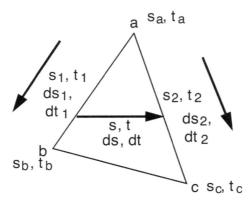

FIGURE 203. Affine texture mapping, linear interpolation

Along with x interpolations, u and v are interpolated along the polygon sides, and along each row. On the left side in the figure, the interpolated values s_1 and t_1 are incremented by ds_1 and dt_1 for every row. On the right side, the same is done with s_2 and t_2, and along each row, the final s and t are calculated by interpolation between s_1, t_1 and s_2, t_2.

Unfortunately, this method results in mappings with highly visible errors. The polygons don't look tilted, only warped. Figure 204 shows an example.

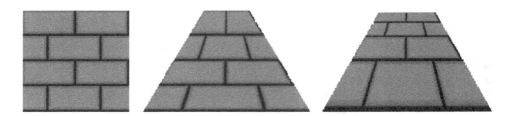

FIGURE 204. A texture, mapped on a polygon with affine and perspective correct mapping, respectively

In the figure, the middle mapping is affine texture mapping, while the right one is the perspective correct one. The difference is obvious, and in animations the effect is particularly bad. So *affine texture mapping is not a fine texture mapping*.

15.14.2 Perspective-correct texture mapping

So, we want perspective correct texture mapping, but a linear interpolation over the texture coordinates did not cut it! So, what can we do? Do you remember how z-buffering worked? When the z value did not vary linearly over the screen, we could use 1/z, which does!

Low-level graphics algorithms

But what we must interpolate are u and v. We can safely assume that s and t vary linearly over the polygon in world coordinates, so that they vary linearly in camera coordinates (x, y, z). Any change in x, y or z will produce a linear change in s, t!

But, again, we want to step from pixel to pixel, in screen coordinates, x_s, y_s!

$$x = x_s \cdot z/f$$

$$y = y_s \cdot z/f$$

Since s and t depend linearly of x and y, they depend linearly of $x_s \cdot z$ and $y_s \cdot z$! You can derive the function $(s, t) = M \cdot (x, y, z)$ (a change of basis from world or camera coordinates to texture coordinates), but that is more work than we need. What we rather want are functions of u and v that vary linearly with x_s and y_s! We find them by division by z as s/z and t/z.

But that doesn't help us! We need (s, t), nothing else, because we will index the texture image with these coordinates! Therefore, we must be able to restore s/z and t/z to s and t. We can do that by also producing the value 1/z. We already know that 1/z is a linear function of x_s and y_s.

So, we can do linear interpolation of u/z, v/z and 1/z! By dividing by z, we eliminate the non-linear variation.

The algorithm is illustrated by Figure 205.

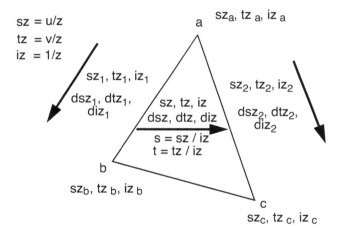

FIGURE 205. Implementation of perspective correct texture mapping

Even though we thus manage to calculate correct s, t values for every pixel, the process is computationally cumbersome. The problem is that it requires at least one division per pixel. You can see two divisions per pixel above, but since both divide by iz, you can calculate 1/iz and use two multiplications instead.

The division bottleneck can be worked around even more. One way is to use piece-wise linear interpolation, that is linear interpolation for something like 8 pixels at a time. Another is to approximate the 1/z function by a polynomial.

Note that sz, tz and iz are all first-order functions of the screen coordinates x and y, so the reasoning in the polygon rendering section is the same, the explicit functions can be derived in the same way, and used to simplify the rendering.

But, why can we interpolate Gouraud shading and Phong shading using linear interpolation? Doesn't that have the same errors? *Yes*, but the eye is much less sensitive to shading errors than it is to texture errors. You can cheat much more when doing shading. An error in a slow variation is hardly noticeable, while a texture where the texels don't stay at the same place in an animation is quite annoying. However, even for these cases, the best result is produced if the mapping is perspective correct, and modern hardware has good support for perspective correct mapping of arbitrary data.

15.15 Clipping texture coordinates

The texture is an image buffer, and just like other image buffers it is limited in size. Therefore, we need some kind of clipping to avoid reading outside the texture.

In texture mapping, this is solved by wrap-around. If you try to read outside the texture, the (s,t) coordinates are wrapped to the other side. If the texture is of a size that is a power of two (32, 64, 128...) this is easily done using a binary AND operation. Here is an example using a 128x128 texture:

dest^ = tex[s & 127, t & 127]

Clearly, this gives a great performance advantage in software and hardware rendering alike, but we are limited to power-of-two sizes. Recent hardware remove the limitation altogether, so in the future we may stop worrying about it.

15.16 Final words on the low-level methods

There are many other low-level algorithms we could study. Most importantly, I have skipped over the midpoint algorithm for circles and splines. We could also look into how a rendering engine works in splitting up work over parts of the image, and many other topics. However, most of these classic low-level operations are hardware accelerated so it seems unlikely that you need to implement them youself very often. In the past, we made much programming on pixel level, in various kinds of software rendering engines. Today, the low level has moved into the shaders. Still, the old methods keep popping up again, in new forms, so don't be surprised when they do.

16. Anti-aliasing

The image displayed on a computer display is sampled; it consists of discrete samples of a continuous signal. A sampled signal can only reproduce signals with frequency components up to half the sampling frequency (the Nyquist frequency). This principle, fundamental in signal processing, is equally true in a 2D signal like a discrete image.

When sampling a 1D signal at a sampling frequency F, the Nyquist frequency is F/2. All frequencies higher than the Nyquist frequency are reproduced onto lower frequencies. Consider a frequency f > F/2. It will be reproduced as a signal at frequency F/2 - (f-F/2) = F - f.

Figure 206 exemplifies how sampling a signal results in lower frequencies, when the original signal contains frequencies above the Nyquist frequency.

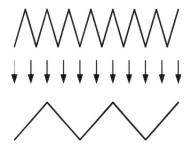

FIGURE 206. Example of how sampling can result in a lower frequency

In this particular case, we have a signal at 1.5 times the Nyquist frequency, which is "mirrored" (folded) over the Nyquist frequency to 1/2 of the Nyquist frequency. Figure 207 illustrates this effect.

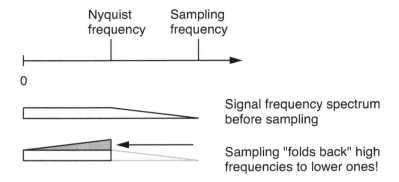

FIGURE 207. Higher frequencies are "folded" over the Nyquist frequency

Computer graphics generates images by sampling signals, be it polygons, textures, or curves. Often this sampling is done with no particular compensation for aliasing. When we draw a line with Bresenham's algorithm, the line has sharp edges, with immediate transitions between 1 and 0. Such a transition contains high frequencies, and will thereby cause aliasing. The most obvious aliasing is the "staircase" look of digital lines.

Ideally, we should filter the line to remove all frequency components above the Nyquist frequency, the ones which are affected by folding, which would smooth the image, eliminating the "staircase" look. This is only possible with an infinite filter kernel, so we must use approximations. There are high quality approximations, but there are also simpler methods that will give an acceptable result, if not perfect, with a small computation cost and trivial math.

16.1 Post-processing

Aliasing can be reduced by low-pass filtering, averaging the image after it is rendered. This will remove some high frequencies, frequencies near N. The most severe aliasing will be in those areas, so this will eliminate most aliasing artifacts. However, we will not only remove most of the errors, but also much of the desired signal, and get a blurred image as result. Bad method!

Filtering removes much of the error - and much of the desired signal!

FIGURE 208. Effects of post-processing filtering in the frequency plane

Figure 208 illustrates the process in a figure much like the previous one. The worst part of the error, the lowest of the folded frequencies, are removed, which is good, but this also filters out much of the desired signal that was below the Nyquist frequency!

16.2 Super-sampling

A similar but much better method is super-sampling. In this case, rendering is done in higher resolution, and the result is sampled down to the desired frequency. The down-sampling is done with averaging, which gives us the same reduction of aliasing as in the previous case, but without eliminating frequencies below the Nyquist frequency.

Suppose that we generate the image at twice the resolution in each direction (that is, 4x the resolution). The sampling frequency as well as the Nyquist frequency are then doubled. The errors from aliasing will still appear, but the most noticeable components will be in the lower frequency range, close to the Nyquist frequency. When sampling down to the final resolution, the aliasing will be greatly reduced, while the desired signal is preserved. Figure 209 shows an example with a line.

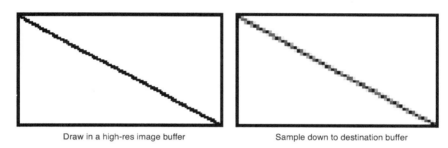

Draw in a high-res image buffer   Sample down to destination buffer

FIGURE 209. A line drawn without anti-aliasing and with super-sampling

In the image, the "staircase" effect should be highly visible in the left image, while the right image, despite being zoomed, has a softer look. In full resolution this will look very good, close to perfect, and it is merely a 2x2 super-sampling.

Super-sampling can be performed in several ways. One is brute force super-sampling (see below), where a large high resolution buffer is used. Another is to compute coordinates at a higher, sub-pixel resolution, but accumulate these values in a temporary buffer for the few pixels that are currently of interest.

An important consideration in super-sampling is how much higher the sampling should be. The practical minimum is 2x2 pixels per destination pixel. When drawing black on white, this gives us as little as 5 possible gray levels, but it is surprisingly good and quite sufficient for many applications. At 3x3, we get 10 grey levels, and at 4x4 we get 17.

Is it possible to say something about how much better the result is, that is by a measure? Let's try. Consider the 1D case. Using one sample per pixel, we have a sampling frequency that is identical to the image resolution. As before, we get the sampling rate F and the Nyquist frequency F/2. All frequencies over F/2 are mirrored down to lower frequencies as aliasing. In all real signals, the amplitude tends to get lower with higher frequencies, so the lowest frequencies over F/2 will dominate the distortion.

Figure 210 is a scaled-up variant of Figure 207 on page 238.

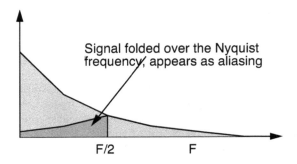

FIGURE 210. Aliasing without super-sampling

Suppose that we sample with twice the frequency. That corresponds to four samples in the 2D case. We sample with 2F, the Nyquist frequency is F. The averaging to lower frequency corresponds to a filtering where all signals above F/2 are eliminated. Since the aliasing was mirrored over F rather than F/2, only frequencies over 3F/2 will end up under F/2 and cause any distortion! This sounds like a very big improvement, and the visual result is really much better. See Figure 211.

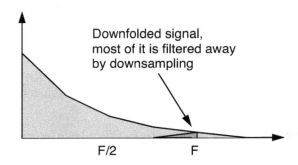

FIGURE 211. Super-sampling significantly reduces aliasing

Depending on our rendering situation, the super-sampling may be done pixel by pixel (see chapter 17), or in a buffer. In the latter case, it may be applied using a temporary buffer covering only a small part of the scene, or a large, full-screen buffer. The implementation is trivial:

Create a temporary image buffer that covers the area in which you want to draw anti-aliased primitives, but in a higher resolution. The higher resolution should, for practical reasons, be in integer steps, like 2x2 times the destination.

- Copy image data from the destination to the temporary buffer, zooming it to the higher resolution. Zooming with nearest neighbor is quite sufficient.

- Draw in the temporary buffer. Any graphics operations can be used.

Anti-aliasing

- Copy from the temporary buffer to the source image, averaging to get the final pixel value.

If you scale by a power of two, e.g. 2x2 or 4x4, the operations are very simple. The averaging can then be reduced to additions and shifts.

16.3 Multisampling

Multisampling is a variant of supersampling, where some optimizations are made possible by assuming that other AA methods are present, especially texture filtering and mip-mapping. Unlike supersampling, where all pixels are rendered individually at a higher resulusion, multisampling will render a group of pixels (the ones that will end up a single pixel) the same.

For example, if we use 3x3 multisampling, a total of 9 pixels are averaged to one. If geometry overlaps the pixel, a number of pixels will be rendered. However, due to individual differences in edges, Z-buffer and stencil buffer, all pixels may not be rendered along edges.

This will give a good anti-aliasing of edges with better performance than supersampling, but the same memory cost, and it will not help against aliasing in textures.

Figure 212 shows an example.

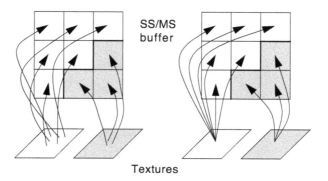

FIGURE 212. Comparison supersampling vs multisampling

The figure shows a 3x3 pixel area, which will be downsampled to one, where to different sub-areas come from different polygons (white and gray, 6 and 3 pixels resp.). For supersampling, every one of the 9 pixel makes it own execution of the fragment shader, with its own light calculations and texture access (illustrated in the figure). For multisampling, however, only a single fragment execution is performed for each, resulting in the same shade for all pixels in each of the two areas. The result is not exactly the same but the error is generally small and the saving in fragment shading is considerable.

16.4 Fast approXimate Anti-Aliasing, FXAA

More recently, *Fast approXimate Anti-Aliasing* (FXAA or FxAA) has become popular [36]. This is a post-processing anti-aliasing algorithm. Despite what I said about post-processing before, this gives quite good result for a very low processing cost. The point is that it does selective filtering, not a global linear filter as I suggested above. Filtering, blurring, is applied only in areas where there are edges. It should be noted that this approach can case some artifacts, like blurring edges in textures, and then we are really back at the problems I mentioned before.

16.5 Anti-aliasing in OpenGL

OpenGL has anti-aliasing built-in, in the form of *full-screen anti-aliasing*. It is so important that it has its own abbreviation, FSAA.

FSAA can be achieved in several ways in OpenGL. The easiest is to use an OpenGL extension, GL_MULTISAMPLE, which is supported on all reasonably modern GPUs. As the name implies, it uses multisampling. You may also plug in FXAA yourself by code available on-line.

Anti-aliasing also appears in some other forms, like texture filtering functions and mipmapping (see chapter 10).

17. Ray-tracing and radiosity

Ray-tracing[1] is the classic method for generating highly realistic images. I will start this description by the sub-problem ray-casting.

17.1 Rays for visible surface detection: ray-casting

Ray-casting is a highly simplified form of ray-tracing. The principle is that you form a ray, that starts at the "lens", that is the PRP, passes through a pixel in the image plane and travels out in the scene until it hits something. See Figure 213. Only objects in front of the camera are taken into account. All intersections with objects are calculated and the closest hit is chosen.

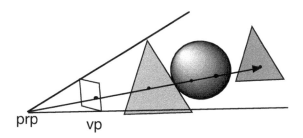

FIGURE 213. Ray-casting in a scene. A ray is formed through prp and a pixel in the image plane.

Then we know what point in the scene that should be reproduced at the pixel in question. If all we need is to show the objects with no or simple lighting, no shadows, transparency or reflections, then we are done. Only calculating the shading from the positions of the light sources will produce fairly nice images, but then we could just as well use the meth-

---

1. "strålföljning" in swedish

ods described earlier. Ray-tracing will provide a general, straight-forward solution to some of the problems that are hard to manage in the real-time case.

The following pseudo code describes the overall ray-casting algorithm:

```
for all pixels in the image
    form a ray through the prp and the pixel
    calculate intersections between this ray and objects in the scene
    if any object was hit
        determine the closest object
        calculate the shading at the intersection
    else
        set the pixel to the background color
```

The ray can be represented at the form $q = p + k \cdot v$. There is really only one step of the algorithm that is complicated, to determine the intersections.

17.2 Ray-casting in a grid, ray-marching

Ray-casting, ray-tracing with only a primary ray, is briefly mentioned above as a method for visible surface detection.

Ray-casting comes in many flavors. Common to all is the principle that you cast rays from the camera into the scene, and find intersections with objects. Most commonly, we discuss casting rays in a world of 3D objects, polygons, quadric surfaces, etc. However, a special case is when you cast rays in a grid. This is called *ray-marching*.

A classic ray-casting in a grid is the ray-casting in the game Wolfenstein 3D. In that game, the world was 2D, and all walls were the same height, aligned with the coordinate axes. They were even the same length, since each wall section corresponded to exactly one grid space.

Wolfenstein 3D was one of the very first texture-mapped 3D games, and this ray-casting is also simple and demands little computation. One ray is cast into the grid for every column in the image. The ray is cast by calculating points where the ray moves to another grid space, and as soon as an occupied grid space (a wall) is found, it returns. The height of the wall is calculated from the distance to the wall found. See Figure 214.

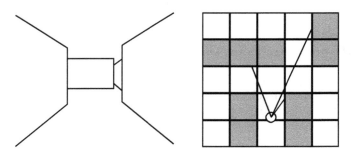

FIGURE 214. Ray casting in a 2D grid

This was combined with scaled sprites, using a one-dimensional Z buffer to make them obscured by walls etc.

It can be tempting to believe that this method is obsolete, now when much more sophisticated graphics is mainstream. However, the same method, but in 3D, is in frequent use for visualization of 3D volumes. This is mostly used in medical applications, to visualize volumes reconstructed from X-rays (by computer tomography).

17.3 Applications of ray-casting

Ray-casting may sound like an insignificant first step of ray-tracing, but that is not the case. It is not just a visible surface detection method, but has several other applications, including the following:

- Picking
- Fairly efficient rendering of 3D scenes defined by a 2D (Wolfenstein 3D style) or 3D grid (Minecraft style world), or a 2D heightmap (Comanche).
- Searching a scene for purposes of illumination.
- Volume visualization of transparent object, where you cast rays through objects, accumulating their density. This is another case of rendering with a 3D grid.
- Visualization computation, typically for game AI. In this case, a 3D scene is typically reduced to a simplified 2D representation, and the problem is reduced to a 2D grid ray-casting problem.

Considering the ray marching, I must note that I do not know exactly how specific games are rendered, like Minecraft, but I do know that there are engines for voxel worlds based on ray-casting, and I once wrote a Wolfenstein-style 2D grid ray-marching engine myself, running smoothly on a 33 MHz computer.

17.4 Multi-level rays: Ray-tracing

In ray-tracing we expand the ray-casting algorithm to allow reflection, mirroring in shiny objects, and refraction through transparent objects. The ray-tracing works in short as follows:

Initiate all needed rays from the synthetic cameras optic center (prp), one ray through each pixel in the image. These rays are now dubbed *primary rays*.

For each ray, call a recursive function which calculates the intersection between the ray and the 3D world and returns the closest intersection. In the point of intersection, we may create new rays, and we may also calculate a contribution from the shading model for that point on that particular surface. Every ray the function creates eventually returns a light value, or rather a vector of three values, <R, G, B>. These light values/vectors are summed together and returned as the return value of the function.

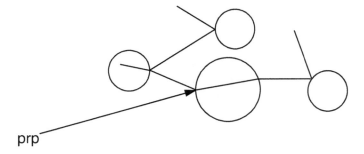

prp

FIGURE 215. A ray is reflected and refracted in mirroring and transparent objects

Thus, when a ray hits an object, we may create up to two rays, one reflected and one refracted ray into the object. The direction for each ray is calculated so they can be traced.

If there are many reflecting objects in a scene, a ray may be reflected many times, as in Figure 215, even to an infinite depth. In order to limit the computational complexity, we should decide upon a maximum recursion depth, the maximum number of times a ray may be reflected or refracted. When the maximum depth is reached, I would suggest that no light at all is returned, that is black. (Why is black better than the background color?)

The pseudo code below roughly describes how a ray-tracer works. The recursive function RayTrace takes three parameters: the starting point **p0**, its direction **u** and the recursion depth **depth**.

```
function RayTrace(p0, u, depth)

if depth > max then return BLACK

μ := FindIntersection(p0, u) // Returns more data, see below

if μ <= 0 then return BACKGROUND_COLOR

Ilocal :=0
IR := 0
IT := 0

if ka ≠ 0 and kd ≠ 0 and ks ≠ 0 then
    Ilocal := ka*Ia + Σ (diffuse shading + specular shading)
// Sum is for all visible light sources

if kR ≠ 0 then
    R := CalculateReflection(u, N)
    IR := RayTrace(p0 + μ*u, R, depth+1)

if kT ≠ 0 then
    T := CalculateRefraction(u, N, h1, h2)
    IT := RayTrace(p0 + μ*u, T, depth+1)
return Ilocal + IR + IT
```

This pseudo code is not complete, but it contains the essentials. Note that the subroutine FindIntersection returns a value μ which tells exactly in which point the ray intersects the object.

The subroutine FindIntersection can be very complex. The task to find the closest intersection implies, in a full-fledged ray-tracer, not only to calculate intersections with single objects, but also to handle a subdivision of the scene that limits the number of intersection tests. It should return some kind of object reference from which we can get all needed information about the closest object, including the parameters kd (reflectivity for diffuse reflection), ks (reflectivity for specular reflection), kR (mirroring), kT (transparency), h1, h2 (material constants for refraction).

Also, the calculation of Ilocal is more complex than what shows in the pseudo code, since it includes *shadow rays* that are needed for determining if a point is shadowed.

The shadow rays, together with the functions CalculateReflection and CalculateRefraction are what makes this a ray tracer rather than merely a ray-caster.

17.5 Reflections

The most typical feature of a ray tracer is that it can handle reflective surfaces. When a ray hits a reflecting surface, the reflected ray is calculated. This is very easy to do, given the normal vector of the surface, as we saw earlier when calculating shading. In this case, instead of an outgoing vector towards the light source, we have an incoming ray. This gives us a slightly modified formula:

$$\mathbf{r} = \mathbf{u} - (2\mathbf{u} \cdot \mathbf{n})\mathbf{n}$$

17.6 Refraction (Transmission)

A feature almost as typical as reflection for demonstrating ray-tracing is refraction, the change in direction for light transmitted into a transparent object. It is very common with things like glass balls in ray-traced images.

Refraction is, however, a more complex problem than reflection. The refraction not only depends on the incoming angle, but also on the speed of light in the materials, which results in different *refraction indices*. The outgoing angle is a function of the incoming angle and the refraction indices. In this section, I will describe a method that derives the transmitted ray in a straight-forward way, known as "Heckbert's method". [9]

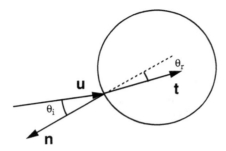

FIGURE 216. Refraction

In Figure 216, **u** is the direction of the incoming ray, **n** is the normal vector of the surface and **t** is the transmitted vector, which is what we want. We also define the angles θ_i as the incoming angle between **-n** and **u**, θ_r is the outgoing angle between **-n** and **t**.

Refraction follows Snell's law, where η_i is the refraction index of the material the light is arriving through and η_r is the index for the material that it enters. The refractive index is defined as the speed of light in vacuum, c, divided by the speed of light in the material, v.

$$\eta = \frac{c}{v}$$

In its simplest form, Snell's law is written:

$$\sin\theta_r = \frac{\eta_i}{\eta_r} \cdot \sin\theta_i$$

Since we only use the ratio between the densities, we can define

$$\eta = \frac{\eta_i}{\eta_r}$$

Note that $\cos\theta_i$ is easy to find; If the incoming direction vector and the surface normal are both normalized, you get cos from the dot product. Similarly, you get the sin from the cross product. So, let $\cos\theta_i = -\mathbf{u}\cdot\mathbf{n}$.

Then we can find the components parallel and perpendicular to **n**:

$$\mathbf{u_{par}} = -\cos\theta_i\mathbf{n}$$

$$\mathbf{u_{perp}} = \mathbf{u} + \cos\theta_i\mathbf{n}$$

Ray-tracing and radiosity

The reflection vector comes for free here:

$$\mathbf{r} = \mathbf{u_{perp}} - \mathbf{u_{par}} = \mathbf{u} - 2 \cos \theta_i \, \mathbf{n}$$

which is the same as mentioned in the previous section. However, we will now use this to create the transmitted ray too. The refracted ray will be in the plane that is defined by $\mathbf{n}$ and $\mathbf{u_{perp}}$. Normalize $\mathbf{u_{perp}}$

$$m = \frac{u_{perp}}{|u_{perp}|}$$

and we have an orthonormal basis vector pair as $\mathbf{n}$ and $\mathbf{m}$. The final result that we are looking for will the vector components along each of these basis vectors.

$$\mathbf{t} = \sin \theta_r \, \mathbf{m} - \cos \theta_r \, \mathbf{n}$$

Since $\sin \theta_i$ is known, $\sin \theta_r$ can be calculated directly from Snell's law (above). Finally, $\cos \theta_r$ is calculated from $\sin \theta_r$ by standard trigonometry:

$$\cos \theta_r = \sqrt{1 - (\sin \theta_r)^2}$$

At this point, we have the solution; we know $\mathbf{m}$, $\sin \theta_r$ and $\cos \theta_r$ so we can calculate $\mathbf{t}$. So we could stop right here.

However, let's go one step further. We can rewrite and get a more compact solution. The vector $\mathbf{m}$ can be rewritten as

$$m = \frac{u_{perp}}{|u_{perp}|} = \frac{u + \cos \theta_i n}{\sin \theta_i}$$

Insert that into the $\mathbf{t}$ formula and we get:

$$t = \frac{\sin \theta_r}{\sin \theta_i}(u + \cos \theta_i n) - \cos \theta_r n$$

Snell's law appears right in front of us, and by replacing the sin ratio by η, we get

$$t = \eta u + (\eta \cos \theta_i - \cos \theta_r) n$$

Snell's law must kick in once more to convert $\cos \theta_r$ to a function of known parameters:

$$\cos \theta_r = \sqrt{1 - \sin^2 \theta_r} = \sqrt{1 - \eta^2 \sin^2 \theta_i} = \sqrt{1 - \eta^2(1 - \cos^2 \theta_i)}$$

and the final formula is

$$t = \eta u + (\eta \cos\theta_i - \sqrt{1 - \eta^2(1 - \cos^2\theta_i)})n$$

Thus, although refraction may seem complicated, it is fairly straight-forward to derive through the geometry.

How about color effects in refractions, rainbow patterns? That happens since the material constant η varies with frequency. In order to produce such effects, you must process different frequences separately and make η a function of the frequency.

Finally, note that it may happen that $\cos\theta_r < 0$. When this happens, no transmitted ray should be created. This is a perfectly valid case of total internal reflection and no error.

17.7 Shadows and shadow rays

One of the most important features of ray-tracing is one that you hardly notice, except when it is missing: shadows. In real-time systems like OpenGL, it is pretty awkward to create shadows. It is possible, but there is no general way that always creates good results. In ray-tracing, however, shadows are easily created with decent quality, and the quality can be improved simply by increasing the processing power.

Whenever a surface has ka, kd or ks $\neq 0$, shading should be calculated from the surface parameters and the light sources. However, if a light source is occluded, it should not contribute. This is tested by creating rays from the surface to every light source that can potentially contribute.

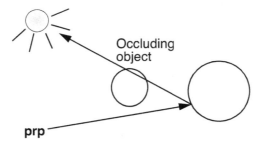

FIGURE 217. The shadow ray tests whether or not a surface point is visible from the light source or not

Such a ray is called a *shadow ray*. See Figure 217. Its only purpose is to test if we have a free line of sight between a point light source and some surface point. It does not provide any means for taking indirect light into account, from neither diffuse objects, mirrors, or even transparent objects. Thus, the shadow of a transparent object will be just the same as for an opaque object. So the model is highly approximative, but still good enough to give

---

Ray-tracing and radiosity

us sharp-edged shadows in a simple way. As we will see in later sections, it can also create soft shadows.

The shadow ray is performed in the following way. Whenever you calculate lighting for a surface point:

- create one shadow ray for each light source
- test if the shadow ray intersects any objects between the surface and the light source, but create no secondary rays!
- only if no intersection was found, calculate the contribution from the light source for the light level in the surface

Note that the amount of calculation grows linearly with the number of light sources. Thus, using many light sources can be computationally cumbersome. This is a problem that the method shares with most shadow calculation methods.

17.8 Numerical problems

When you create a ray from a surface, you can do that in the form $q = p + k \cdot u$, where k=0 at the starting point. Then it seems simple to detect the next surface, once you calculate the intersection with all possible candidates. Isn't that just to pick the smallest one that is larger than zero? If you do that, you may get some strange false hits. The problem is simply numerical errors that causes you to sometimes find the originating surface itself, with a k value that may be 10^{-15} or something similar. This should not be an unexpected problem, but the problem is where to put the limit between calculation errors and real hits. You may pick some more or less arbitrary minimal level for k (possibly after analyzing how large the errors really are). You may be tempted to simply ignore the originating object, which is just fine for a reflecting object, but less so for a transparent one!

17.9 Speed optimizations

The most obvious drawback with ray tracing is that it is computationally demanding. Real-time ray-tracing was for a very long time a completely unreasonable dream. Today, with modern shaders, it is not as unreasonable any more, but only if great attention is paid on speed optimizations. In particular, any serious ray-tracer must include some kind of method of limiting the number of intersection tests that are needed for every ray. Generally speaking, this involves some kind of partitioning of 3D space so that objects can be grouped and discarded collectively, a problem that appears in several other places in computer graphics (collision detection, VSD). A common method is to subdivide the world into an octree.

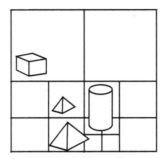

FIGURE 218. Subdivision of space into a quadtree to simplify searches

In Figure 218, you see a simple scene subdivided into a quadtree, the 2D version of octrees. The principle is the same; the scene is split at the highest level into 4 parts (8 in octrees). Every part (node) that contains more than one object is split again, recursively, until the leaves of the tree have reached a smallest allowed size or only contain one object.

There are other approaches to this problem, like binary trees (e.g. BSP trees), grouping of nearby objects with enclosing spheres, and many other methods.

17.10 Multiple rays for anti-aliasing and effects

Ray-tracing, like other computer graphics, is plagued by aliasing problems. If you only send one ray for each pixel, you will get highly noticeable aliasing, especially in areas with high frequency textures. Also, edges will appear jagged.

As mentioned in section 16.2 on page 239, super-sampling is an easy and efficient way to reduce aliasing problems in computer graphics. This is easy to do in ray-tracing; simply send several rays in a regular pattern, as in Figure 219.

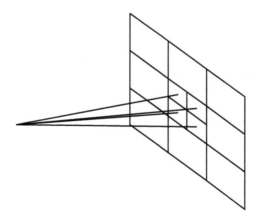

FIGURE 219. Super-sampling, e.g. 4 rays in a regular pattern

Ray-tracing and radiosity

Four rays will reduce aliasing considerably, 9 rays even more. This is fully equivalent to generating an image in a higher resolution. Thus, it is super-sampling, but not the "brute force" super-sampling mentioned earlier, since we never have a higher resolution image.

For best result, some care must be taken in designing the filter function for the down-sampling, but this is actually of minor importance. What is more interesting is that a significant quality improvement can be achieved by not sending the rays in a regular pattern, but instead sending them in a random pattern! See Figure 220.

FIGURE 220. Ray-traced image, detail. Left: no anti-aliasing. Middle: 2x2 super-sampling. Right: 2x2 distributed ray-tracing, 4 random rays

What happens here is that the randomness very efficiently "drowns" the aliasing in noise! If you live in the delusion that noise is something bad, remember that noise is always present, we are used to seeing it all the time, while aliasing is a much bigger problem. Noise is good up to a certain degree, as mentioned earlier. Only when the noise is higher than the signal, the message fails and we perceive a bad image. Otherwise, *noise is beautiful*!

This technique, to send many rays with random variations in direction, is called distributed ray-tracing or *jittering*. So, jittering a ray means that we vary its direction. It is not only used for anti-aliasing, but also for many other effects. It all depends on where you make the variation, where you split the ray in many and how the direction is varied. Some effects that can be achieved this way include:

- (1) Depth-of-field effects. Lock the primary ray at a certain distance from the camera, vary the direction but always pass through this point.

- (2) Gloss, fuzzy reflections (diffuse reflections with mirroring): Jitter the reflected ray.

- (3) Fuzzy translucency: Jitter the refraction ray.

- (4) Soft shadows: Jitter the shadow ray.

- (5) Motion blur: For different rays, vary positions of objects over time.

The numbers above correspond to the numbers in Figure 221.

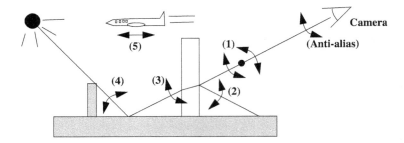

FIGURE 221. Jittering effects. See text for numbers.

We do not go deeper into this, we only note that they are achieved in a way that is similar to anti-aliasing, above. Also note that many of these effects apply equally well to real-time rendering. If you have time to render several images for each frame (which is perfectly realistic today) you can generate several images with variations in one or more parameters. The easiest ones are probably motion blur, depth-of-field and anti-aliasing.

17.11 More realism: Radiosity

And now for something completely different[1]. The citation aside, it really is. Radiosity is a fundamentally different concept for rendering highly realistic images. This method is based on a more realistic light model than what we have been using so far. The model describes the light exchange between diffusely reflecting surfaces. Unlike both ray-tracing and the three-component model, radiosity models indirect light. In radiosity all surfaces are distributed light sources, no more point light sources! The light intensity emitted from each surface is calculated as a function of all incoming light, plus any self-emission in the case that the surface is a "real" light source. The primitive ambient light parameter from the three-component model is replaced by a much more complete model of the complex light exchange in a scene.

Radiosity is a very important model, which apart from the obvious, to use it for rendering realistic scenes, is also used for pre-process scenes for real-time rendering, to calculate light mapping.

17.12 The radiosity model

To keep the situation reasonably simple, we assume that all surfaces are Lambertian surfaces, perfectly diffuse surface elements. The energy emitted from one surface element is proportional to its area, and varies linearly with the solid angle that the surface element fills in any given angle.

A surface element emits energy which is the sum of reflected energy and the emission of the surface:

---

1. Famous quote from Monty Python. All university lecturers over-use it, always.

$$\text{Energy} \cdot \text{area} = \text{emitted} + \text{reflected}$$

Imagine a small number of surfaces that form an enclosure, a kind of box where all sides but one are thick, opaque ones, and one is a thin paper with a lamp nearby. The paper emits light into the box while the other surfaces only emit reflected light. We know exactly how much light that enters the system, and we disregard all light exchange with the outside. Then, how much light is emitted from each surface inside the box?

Apparently, the problem is to model the reflection of incoming light, from all surfaces that are visible from each surface, and through them indirect contribution from other surfaces. The whole exchange can be described by the following equation:

$$B_k \cdot dA_k = E_k \cdot dA_k + R_k \cdot \int B_j \cdot F_{jk} \cdot dA_k$$

The equation describes how the emitted light from a surface k, B_k, can be calculated from the surface emission E_k and the light exchange with all other surfaces j, their emitted light B_j, by using the form factors F_{jk}. R_k is the reflectivity of the surface. In practice, we do this with a limited number of discrete surface elements. Thus, we switch to a discrete form.

The emitted light from a surface is the sum of its emission E_k and the sum of all incoming energy H_k times the reflectivity of the surface:

$$B_k = E_k + R_k H_k$$

The sum of incoming energy is written:

$$H_k = \sum B_j \cdot F_{jk}$$

which gives us the radiosity equation:

$$B_k = E_k + R_k \cdot \sum B_j \cdot F_{jk}$$

See Figure 222.

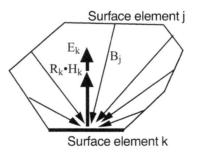

Surface element j

E_k

B_j

$R_k \bullet H_k$

Surface element k

FIGURE 222. The light energy emitted from k is given by its own emission E_k and incoming light energy H_k

If the model consists of N surface elements, this equation leads to an equation system with N equations and N unknown variables (B). Thus, the equation system can be very large, but it appears to be solvable with straight forward equation solving methods. For scenes that are very complex, many surfaces are often obscured. That leads to a sparse matrix with many zeroes, and in such a case there are more efficient methods for solving the equation system. We will not go into them here though.

The result is the radiosity, the emitted light energy, for each surface. Light energy is not necessarily the same as light intensity, but we can assume that for our purposes.

As several times before, I have only described how to solve the problems for grayscale. For full color, the system is split into a red, green and blue system that are solved separately. Note that any inter-dependency between the channels is then ignored. It is a simplification that will rarely be noticeable.

When the light energy, and thereby the intensity, is calculated, all items in the scene can be rendered. They must be rendered with some kind of interpolation to avoid visible edge artifacts, that is, not with flat shading. A suitable choice is Gouraud shading. This can sound odd for anyone who knows that Gouraud shading is a very rough approximation, but it is often quite enough since surfaces are diffuse (no sharp highlights) and the difference between neighboring surface elements thus tends to be small.

17.13 Calculation of form factors

The biggest problem is to calculate the form factors F_{jk}. All the form factors F_{jk} define a large matrix, with one element for each possible pair of two surface elements j and k, which tells how much of the energy that is emitted from j that hits k. It is defined as:

$$F_{jk} = \text{energy to k from j / total energy from j.}$$

F_{jk} depends on how much of k's surrounding that is filled by j, depending on its solid angle and obscuring surfaces.

Except for obscuring surfaces, this is basically a matter of calculating the solid angle, which is relatively simple. However, obscuring surfaces in a complex scene is a hard problem, in general one of the most complicated problems in computer graphics, especially for very large scenes. (See chapter 13.)

One method for calculating form factors is based on rendering the scene with flat shading. (Note how outdated, useless methods tend to show up as useful tools in other contexts!) Consider a virtual half cube, with five sides, placed around a surface k for which we wish to calculate all form factors F_{jk}. We set up the camera with the prp in the center of the surface k, and the viewing plane in one of the five surfaces. Now, render the scene as an image on one surface at a time. It is done with flat shading, no anti-aliasing, and with one unique color for each surface element j! The procedure results in five images. Make a histogram for all these images, that is a count of the number of pixels with each possible color. The count tells how many pixels that each surface element j has contributed with, and this can be used as an approximation of the actual visibility. See Figure 223.

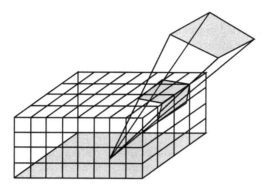

FIGURE 223. Enclosing half cube for approximation of form factors

You might recognize this method as related to a method for calculating the PVS, *potentially visible set*, page 173.

17.14 Splitting surface elements

For producing good results with the radiosity model, it is of high importance that there is not too much light variations on one single surface element. A surface element is rendered in one specific color, and the only variation that is allowed is interpolation to neighboring elements. Thus, areas with strong variations need to be split into several parts, as in Figure 224. This typically happens at edges of shadows and similar situations.

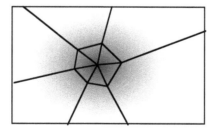

FIGURE 224. An area with much variation must be split into many

Obviously, this makes the rendering more complicated, and the whole splitting procedure must be redone if objects are moved.

In practice you can start with a rough subdivision, with a small number of surface elements per surface, and do step-wise refinement, iteratively, after some kind of check for what areas that need more detail. For example, one can check the difference intensity between neighboring surface elements, and split if the difference is too large.

17.15 Radiosity through step-wise refinement

One method for solving the radiosity equation system is calculating through step-wise (progressive) refinement. In the first iteration, light from light sources (surface elements with emission) is transported to elements lit by those elements. The light then passes from surface to surface until a certain depth, or a sufficiently good approximation results. When the incoming light to a surface is small enough, that part of the process can be stopped since it will no longer make significant contributions. An interesting advantage with this method is that it is possible to display a preview practically immediately.

17.16 More global illumination

With this chapter, we introduce methods for higher realism, and touch upon the exciting subject of *global illumination*. Global illumination methods are methods for getting a more realistic illumination, which must be more or less based on the bidirectional nature of light exchange. Radiosity is only one such method, and new variants are being actively researched, on the quest for true real-time global illumination. Here, we present these methods as off-line methods, not expected to run animations in real time, but this is about to change. Computer Graphics has been predicted some big changes, and this may be the biggest challenge.

18. More about shader programming with GLSL

Shader programming has moved from advanced cutting-edge technology in 2001 to mainstream and a must for modern computer graphics. In my courses, it debuted in the advanced course, moved to the advanced end of the main course in 2008, and now it has moved to be an integrated part of all computer graphics programs.

We have been discussing GLSL many times through the book. This chapter is a container for all odds and ends that have been left or not discussed in detail. There are no examples here, they have all moved to relevant parts of the book.

Until 1996, many computer graphics programmers were busy optimizing software implementations, especially implementing texture mapping and Gouraud shading in real-time polygon renderers. Then came 3dfx with the Voodoo 1 board, and the software path quickly got scrapped. What was worse, the fixed functionality of the hardware pipeline, with its limitations, was then the only way, and you could ask why you would need to know low-level graphics any more.

But in 2001, the tide turned again, with the GeForce 3 that introduced programmable shaders. Since then, the power of the shader programs has grown to compete with the CPUs themselves. The current GPUs are powerful massively parallel processors. They can be programmed in special languages. One of those languages is GLSL, OpenGL Shading Language. Thereby, a new kind of low-level control was provided to graphics programmers.

In this book, shaders and GLSL are used to illustrate and apply computer graphics, and the coverage is as needed for our purposes. For a more thorough description and reference, there is documentation available on-line from OpenGL.org. The physical reference is a big book called "OpenGL Shading Language", the so-called "orange book". [2]

Originally, there were two separate sets of shader processors in the GPU. Starting with the GeForce 8000 series, we got a *unified architecture*, where all shader processors are alike, they are only assigned the task of vertex or fragment processing. The model with two kinds of shaders, presented here, still holds but is no longer describes the hardware as it used to, but rather describes the tasks.

When I originally assembled this information, I was working with GLSL 1.0 and OpenGL 1.5. With OpenGL 2.0, GLSL became an official part, and with OpenGL 3.2 we focus even more on shaders. The Fermi architecture arrived in 2010 and changed the rules again. Things are changing rapidly.

18.1 Shading languages

There are no less than four different shading languages for modern GPUs.

Assembly language: This was common in the early days of shader programming, but has been phased out. The support for it is no longer updated.

Cg: Cg stands for "C for graphics" and is developed by NVidia.

HLSL: HLSL stands for "High-level shading language", developed by Microsoft

GLSL: GLSL stands for "OpenGL shading language" and is a part of the OpenGL standard.

The assembly language is best avoided for new development. The choice between the others depend on platform as well as practical need (and taste). GLSL is part of an open standard, and highly portable. The choice is not obvious, but GLSL is a very strong candidate.

18.2 GLSL - OpenGL Shading Language

GLSL is a language that is reminiscent of C. This is not necessarily a good thing, but the design of GLSL avoids most negative sides of C and makes it very nice and easy to learn. You may have heard people making sour comments about technologies "made by a committee", as if that was bad. This is one such technology, and in my opinion, the result speaks in favor of "committee designs".

The syntax is somewhere between C and C++. Syntax is just syntax, though, and it has few of the most central parts of C and C++. C is mainly a pointer processing language, and GLSL has no pointers. C++ is C plus object-orientation additions. GLSL has no classes. So which are then the similarities?

So there are no classes, and no need for any. Since the processors the programs run on are limited, the code tends to be straight-forward and simple, understandable both by language design and the problems that it should be applied to.

Rather than comparing only to C/C++, I would say that GLSL is one of the many descendants of Algol. Even though almost nobody uses the original Algol language today, most languages are based on it and it is easy to move between them. We all use Algol, without knowing it!

18.3 A summary of the GLSL language

It is unreasonable to try to fit a full specification of the GLSL language in a book like this. What you have here is more intended as an introduction and quick reference. I will, in rather brief terms, deal with

- the character set
- preprocessor directives
- comments
- identifiers
- types
- modifiers
- constructors
- operators
- built-in functions
- built-in variables
- how to activate shaders from OpenGL
- communication with OpenGL

18.4 Character set

Alphanumeric characters: a-z, A-Z, _, 0-9

. + - / * % < > [ ] { } ^| & ~ = ! : ; ?

for preprocessor directives (!)

space, tab, FF, CR, FL

Note that it accepts all line-breaking standards, CR, LF and CRLF! The language is case sensitive.

Characters and string variables do not exist! You can not use 'a', "Hello" etc.

18.5 The preprocessor

To me, it is somewhat alarming that GLSL has such an arcane concept as a preprocessor. However, its use is limited to fairly good purposes. It accepts #define, #undef, #if etc.

VERSION is useful for handling version differences. It will hardly be possible to avoid in the long run.

#version is used to specify what GLSL version the shader uses, so the driver can compile accordingly.

#include does not exist!

18.6 Comments

This is nicely shown by example:

```
/* This is a comment
   that spans more than one line */
// but I usually prefer single-line comments
```

So this is just as usual. So use comments to document your code well!

18.7 Identifiers

Identifiers are mostly like C: they consist of a range of alphanumeric characters, and may not start with a digit. However, there are many predefined identifiers. These use gl_ as prefix. You can not use the gl_ prefix for any variables that you declare yourself!

18.8 Types

There are some well-known scalar types:

- void: return value for procedures
- bool: Boolean variable, that is a flag
- int: integer value
- float: floating-point value.

However, long and double do not exist.

Vector types are more interesting. There are a number of standard types for vectors and matrices.

- vec2, vec3, vec4: Floating-point vectors with 2, 3 or 4 components
- bvec2, bvec3, bvec4: Boolean vectors
- ivec2, ivec3, ivec4: Integer vectors
- mat2, mat3, mat4: Floating-point matrices of size 2x2, 3x3, 4x4

18.9 User defined functions

You can, like in most languages, define functions in order to encapsulate code parts that you need to reuse, or only to structure the code. Surprisingly, this feature is not very important in shaders.

Your functions look almost like a C function, except that you can't use a pointer to a variable, like C does to define variable output parameters. Instead, the keywords in, out and inout are used.

in: input only parameter, read-only (default)

out: output only parameter, not readable until we have written something to it

inout: both input and output, read and write allowed

Thus, a function can look like this:

```
void MyFunction(in vec3 someInputData, float alsoInputData, out vec4
someOutputData, inout variableData)
{
    (code here)
}
```

However, user defined functions are not as useful as they seem. Shaders tend to be fairly small. There is relatively little need to reuse code within a shader. Also, recursive functions are not allowed!

18.10 Modifiers

So far things were simple. Now let us look at something of greatest importance: modifiers. Modifiers declare how variables are meant to be used. In standard C we have modifiers like *static* and *extern*. In GLSL the needs are very different. There are a number of modifiers to choose from. This set differs between older and newer versions of GLSL. I will focus on the syntax used in OpenGL 3.2 and up, but we can not totally ignore the older syntax.

The most important modifiers are. They are: *const, in/out* and *uniform*. If a variable is declared without any of these, then its usage depends on whether it is declared inside a function or not, that is it is local or global over the file, and can be read and written as desired. It should be noted that older OpenGL uses *attribute* instead of *in* for attribute arrays.

const denotes a constant, set at compilation time and can not be changed.

Arguments from OpenGL are called attribute and uniform variables. An attribute is information defined per vertex (passed from the host as arrays, e.g. the vertices themselves, normal vectors, texture coordinates...), while a uniform is information defined per primitive. Thus, attributes can be different for different vertices within a primitive while a uniform must be the same throughout a primitive. Uniform variables are declared **uniform**. Attribute variables are declared **in**.

Variables that are interpolated between vertices, written in the vertex shader and read by the fragment shader, are declared **out** in the vertex shader and **in** in the fragment shader.

Examples of interpolated variables include texture coordinates, normal vectors for Phong shading, vertex colors, light intensities for Gouraud shading...

18.11 More types

There are no pointers!

There are data structures, records. They are called "struct" and are used essentially as in C. Arrays, too, work mostly as in C, except that the pointer/array confusion is gone. You declare and use them with brackets: "[" and "]".

18.12 Communication with the host program

If your shader program has no other data than the built-in variables, such as vertices and normals, you can do many interesting things, but have no means of adjusting the behavior with other parameters. In order to send arbitrary data from OpenGL to GLSL, the host program can set uniform and attribute variables that GLSL can read, and that can change at run-time.

There is, however, no communication in the other direction. The only output from GLSL are the fragment colors. So let us return to the passing of data from OpenGL. What you do in your OpenGL program is to send names and addresses of your variables to GLSL through special calls. For example, let us take the case that you want to pass a float as a uniform variable. This is done like this:

```
float myFloat;
GLint loc;

loc = glGetUniformLocation(p, "myFloat");
glUniform1f(loc, myFloat);
```

In this example, p is a reference to the shader program. (How to get this will be explained in section 18.18 on page 267.) The call glGetUniformLocation gets a reference to the location of the variable in the shader's memory space, the information that glUniform needs to pass on the value to GLSL. Then the matching variable in GLSL will get the value. In GLSL, it is declared:

```
uniform float myFloat;
```

Note that the variable name can be different in your OpenGL code and your GLSL code. The string that you pass to glGetUniformLocation is the connection, it must match the name that you use in GLSL!

18.13 Constructors

As I mentioned before, there are no objects in GLSL. It may then seem strange that the concept of constructors, which is an OO concept, exists, but that is a matter of words more than computer science. A constructor in GLSL is rather a matter of type casting and initializing of variables. Thus, you can not write your own constructors. Some examples:

More about shader programming with GLSL

```
a = int(b);
b = float(a);
c = bool(a);
```

These examples simply cast between types. In my humble opinion, it is a nicer, more readable way of expressing type casting.

Constructors get more interesting when we move to vectors. When you assign a vec4 by passing four floating-point values, it is perfectly natural:

```
vec4 color = vec4(1.0, 0.5, 0.0, 1.0);
```

However, what is not quite as obvious is that you can use constructors to go between different number of components, and it does not have to be by passing exactly the components in question, but GLSL also supports a lot of shortcuts. For example, you can "cast" a single float to a vec4. This looks just like in C++ or Java!

```
color = vec4(1.0);
```

What is that supposed to mean? It sets all components to 1.0! And then we have this case:

```
vec3 a = vec3(color);
```

It copies the three components that fit and skips the fourth one.

18.14 More vector operations

Since vector operations are so important, the shortcuts in constructors is just the beginning. Vectors can be accessed one component at a time, or collectively:

```
a = b + c;
```

or

```
a.x = b.x + c.x;
a.y = b.y + c.y;
a.z = b.z + c.z;
```

There are three synonymous sets of names for the components, x, y, z, w - r, g, b, a - s, t, p, q. Obviously, xyzw are meant for spatial coordinates (where w is the homogeneous coordinate), rgba are meant for color information, and stpq are meant for texture coordinates. However, using the wrong set is not necessarily forbidden. Rather, it is generally allowed. GLSL does not know what you want to do with your data.

A particularly neat, but somewhat strange, feature is the *swizzling* feature. With swizzling, you can create a vector from the parts of another, without constructor:

```
vec2 v2 = v4.rg;
vec3 v3 = v4.xyz;
v2 = v4.st;
```

It is even allowed to make the components change order:

```
v3 = v3.bgr;
```

and you can duplicate components as desired:

```
vec4 v4 = v3.barb;
```

The most obvious use for swizzling is the case where you want a part of a vector (e.g. st) but converting between texture formats (like rgba to abgr) can also be useful. But less obvious is the possibility to move data around for more advanced algorithms. There are cases when you want to pack non-image data into textures, and reading that out in the proper way may benefit from this kind of features.

Most vector operations do what you expect.

```
vec3 v3 = {1.0, 2.0, 3.0};
float f = 1.0;

v3 = v3 + f;
```

produces {2.0, 3.0, 4.0}

Multiplication of two vectors multiply them component by component, returning a vector.

Multiplication of matrices and vectors work as expected.

Dot and cross product are performed by built-in functions, dot() and cross().[1] The function length() returns the length of a vector, its norm. The function normalize() returns a normalized version of the vector. And finally, there is even a function called reflect(), which calculates a mirrored vector!

18.15 Predefined functions in GLSL

GLSL has plenty of predefined functions, primarily mathematical functions. If you expect it to be there, it usually is there. And there are plenty of things that you might not have expected.

Trigonometry: sin, cos, atan...

More math: pow, exp, abs, fract, mod, min, max, clamp...

Geometry: length, dot, cross, normalize, reflect...

Local derivative (for bump mapping): dFdx, dFdy

18.16 Predefined variables in GLSL

A few built-in variables exist that are worth mentioning.

Vertex shader, output data:

---

1. Guess why I prefer using a dot for dot product when the name is "dot" even in GLSL?

More about shader programming with GLSL

Most important, must be written:

```
gl_Position
```

You may also want to write:

```
gl_PointSize
```

Fragment shader, input data:

There are some special input variables for the fragment shader:

```
gl_FragCoord, gl_FrontFacing
```

Fragment shader, output data:

And there are also special outputs:

```
gl_FragColor, gl_FragDepth
```

There is also "discard", which is not a variable but a control statement, which signals that the fragment is not to be written to the frame buffer.

Constants:

Again, a selection:

```
gl_MaxTextureImageUnits (at least 16 exists)
```

18.17 Noise functions

Noise is, as I have mentioned in chapter 17, not a problem but a feature. Real life is noisy, so we want noise. In order to simulate real-life structures, one of the most essential ingredients is noise. The applications are simply too many to mention, they include waves on water, they include a layer of fine-grained noise to make a low-res texture look right, and they include the random parameters in the creation of a plant by a fractal. Not least, we often need static noise, random sets of data that will not change over time.

GLSL includes noise functions, but I would claim that these functions are not quite trust-worthy yet in my experience. On many reasonably modern systems, they return nothing. By all means test them, but there are two other ways to add a little noise to your life:

• Random generators written in GLSL

• Noise textures

The latter is very easy to control. Its main drawback is that they take up precious VRAM.

18.18 Compiling and running shaders from OpenGL

Now it is time to move back to OpenGL. When you want to run a shader program, you need to load it into memory, compile and execute. This is done in two steps:

1) Initialization and compilation

You should do this before your animation is running. First you create a "program object" and "shader objects", pass source to them and compile.

```
PROG = glCreateProgram();
// Vertex shader:
VERT = glCreateShader(GL_VERTEX_SHADER);
text = readTextFile("shader.vert");
glShaderSource(VERT, 1, text, NULL);
glCompileShader(VERT);
// Fragment shader:
FRAG = glCreateShader(GL_FRAGMENT_SHADER);
text = readTextFile("shader.frag");
glShaderSource(FRAG, 1, text, NULL);
glCompileShader(FRAG);
// Attach and link
glAttachShader(PROG, VERT);
glAttachShader(PROG, FRAG);
glLinkProgram(PROG);
```

2) Activation

You activate your shader like this:

```
glUseProgram(PROG);
```

and then it is used for following rendering. When you don't want it any more (when you move to surfaces that do not use your shader), you can deactivate it with:

```
glUseProgram(0);
```

Together with the variable communication, section 18.12 on page 264, this is pretty much what you need to add to your OpenGL toolbox.

18.19 Debugging shader programs

Debugging your shader is a somewhat special experience. You are probably used to debugging either with a debugger, single-stepping, setting breakpoints, inspecting variables etc., or with the glorious[1] "printf debugger", that is adding temporary debugging output on stdout/stderr. None of these work here.

Just imagine if GLSL had a printf! What would it do with it? For a 1024x1024 image, a single printf in your shader will output over a million lines per frame. And how should they reach you? There is no output for text!

Thus, we use other tricks.

- Compiler error messages, the InfoLog
- Signalling with the vertex shader

---

1. Irony

- Signalling with the fragment shader
- Use simple geometry

The *InfoLog*, which you get with glGetProgramInfoLog() and getShaderInfoLog(), is simply the output from the compiler, where you get messages about compilation and linking results. There may be error messages, warnings and more. The exact content depends on the GPU manufacturer. In any case, do not pass on this information. This is where you start when compiling ordinary programs, so start there here too.

Signalling with the shaders is a powerful technique that is the closest we get to printf debugging. When you want to know if a certain statement holds, make an if statement and make some highly visual change depending on the result. Set the color to bright red, move a vertex dramatically... If you need many pieces of data, test what pixel coordinates you work on and do different tests for different pixels.

When testing a shader, don't do it on a complex shape. When you have problems, they are often easier to analyze on a cube than on the Stanford Bunny.

18.20 Development tools

It is highly impractical to develop shaders in a big application. Like any complex algorithm, you should debug it properly in a "sandbox" environment where you get to the point right away. You don't put a glittering diamond with a nice shader for translucency effects at the end of a game level so it takes 15 minutes to get there after every change! You put it there once the shader is perfect.

A shader development tool is really something pretty simple. It will typically include

- An editor for editing the shader source-code
- A command for compiling
- Running the shader on some model
- Display the InfoLog

Two such shader development tools are Rendermonkey and OpenGL Shader Builder, However, making a small application that does all or most of this yourself is not a very complex task at all.

This covers the essentials of GLSL. You are encouraged to find the GLSL specifications and the OpenGL quick reference card on-line.

More about shader programming with GLSL

19. Final words

The book is near its end, and every good story should have an ending.

19.1 What did not fit here

Since this is a course book intended for students who do not have to have taken any other graphics courses before this, and the course is limited in size, a number of quite interesting topics have been skipped, only briefly mentioned, or introduced with little detail. Since I have no intention of keeping them secret from you, I want to mention them here. I deal with these in the second volume, which is the course book for the advanced game programming course. Just as with this book, there are plenty of good, bulky, expensive books that could be used for that course... except that they are just that.

Some of these additional topics are not at all hard to learn. I do not in any way claim that all of them are necessarily very advanced, I just say that they did not fit in this course, so you do not have to learn them to pass this course.

So here is a list of topics that are to come:

- Real-time shadows including ambient occlusion
- Stencil buffers
- Framebuffer objects
- Skin & bones animation
- Deformable objects
- Collision handling and game physics
- Advanced shader programming
- HDR, high dynamic range
- A closer look at bump mapping and its extensions
- GPGPU - general purpose GPU programming with GLSL and CUDA
- Game networking

- Game AI

- Quaternions for rotations

The title of the second volume is

"...so how can we make them scream?"

19.2 The actual final words

In 2013, computer graphics may seem like a solved problem, but like many other fields, every exciting breakthrough leads to new problems, and I believe computer graphics will continue to be both interesting and useful for many years to come. The jobs are there, all we need are people who know the subject. I hope this book can help a few people who want to go there. Whether you do it for fun, as a hobby, or by profession, that doesn't matter.

Let me end the book by the same words with which I end my lecture series, inspired by the great Povel Ramel (1922-2007):

If you like the book...

tell your friends.

If you don't like...

your friends...

this book may help you create new, virtual ones.

20. References

References are important, and this list is really too short for a book like this. For an extensive reference list, [7] is particularly good. (846 references!)

[1]   OpenGL ARB, "OpenGL Programming Guide", (known as the "Red Book") seventh edition, Addison-Wesley 2010.

[2]   R. Rost, "The OpenGL Shading Language", third edition, Addison-Wesley 2010.

[3]   Samuel R. Buss, "3-D Computer Graphics, A Mathematical Introduction with OpenGL", Cambridge University Press 2003.

[4]   Christer Ericson, "Real-time Collision Detection", Morgan Kaufman/Elsevier, 2005.

[5]   McCormack, Ragnemalm, Celestin, "Tricks of the Mac Game Programming Gurus", Hayden Books/MacMillan, 1995.

[6]   D. Hearn, M. P. Baker, W.R.Carithers, "Computer Graphics with OpenGL", fourth edition, 2011.

[7]   T. Akenine-Möller, E. Haines, "Real-Time Rendering", 2nd edition, AK Peters, 2002

[8]   D. Luebke, "Level of detail for 3D graphics", Morgan Kaufman 2004.

[9]   A.S.Glassner, "An Introduction to ray-tracing", Academic Press, 1989.

[10]   M. Abrash, "Graphics Programming Black Book", Corolis Group, 1997.

[11]   B-T Phong, "Illumination for Computer Generated Pictures", *Communications of the ACM*, 18(6), pp 311-317, 1975.

[12]   H. Gouraud, "Continuous shading of curved surfaces", *IEEE Transactions on Computers*, 20(6), pp 623-629, 1971.

[13]   J.E. Bresenham, "Algorithm for Computer Control of a Digital Plotter", *IBM Systems Journal*, 4(1), pp 25-30, 1965.

[14]   E. Catmull, R. Rom, "A Class of Local Interpolating Splines", *Computer Aided Geometric Design*, Academic Press, pp 317-326, 1974.

[15]   W.H. de Boer, "Fast Terrain Rendering Using Geometrical Mipmaps", *www.flipcode.com/articles/article_geomipmaps.pdf*.

[16] J.T. Klosowski, et al, "Efficient Collision Detection Using Bounding Volume Hierarchies of k-DOPs", *IEEE Trans. on Visualization and Computer Graphics*, 4(1), 1998.

[17] Open GL home page: *www.opengl.org*.

[18] OpenGL Utility Toolkit: *www.opengl.org/resources/libraries/glut.html*.

[19] SDL, Simple DirectMedia Layer: *www.libsdl.org*.

[20] libJPEG: *www.ijg.org*.

[21] NVIDIA: *www.nvidia.com*.

[22] Teddy, *http://www-ui.is.s.u-tokyo.ac.jp/~takeo/teddy/teddy/teddy.html*

[23] Stanford 3D Scanning Repository: *graphics.stanford.edu/data/3Dscanrep*

[24] Foley, van Dam, Feiner, Hughes, "Computer Graphics, Principle and Practice", second edition, Addison-Wesley, 1990.

[25] libpng: www.libpng.org/pub/png/libpng.html

[26] pnglite: github.com/dankar//pnglite/

[27] Alan Watt, "3D Computer Graphics", Addison-Wesley, 2000.

[28] D. Astle, K. Hawkins, "Beginning OpenGL Game Programming", Thomson 2004.

[29] OpenGL.org, "Survey Of OpenGL Font Technology". http://www.opengl.org/resources/features/fontsurvey/

[30] Ken Perlin, "An Image Synthesizer", Computer Graphics 19(3), pp 287-296, 1985

[31] Paul Bourke's cube maps, http://local.wasp.uwa.edu.au/~pbourke/

[32] Valve software, http://developer.valvesoftware.com/wiki/Phong_materials

[33] A. Vlachos, J Peters, C. Boyd, J.L. Mitchell, "Curved PN Triangles", I3D '01 Proc of the 2001 symposium on Interactive 3D graphics, 2001, pp 159-166.

[34] S. Gustavsson, "Simplex noise demystified", http://webstaff.itn.liu.se/~stegu/simplexnoise/simplexnoise.pdf

[35] K. Perlin, "Ken's Academy Award", http://www.mrl.nyu.edu/~perlin/doc/oscar.html

[36] T. Lottes, "FXAA", NVidia white paper, 2009. http://developer.download.nvidia.com/assets/gamedev/files/sdk/11/FXAA_WhitePaper.pdf

[37] J. Blinn, "Simulation of wrinkled surfaces", proc SIGGRAPH, 1978, pp 286-292.

[38] P. Hanrahan, P. Haeberli, "Direct WYSIWYG Painting and Texturing on 3D Shapes", Computer Graphics, Volume 24, Number 4, 1990

[39] M. Garland, P. Heckbert, "Surface simplification using quadric error metric", 1proc SIGGRAPH '97, pp 209-216, 1997

21. Index

F

G

www.ingramcontent.com/pod-product-compliance
Lightning Source LLC
Chambersburg PA
CBHW080550060326
40689CB00021B/4811